HUDSON'S BAY

TADOUSAC

HUDSON'S BAY

OR

EVERY-DAY LIFE IN THE WILDS

OF

NORTH AMERICA

DURING SIX YEARS' RESIDENCE IN THE TERRITORIES OF
THE HONOURABLE HUDSON'S BAY COMPANY

With Illustrations

BY

ROBERT M. BALLANTYNE

CHARLES E. TUTTLE COMPANY
Rutland, Vermont & Tokyo, Japan

Representatives
Continental Europe: BOXERBOOKS, INC., *Zurich*
British Isles: PRENTICE-HALL INTERNATIONAL, INC., *London*
Australasia: PAUL FLESCH & CO., PTY. LTD., *Melbourne*
Canada: M. G. HURTIG LTD., *Edmonton*

Published by the Charles E. Tuttle Company, Inc.
of Rutland, Vermont & Tokyo, Japan
with editorial offices at
Suido 1-chome, 2-6, Bunkyo-ku, Tokyo, Japan

© *1972 by M. G. Hurtig Ltd.*

Library of Congress Catalog Card No. 71-170102

International Standard Book No. 0-8048-1004-4

First Tuttle edition published 1972

PRINTED IN JAPAN

TABLE OF CONTENTS

LIST OF ILLUSTRATIONS

INTRODUCTION TO THE
NEW EDITION

BEFORE Ballantyne, or so it seems to me in recollection,
lie nursery rhymes and the mists of infancy. For his
are the first novels of which I have a clear memory
extending out of childhood: a memory of pristine worlds
which enveloped the actual adventures that provided
ways for the mind to enter. The setting, now at least,
seems all important; I am aware of an empty and un-
spoilt world—as of course Ballantyne's world of the
nineteenth century was in comparison with our own—
and the dominant image is a crystalline one, of the ice
world of the Canadian North, of underwater luminosi-
ties in *The Coral Island*. After many years one forgets
the details of such books—the action and even the
characters grow vague—but their atmosphere curiously
remains, with the sense of excitement at realizing that
other self-consistent worlds could exist outside one's
own, and that it did not really matter if their existence
was literal. Later the reading of Ballantyne led to the
reading of actual travellers' narratives, to the reinforcing
of the fiction of adventure with the solidity of scientific

journeyings in such books as Bates's *Naturalist on the River Amazons* or Darwin's inimitable *Voyage of the Beagle*.

But Ballantyne was not merely the creator of fictional worlds in books that set young readers travelling in the mind and longing to travel in the flesh, not merely the principal founder of a tradition of writing for boys carried on vigorously by Henty and Stevenson and diluted into that diet of imperial pabulum provided so regularly and over so many years by the recently deceased *Boy's Own Paper* and its lesser rivals. He was a man who had experienced, as a boy, at least one of the primitive worlds of which he wrote, and *Hudson's Bay* is the record of that experience.

As the reader, his antennae attuned to mid-Victorian tastes, becomes quickly aware, *Hudson's Bay* is not a book intended primarily for boys. There is too much drinking (in which the writer-hero indulges without moralizing) for that, and it is significant that, though the adventures described in this book resemble those narrated in such juvenile novels as *Ungava* and *The Young Fur Traders*, it is not one of the books by Ballantyne that were reprinted regularly and still are today. For many years, indeed, it has been out of print.

Yet *Hudson's Bay* is the most readable, because it is the most concerned with personal adventure, of a number of non-fictional books that resulted from Ballantyne's lasting interest in North America. He put together in 1853 a compilation—rather like those done more recently by Farley Mowat—of accounts of Arctic voyages entitled *The Northern Coasts of America, and the Hudson's Bay Territories*, and in 1858, when British Columbia sprang into being and fame, he seized the moment to prepare a topical *Handbook to the New Gold Fields*. These were ephemeral works, and there is no reason to revive them. *Hudson's Bay* is another matter. It is interesting as the first book of an afterwards celebrated author, containing much that anticipates his later and more popular works. And in its own right it is a vigorous and informative account of the fur trade at a time—midway between the union of the Hudson's Bay and North West companies in 1820 and the surrender of the Northwest in 1870—about which little of enduring interest was written.

Unlike Palliser, Butler and other writers of the 50s and 60s who described the Northwest as travellers unattached to its regular life, Ballantyne actually lived and worked in the Canadian North as a member of the aristocracy of fur traders which gave the country what slight simulacrum of government it possessed. Yet he differed from most of his fellow Hudson's Bay men because of the background that made writing come easily to him—more easily perhaps than fur trading, as his narrative suggests. He came from one of the distinguished literary families of Scotland. Two of his uncles were noted Edinburgh publishers and one of them, James, was the friend as well as the printer of Sir Walter Scott. His elder brother, another James

Ballantyne, balanced Robert Michael's passion for the wild and uncrowded portions of the earth by an interest in ancient India and, after a period teaching in Benares, he returned to become a leading authority on Sanskrit literature.

It seems likely from R. M. Ballantyne's later career—for most of his twenties were spent in publishing and his life thereafter became that of the hard-working professional writer—that he never intended to stay permanently in the fur trade and to follow the long ladder of promotion which led to a chief factorship and a share in the company's profits. His period in the North was a kind of education, the equivalent of those wander years of the Grand Tour which his less enter-prising contemporaries were still taking on the well-trodden paths of Europe and the Levant. And, though he was only sixteen when he set off from London on the company's ship *Prince Rupert* for the long voyage via Stornoway to York Factory on Hudson's Bay, he appears already to have developed literary aspirations; from the beginning he kept a diary of his experiences, and before leaving the company's service he beguiled the solitude of the remote St. Lawrence post of Sept-Iles by writing the first chapters of *Hudson's Bay*.

In a double sense, in fact, *Hudson's Bay* is a work of youth. Leaving home as a boy less than five feet tall, Ballantyne returned in 1847 as a young man of 22; he completed his book immediately and published it in 1848, first in a special edition for private circulation (from which this text is reproduced) and then in a general edition. It was not the work of an older man looking back on his youth, and this fact explains both the main virtue of *Hudson's Bay*—its sense of vigorous immediacy—and its principal weakness, the lack of a real sense of the historical forces that were already reshaping the old dominion of Prince Rupert's successors.

For by the time Ballantyne arrived, the Northwest was already in a process of change whose impetus was mounting from year to year. To the young clerk, impressed by the vast emptinesses of the country, by the fact that three fur-trading posts with a handful of white men might represent British power in an area as large as the whole United Kingdom, that process was not so evident as it is to us in hindsight or as it already was to politicians in Upper Canada and to the more astute of the company's own factors and traders. Under the ruthless hand of Sir George Simpson, who still reigned at Lachine as the company's governor-in-chief, the multitude of posts (often set up out of mere rivalry) which existed at the time of the union of the companies in 1820 had been drastically reduced in number. Apart from the Columbia region on the Pacific Coast, and the posts along the St. Lawrence, the main body of the company's trade was now directed through York Factory on Hudson's Bay; and the great route from Montreal to the Saskatchewan country through the Great Lakes and the Shield country which the North West Company had established was now almost abandoned. No brigades

followed it any longer, and when Ballantyne passed
that way from Norway House to Montreal in 1845 even
the portages were falling into decay.

Far to the west, beyond Ballantyne's journeyings, the
company's power had vanished and its trade was waning
in the Oregon Territory. Up the Ottawa River, once a
wilderness thoroughfare of Indians and fur traders,
the lumbermen were steadily advancing and in the
clearings they made, agricultural villages were established, while along the Red River, in the very heart of
Rupert's Land, Lord Selkirk's colony had endured and
grown into a chain of settlements that soon would
tempt the hungry land hunters of Upper Canada. The
company's dominion, which had survived French
challenges on the bay and had remained undiminished
for more than a century and a half, was at last waning.
Even the fur trade itself was changing, for beaver hats
were going out of fashion in Europe and other furs were
taking the place of what had once been the great staple
of the Canadian economy.

Ballantyne, unlike other fur traders who claim their
place in literature, did not have the opportunity to
become a great traveller. Most of his time was spent on
desk work in York Factory, Norway House and Fort
Garry, and his leisure was occupied in wandering in the
immediate environs of those posts. But he did journey
more than once between York Factory and Norway
House; he travelled on the Red River, and he followed
the old North West route from the Red over the height

of land and by the Great Lakes to Montreal, continuing afterwards, by sleigh and boat and snowshoe, along the St. Lawrence, first to Tadousac and then to what seemed to him the end of the world at Sept-Iles. He never reached the prairies or the Rockies or the Pacific Coast, and though his travelling was often hard, it was rarely dangerous. Always he was following established routes, and there is nothing in his travels that can be graced with the title of exploration.

Indeed, there is little Ballantyne tells us except in terms of personal incident that we cannot find elsewhere, scattered in various pages of other books on the Northwest. What really distinguishes *Hudson's Bay* is, first, that it brings together in an interesting single pattern enough information to give us a vivid picture of fur-trading life at a time when vast transitions were impending; secondly, that Ballantyne brings to his narrative a youthful zest, a sense of action and how to render it in prose and a power of describing the physical environment which one finds among none of his contemporaries. He brings a skill that is sophisticated in terms of his age and times, and applies it to what—by Mackenzie and Fraser and the other writers of fur-trade journals—was usually described in such laconic and utilitarian terms. The result is pleasing and evocative. Scenes take on the sharpness and depth of vignettes in the mind. Episodes are highlighted into comedy or pathos.

Not least important, a personality is projected, and

a developing one at that. One follows the mental growth of Ballantyne from a boy given to horseplay and thrilled by shooting his first duck in the early days at Norway House, to the responsible and observant young man commanding small boats and minor trading posts on the St. Lawrence during the last months of his service in 1847.

In many ways, of course, the book is marked by its period, by attitudes that seem alien in a post-imperial age but which did not seem so as recently as my own boyhood. Ballantyne and his fellow clerks, and even more the senior officers of the company, had no doubt at all that they were, in the words of the company's charter, "True and absolute Lordes and Proprietors" of the land they so thinly occupied. The canoemen and other servants—whether Orkneymen or French Canadians or Métis—were regarded as something like feudal retainers, and towards the Indians, Ballantyne (and doubtless his companions) maintained the attitude of condescension that goes with suzerainty, a facetious condescension that will refer to an Indian elder as a "dingy gentleman" and exaggerate immoderately the incidence of cannibalism in Indian life.

There is also at times a callousness which a modern writer would allow himself only if he were writing deliberately for sadistic effect. Ballantyne tells nonchalantly of shooting birds with no intention of eating them; he recounts a gruesome little tale of gull eggs being hatched in hot water and the young birds boiled

alive; and when he goes on a seal-clubbing expedition
he strives for comic effect by emphasizing the laughable
antics of an inexperienced tailor, though in the end he
admits it was a cruel little incident.

What strikes one most, however, are the vast areas of
Ballantyne's incuriosity. He describes vividly what he
actually sees or experiences; what he learns from others
on matters that interest him is well recounted. Details
of the fur trade, the lore of hunting and fishing, the
practicalities of travelling and living in the wilderness
are all presented copiously and accurately, and Ballantyne also shows a lively interest in exploration, demon-
strated particularly in his description of a chance
meeting on a lonely portage with the explorer, Dr. John
Rae. This was in 1845, before Rae had carried out the
great journeys that resulted in the first discoveries
regarding the fate of Franklin. But Ballantyne was
already able to assess and to contrast the importance of
Rae's method of travelling unencumbered and living
like the native peoples off the land, with what he calls
the "vague and uncertain notions of Back and Franklin";
a few years later the failure of Franklin's last expedition proved Ballantyne's point.

Yet it is still amazing how little Ballantyne learned
about the people who were native to the country where
he lived for six years. Admiring Rae, he did not imitate
him. For the most part he was content to learn about
Indian customs so far as they affected the fur trade—
ways of trapping, fishing, etc.—but very little further.

He never appears to have learned an Indian language enough to speak it, and he has nothing to tell about the social organization of native peoples or—except in the vaguest terms—about their beliefs. Even about the voyageurs with whom he travelled he appears to have known amazingly little. Officers and servants of the company, even on journeys, ate apart, and appear rarely to have conversed; thus, though Ballantyne tells us of the traditional French Canadian songs with which the voyageurs lightened their labors, one never has the feeling that he is interested in the working of their minds or curious about the part of their lives that had been lived away from canoes.

In other words—as the sentimentality which at times mars his otherwise functional prose may demonstrate —Ballantyne was a typically Victorian man who happened to have lived during the years of adolescence with a special intensity. And this, undoubtedly, was why he was so successful as a writer for boys. He shared the conservatism and the practicality which so many adolescents display; he was able to transfer to young people in an adult world the sense of importance and self-reliance he himself had developed on Hudson's Bay (for unusual resourcefulness is a dominant characteristic among his young heroes). Above all, he could translate that vision of a pristine world which is already present in *Hudson's Bay* into the crystalline images which stay in the mind for decades as the residues of books like *Snowflake and Sunbeams; or, the Young Fur*

Traders (his first story, written nine years after his return from Canada), and those masterpieces (out of eighty other novels) *Ungava* and *The Coral Island*. Apart from *The Coral Island*, which was a rare and unique work of escapist fantasy, Ballantyne remained at his best in writing of the Canadian North, and best of all in those early books which he wrote within the decade from 1848 to 1858 following his return to Scotland, when his recollections were still as sharp and clear as they appear in *Hudson's Bay*.

GEORGE WOODCOCK

PREFACE

In venturing to bring out the present work, the author rests his hope of its being in any measure favourably received, entirely upon the fact, that the subject of which it treats is, comparatively speaking, a new one.

It is true that others have slightly sketched the same subject, in books upon Arctic discovery, and in works of general information; but the very nature of these publications prohibits their entering into a lengthened or minute description of EVERY-DAY LIFE, which is the leading feature of the present work.

The illustrative wood-cuts were executed from drawings made on the spot by the author,—who has slightly changed his plan regarding them,

since the first sheets of the contents were issued
to his subscribers ; being of opinion, that a number of small cuts, illustrative of several parts of
Indian costume, &c., intermingled with three or
four landscapes, will prove more interesting to
the general reader than a number of drawings
representing eight or ten of the Hudson's Bay
Company's forts and establishments, which was
his first intention.

HUDSON'S BAY

HUDSON'S BAY.

CHAPTER I.

EADER, — I take it for granted that you are tolerably well acquainted with the different modes of life and travelling peculiar to European nations. I also presume that you know something of the inhabitants of the East; and, it may be, a good deal of the Americans in general. But I suspect, at least I would fain hope, that you have only a vague and indefinite knowledge of life in those wild, uncivilised regions in the northern continent of America, around the shores of Hudson's Bay. I would fain hope this, I say, that I may have the satisfaction of giving you information on the subject, and of showing you that there is a body of civilised men who move, and breathe, (pretty cool air, by the way!) and spend their lives in a quarter of the globe as totally different, in most respects, from the part you inhabit, as a beaver, roaming among the ponds and marshes of his native home, is from that sagacious animal when converted into a fashionable hat.

About the middle of May, eighteen hundred and forty-one, I was thrown into a state of extatic joy by the arrival of a letter appointing me to the enviable situation of apprentice clerk in the service of the Honourable Hudson's Bay Company. To describe the immense extent to which I expanded, both mentally and bodily, upon the receipt of this letter, is impossible; it is sufficient to know, that from that moment I fancied myself a complete man-of-business, and treated my old companions with the condescending suavity of one who knows that he is talking to his inferiors.

A few days after, however, my pride was brought very low indeed, as I lay tossing about in my berth on the tumbling waves of the German ocean, eschewing breakfast as a dangerous meal, and looking upon dinner with a species of horror utterly incomprehensible by those who have not experienced an attack of sea-sickness. Miseries of this description, fortunately, do not last long. In a couple of days we got into the comparatively still water of the Thames; and I, with a host of pale-faced young ladies, and cadaverous-looking young gentlemen, emerged for the first time from the interior of the ship, to behold the beauties and wonders of the great metropolis, as we glided slowly up the crowded river.

Leave-taking is a disagreeable subject, either to reflect

upon or to write about, so we will skip that part of the business and proceed at once to Gravesend, where I stood (having parted from all my friends) on the deck of the good ship Prince Rupert, contemplating the boats and crowds of shipping that passed continually before me, and thinking how soon I was to leave the scenes to which I had been so long accustomed, for a far distant land. I was a boy, however, and this, I think, is equivalent to saying that I did not sorrow long. My future companion and fellow-clerk, Mr W——, was pacing the deck near me. This turned my thoughts into another channel, and set me speculating upon his probable temper, qualities, and age; whether or not he was strong enough to thrash me, and if we were likely to be good friends. The captain, too, was chatting and laughing with the doctor with as much carelessness as if he had not the great responsibility of taking a huge ship across a boundless waste of waters, and through fields and islands of ice, to a distant country some three thousand miles to the nor'-west of England! So, under the influence of these favourable circumstances, my spirits began to rise, and, when the cry arose on deck that the steamer containing the committee of the Honourable Hudson's Bay Company was in sight, I sprang up the companion-ladder in a state of mind, if not happy, at least as nearly so as, under the circumstances, could be expected.

Upon gaining the deck, I beheld a small steam-boat passing close to us, filled with a number of elderly consequential-looking gentlemen, who eyed us with a very critical expression of countenance. I had a pretty good guess who these gentlemen were ; but, had I been entirely ignorant, I should soon have been enlightened by the remark of a sailor, who whispered to his comrade, " I say, Bill, them's the great guns !"

I suppose the fact of their being so had a sympathetic effect upon the guns of the Company's three ships, the Prince Rupert, Prince Albert, and Prince of Wales, which fired a number of blank cartridges at the steamer as she passed them in succession. The steamer then ranged alongside of us, and the elderly gentlemen came on board and shook hands with the captain and officers, smiling blandly as they observed the neat, trim appearance of the three fine vessels, which, with every thing in readiness for setting sail on the following morning, strained at their cables, as if anxious to commence their struggle with the waves.

It is a custom of the directors of the Hudson's Bay Company, to give a public dinner to the officers of their ships upon the eve of their departure from Gravesend ; and, ere the gentlemen of the committee left the vessel, one of them invited the captain and officers to attend, and, to my astonishment and delight, also *begged me* to honour them with my company. I accepted the invitation with extreme politeness ; and, from inability to express my joy in any other way, winked to my friend W——, with whom I had become, by this time, pretty familiar. He, having been also invited, winked in return to me; and, having disposed of this piece of juvenile free-masonry to our satisfaction, we assisted the crew in giving three hearty cheers as the little steamer darted from us and proceeded to the shore.

The dinner, like all other public dinners, was as good and substantial as a lavish expenditure of cash could make it; but really my recollections of it are very indistinct. The ceaseless din of plates, glasses, knives, forks, and tongues, was tremendous; and this, together with the novelty of the scene, the heat of the room, and excellence of the viands, tended to render me oblivious of much that took place. Almost all the faces present were strange to me. Who were, and who were not, the gentlemen of the committee, to me was matter of the most perfect indifference; and as no one took the trouble to address me in particular, I confined myself to the interesting occupation of trying to make sense of a conversation held by upwards of fifty pairs of lungs, at one and the same time. Nothing intelligible, however, was to be heard, except when a sudden lull in the noise gave a bald-headed old gentleman, near the head of the table, an opportunity of drinking the health of a red-faced old gentleman near the foot, upon whom he bestowed an amount of flattery perfectly bewildering; and, after making the unfortunate red-faced gentleman writhe for half an hour in a fever of modesty, sat down amid thunders of applause. Whether the applause, by the way, was intended for the speaker, or the *speakee*, I do not know; but, being quite indifferent, I

clapped my hands with the rest. The red-faced gentleman, now become purple with excitement, then rose, and
during a solemn silence, delivered himself of a speech,
to the effect, that the day then passing was certainly the
happiest in his mortal career, and that he felt quite
faint with the mighty load of honour just thrown upon
his delighted shoulders by his bald-headed friend. The
red-faced gentleman then sat down to the national air
of Rat-tat-tat, played in full chorus, with knives, forks,
spoons, nutcrackers, and knuckles, on the polished surface
of the mahogany table.

We left the dinner-table at a late hour, and after
I, in company with some other youngsters, had done as
much mischief as we conveniently could without risk-
ing our detention by the strong arm of the law, we
went down to the beach and embarked in a boat with
the captain, for the ship. How the sailors ever found
her in the darkness is a mystery to me to this day.
Find her, however, they did, and in half an hour I was
in the land of Nod.

The sun was high in the heavens next morning when
I awoke, and gazed around for a few moments to discover where I was ; but the rattling of ropes and blocks,
stamping of feet over-head, and above all, a certain
strange and disagreeable motion in my dormitory, soon
enlightened me on that point. We were going rapidly
down the Thames, with a fair breeze, and had actually
set sail for the distant shores of Hudson's Bay. What
took place during the next five or six days, I know not,

for the demon of sea-sickness had again completely pro-
strated my faculties, bodily and mental. Some faint recollections I have of stormy weather, horrible noises,
and hurried dinners ; but the greater part of the time is
a miserable blank in my memory. Towards the sixth day,
however, the savoury flavour of a splendid salmon-trout
floated past my dried-up nostrils, like " Afric's spicy
gale," and caused my collapsed stomach to yearn with
strong emotion. The ship, too, was going more quietly
through the water, and a broad stream of sunshine shot
through the small window of my berth into my breast,
and through that into my heart, filling it with a calm
but melancholy pleasure, quite indescribable. Sounds,
however, of an attack upon the trout roused me, and
with a mighty effort I tumbled out of bed, donned my
clothes, and seated myself, for the first time, at the
table.

Our party was composed of the captain, Mr C——, a
chief factor in the Company's service, the doctor, two apprentice clerks, the first and second mates, and myself ;
all excellent fellows in their way. Soon after this, we
anchored in the quiet little harbour of Stornoway. The
bay is surrounded by high hills, except at the entrance,
where a passage, not more, I should think, than three
hundred yards wide, admits vessels of any tonnage into
its sheltering bosom. Stornoway, a pretty, modest-
looking little village, apparently pleased with its lot, and
contented to be far away from the busy and bustling
world, lies snugly at the bottom of the bay. Here we

remained upwards of a week, engaging men for the
wild Nor'-west, and cultivating the acquaintance of the
villagers, who were extremely kind and hospitable.
Occasionally, I amused myself with fishing excursions to
the middle of the bay in small boats, in which excursions
I was usually accompanied by two or three very ragged
little boys from the village. Our sport was generally
good, and rendered extremely interesting by our un-
certainty as to which of the monsters of the deep would
first attack our hooks. Rock-codlings and flounders
appeared the most voracious, and occasionally a skate
or long-legged crab came struggling to the surface.

Just before leaving this peaceful little spot, our captain gave a grand ball on board, to which were invited
the *élite* of Stornoway. Great preparations were made
for the occasion. The quarter-deck was well washed
and scrubbed; an awning was spread over it, which
formed a capital ceiling, and representatives of almost
every flag that waves formed the walls of the large and
airy apartment. Oil lamps, placed upon the sky-lights,
companion, and capstan, shed a mellow light upon the
scene, the romantic effect of which was greatly height-
ened by a few flickering rays of the moon, which shot
through various openings in the drapery, and disported
playfully upon the deck. At an early and very un-
fashionable hour on the evening of the appointed night,
the guests arrived in detachments; and, while the gentlemen scrambled up the side of the vessel, the ladies, amid
a good deal of blushing and hesitation, were hoisted on

board in a chair. Tea was served on deck ; and, after half an hour's laughing and chatting, during which time our violin-player was endeavouring to coax his first string to the proper pitch without breaking, the ball opened with a Scotch reel.

Great was the fun, and numerous the ludicrous incidents that happened during that mirthful night; and loud the noise and merriment of the dancers as they went, with vigorous energy, through the bewildering evolutions of country-dance and reel. Immense was the delight of the company when the funniest old gentleman there volunteered a song ; and extatic the mirth, when he followed it up by a speech upon every subject that an ordinary mind could possibly embrace in a quarter of an hour. But who can describe the scene that ensued, when supper was reported ready in the cabin ! Such pushing, squeezing, laughing, shrieking, and joking, in the vain attempt made to get upwards of thirty people crammed into a room of twelve feet by ten ! Such droll, and sometimes cutting remarks as were made when they were at last requested to sup in detachments ! All this, however, was nothing to the fun that ensued after supper, when the fiddler became more energetic, and the dancers more vigorous and active. But it is useless trying to describe the merry scene, and I blush to think I have had the audacity to attempt it. The first grey streaks of morning glimmered in the east ere the joyous party tumbled down the sides and departed to their homes.

There is a sweet, yet melancholy pleasure, when far away from friends and home, in thinking over happy days gone by, and dwelling on the merry scenes and pleasures that have passed, perhaps for ever. So I thought and felt, as I recalled to mind the fun and frolic of the Stornoway ball, the graver mirth of the Gravesend dinner, and the peaceful time when I lived in sweet P——, surrounded by the gentle inmates of my happy home. We had now left the shores of Scotland, and were ploughing through the heaving waves of the wide Atlantic; and, when I turned my straining eyes towards the faint blue line of the lessening hills, " a tear unbidden trembled," as the thought arose that I looked, perhaps, for the last time, upon my dear native land.

The sea, for ages back, has been an inexhaustible subject for the pens of all writers. The poet, the traveller, and the novelist, have each devoted a portion of their time and talents to the mighty ocean; but alas! that part of it which it has fallen to my lot to describe, is very different from those about which the poets have sung with rapture. Here, none of the many wonders of the tropical latitudes beguile the tedium of the voyage; no glittering dolphins force the winged inhabitants of the deep to seek shelter on the vessel's deck; no ravenous sharks follow in our wake to eat us if we chance to fall overboard, or amuse us by swallowing our baited hook; no passing vessel cheers the passenger with the knowledge that there are others besides himself roaming over the interminable waste of waters. All was dreary and monotonous; the same view of sky and water met our gaze each morning as we ascended to the deck to walk for half an hour before breakfast; except when the topsails of our accompanying vessels fluttered for a moment on the distant horizon. Occasionally we approached closer to each other, and once or twice hailed with the trumpet; but these breaks in the gloom of our existence were few and far between.

Towards the end of July we approached Hudson's Straits, having seen nothing on the way worth mentioning, except one whale, which passed close under the stern of the ship. This was a great novelty to me, being the first whale I had seen, and it gave me something to talk of and think about for the next four days.

The ships now began to close in, as we neared the entrance of the straits, and we had the pleasure of sailing in company for a few days. The shores of the straits became visible occasionally, and we soon sailed, with perfect confidence and security, among these narrow channels and mountains of ice that had damped the ardour and retarded the progress of Hudson, Button, Gibbons, and other navigators in days of yore.

One day, during a dead calm, our ship and the Prince of Wales lay close to each other, rolling in the swell of the glassy ocean; and, there seeming to be no prospect of a breeze, the captain ordered his gig to be launched, and invited the doctor, Mr C——, and myself, to go on board the Prince of Wales with him. We accepted his offer joyfully, and were soon alongside.

Old Captain R——, a veteran in the Company's service, received us kindly, and prevailed on our captain to stay tea. The passengers on board were Mr F——, a chief factor, (the highest rank attainable in the service,) who had been home on leave of absence, and was returning to end his days, perhaps, in the north-west; and Mr John M——, a young apprentice clerk, going, like myself, to try his fortune in Hudson's Bay. He was a fine, candid young fellow, full of fun and frolic, with a kind, engaging disposition, and I formed a great friendship for him the moment I saw him, which was destined to ripen into a lasting one many years after. Yes, little did I think, when I parted from him that evening on the bosom of the sea, that I should ever meet him again; yet so it was. About six years from the time I parted from him in Hudson's Straits, I again grasped his hand on the shores of the mighty St Lawrence, and renewed that friendship which afforded me the greatest pleasure I enjoyed in the country, and which, I trust, neither time nor distance will ever lessen.

We spent the evening delightfully, the more so that we were not likely to have such an opportunity again, as the Prince of Wales would shortly part company from us, and direct her course to Moose factory, in James's Bay, while we should proceed across Hudson's Bay to York factory. We left the ship just as a few cat's-paws on the surface of the water gave indications of a coming breeze.

Ice now began to surround us in all directions, and

soon after this I saw, for the first time, that monster of
the Polar Seas, an iceberg. We passed quite close,
and had a fine opportunity of observing it. Though
not so large as they are frequently seen, it was
beautifully and fantastically formed. High peaks rose
from it on various places, and down its sides streams of
water and miniature cataracts flowed in torrents. The
whole mass was of a beautiful greenish-white colour, and
its lofty pinnacles sparkled in the moonbeams as it
floated past, bending majestically in the swell of the
ocean. About this time, too, we began to meet with
numerous fields and floes of ice, to get through which,
we often experienced considerable difficulty.

My favourite amusement, while thus threading our
way through the ice, was to ascend to the royal-yard,
and there, while gazing on these most romantic scenes,
cogitate on the wonders of creation.

It is impossible to convey a correct idea of the beauty,

the magnificence, of some of the scenes through which
we passed. Thousands of the most grotesque, fanciful,
and beautiful little icebergs, and fields, surrounded us
on all sides, intersected by numerous serpentine canals,
which glittered in the sun, (for the weather was fine all
the time we were in the straits,) like threads of silver,
twining round ruined palaces of crystal. The masses
assumed every variety of form and size, and many of
them bore such a striking resemblance to cathedrals,
churches, columns, arches, and spires, that I could almost
fancy we had been transported to one of the floating
cities of Fairy-land. The rapid motion, too, of our ship,
in what appeared a dead calm, added much to the
magical effect of the scene. A light but steady breeze
urged her along, with considerable velocity, through a
maze of ponds and canals, which, from the immense
quantity of ice that surrounded them, were calm and
unruffled as the surface of a mill-pond,

Not a sound disturbed the delightful stillness of nature,
save the gentle rippling of the vessel's bow as she sped
on her way, or the occasional puffing of a lazy whale,
awakened from a nap by our unceremonious intrusion
on his domains. Now and then, however, my reveries
were disagreeably interrupted by the ship coming into
sudden contact with huge lumps of ice. This happened
occasionally when we arrived at the termination of one
of those natural canals through which we passed, and
found it necessary to force our way into the next.
These concussions were sometimes very severe, and even

made the ship's bell ring; but we heeded this little, as the vessel was provided with huge blocks of timber on her bows, called ice-pieces, and was besides built expressly for sailing in the northern seas. It only became annoying at meal-times, when a spoonful of soup would sometimes make a little private excursion of its own, over the shoulder of the owner instead of into his mouth.

As we proceeded, the ice became more closely packed, and at last compelled us to bore through it. The ship, however, was never altogether detained, though much retarded. I recollect, while thus surrounded, filling a bucket with water from a pool on the ice, to see whether it was fresh or not, as I had been rather sceptical upon this point. It was excellent, and might almost compete with the water from the famous spring of Crawley! In a few days we got out of the ice altogether, and in this, as the ships are frequently detained for weeks in the straits, we considered ourselves very fortunate.

I experienced at this time a severe disappointment in the non-appearance of the Esquimaux upon the coast. The captain said they would be sure to come off to us, as they had always been in the habit of doing so, for the purpose of exchanging ivory and oil, for saws, files, needles, &c., a large chest full of which is put on board annually for this purpose. The ivory usually procured from them is walrus tusks. These are not very large, and are of inferior quality.

As we approached the shores of the straits we short-

ened sail and fired three or four guns, but no noisy
" *chimo*" floated across the water in answer to our salute ;
still we lingered for a while, but, as there was no sign of
the natives on shore, the captain concluded they had
gone off to the interior, and steered out to sea again.
I was very much disappointed at this, as it was wholly
unexpected, and I had promised myself much pleasure in
trading with them, for which purpose all the buttons of
my old waistcoats had been amputated.   It was useless,
however, to repine, so I contented myself with the hope
that they would yet visit us in some other part of the
straits.   We afterwards learned that our guns had
attracted them to the coast in time to board the Prince
Albert, (which was out of sight astern,) though too late
for us.

Our passage across Hudson's Bay was stormy, but
no one on board cared for this, having become quite
accustomed to it.   For my part, I had become quite a
sailor, and could ascend and descend easily to the truck,
without creeping through the *lubber's hole*.   I shall not
forget the first time I attempted this : our youngest
apprentice had challenged me to try it, so up we went
together—he on the fore, and I on the main-mast.   The
tops were gained easily, and we even made two or three
steps up the top-mast shrouds with affected indifference ;
but, alas ! our courage was failing, at least *mine* was,
very fast.   However, we gained the cross-trees pretty
well, and then sat down for a little to recover breath.
The top-gallant-mast still reared its taper form high

above me, and the worst was yet to come. The top-gal-
lant shrouds had no rattlins on them, so I was obliged to
shin up; and, as I worked myself up the two small ropes,
the tenacity with which I grasped them was fearful.
At last I reached the top, and with my feet on the small
collar that fastens the ropes to the mast, and my arms
circling the mast itself—for nothing but a bare pole, and
the signal halyards, now rose above me—I glanced upwards. After taking a long breath, and screwing up my
courage, I slowly shinned up the slender pole, and, standing on the royal-yard, laid my hand upon the *truck*.
After a while I got accustomed to it, and thought nothing of taking an airing on the royal-yard after breakfast.

About the 5th or 6th of August, the captain said we
must be near the land. The deep-sea lead was rigged
and a sharp look-out kept, but no land appeared. At
last one fine day, while at the mast-head, I saw something like land on the horizon, and told them so on
deck. They saw it too, but gave me no answer. Soon
a hurried order to dowse top-gallant-sails and reef topsails made me slide down rather hastily from my elevated position; and I had scarcely gained the deck when
a squall, the severest we had yet encountered, struck the
ship and laid her almost on her beam-ends, and the sea,
which had been nearly calm, foamed and hissed like a
seething cauldron, and became white as snow. This, I
found, was what sailors call a *white squall*. It was as
short as it was severe, and great was my joy when the

ship regained her natural position in the water. Next day we saw land in earnest, and in the afternoon anchored in " Five Fathom Hole," after passing in safety a sand-bar which renders the entrance into this roadstead rather difficult.

Here, then, for the first time, I beheld the shores of Hudson's Bay; and truly their appearance was any thing but prepossessing. Though only at the distance of two miles, so low and flat was the land that it appeared ten miles off, and scarcely a tree was to be seen. We could just see the tops of one or two houses in York factory, which was seven miles up the river from where we lay. In a short time, the sails of a small schooner came in sight, and in half an hour more the Frances, (named after the lady of the governor, Sir George Simpson,) was bobbing alongside.

Mr P——, the skipper, came on board, and there commenced between him and the captain a sharp fire of questions and answers, in the midst of which I left them and went on deck. Here the face of things had changed. The hatches were off and goods scattered about in all directions ; another small schooner had arrived, and the process of discharging the vessel was going rapidly forward. A boat was dispatched to the factory with the packet-box and letter-bag, and soon after the Frances stood in for the shore.

The Prince Albert had arrived almost at the same moment with us, and was now visited by the second schooner, which soon returned to our own ship to take the passengers on shore. Those of our consort, Messrs G—— and R——, with the wife of the former, were already on board. These gentlemen were missionaries bound for Red River Colony, and as I had some prospect of going there myself, I was delighted to have the probable chance of travelling with such agreeable companions.

Mr C——, Mr W——, and myself, now bade adieu to the Prince Rupert, which had been our home for such a length of time, (but I must say I did not regret the parting,) and followed our baggage on board the schooner, expecting to reach the factory before dusk. But alas! "there's many a slip 'twixt the cup and the lip," and we had not been long under weigh before the ebb tide began to run so strong against us as to preclude the possibility of our reaching the shore that night. There was no help for it, however, so down went the anchor to the bottom, and down went I to the cabin. Such a cabin! A goodly sized trunk, with a small table in it, and thé lid shut down, had about as much right to the name. It was awfully small; even *I* could not stand upright in it, though at the time I had only attained to the altitude of four feet eleven inches; yet here we were destined to pass the night; and a wretched night we did pass! We got over the first part tolerably, but when it began to grow late, our eyes began to grow heavy; then we yawned, and fidgeted, and made superhuman efforts to keep awake and seem happy; but it would not do. There were only two berths in the cabin; and, as so many gentlemen were present, Mrs G—— would not get into one of them, and declared she would sit up all night.   The gentlemen, on the other hand, could not be so impolite as to go to sleep while the only lady present sat up.   The case was desperate, so I went off to the hold, intending to lie down on a bale if I could find one. In my search, I tumbled on Mr W——, who had anticipated me, and found a convenient place whereon to lie. My search, however, was less successful ; not a place big enough for a cat to sleep in was to be found, so I was obliged to return to the cabin, where I found the unhappy inmates all winking and blinking at each other like owls in the sunshine.

These good folks, compassionating, I fancy, the sleepy " youngster," urged me to get into one of the berths ; but, feeling my dignity as a new-made man-of-business considerably compromised by their friendly advice, I would not think of so ungallant an action, and determined manfully to sit it out with the rest.   Nod went my head, bang against the wall, wakening them all up suddenly ; and then, after smiling faintly at the accident, I made another attempt at sleep again.   Flesh and blood could not stand this : I would have lain down on the floor, but alas ! it was too small.   At last I began to reason thus with myself : " Here are two capital beds with nobody in them ; it is the height of folly to leave them empty : but then what a selfish-looking thing to leave Mrs G—— sitting up !   After all, she *won't* go to bed.   Oh dear ! what *is* to be done ?" (Bang goes the head again.)

" You'd better turn in," says Mr G——. Again I
protest that I cannot think of it; but my eyes won't
keep open to look him in the face. At last my scruples,
I blush to say it, were overcome, and I allowed myself
to be half forced into the berth, while Mr R——, taking
advantage of the confusion thus occasioned, vanished into
the other like a harlequin. Poor Mr and Mrs G——
laid their innocent heads side by side upon the table,
and snored in concert.

How long I slept I know not; but, long before day,
a tremendous thumping awoke me, and after I had
collected myself enough to understand it, I found that
the schooner was grounding. "Oh!" thought I, and,
being utterly incapable of thinking or saying more, I
fell back on the pillow again sound asleep, and did not
awake till long after day-break.

The morning was beautiful; but we were still aground,
and from what the skipper said, there appeared to be
no prospect of getting ashore till the afternoon. Our
patience, however, was not tried so long; for, early in
the day, a boat came off from the factory to take us
ashore, but the missionaries preferred remaining in the
schooner. Mr C——, young W——, and I, gladly availed ourselves of the opportunity, and were soon sailing
with a fair breeze up Hayes River. We approached to
within a few yards of the shore; and I formed, at first
sight, a very poor opinion of the country which, two years
later, I was destined to traverse full many a weary hour
in search of the feathered inhabitants of the marshes.

The point of marsh, which was the first land we made,
was quite low, only a few feet above the sea, and studded
here and there with thick willows, but not a single tree.
Long lank grass covered it in every place, and afforded
ducks and geese shelter in the spring and autumn.   In
the centre of it, the ship-beacon, a tall ungainly looking
pile, rose upwards like a monster in the water: altogether,
a more desolate prospect could not well be imagined.

The banks of Hayes River are formed of clay, and
they improved a little in height and verdure as we
ascended; but still, wherever the eye turned, the same
universal flatness met the gaze.   The river was here
about two miles wide, and filled with shallows and sand-
banks, which render the navigation difficult for vessels
above fifty tons.

As we proceeded, a small bark canoe, with an Indian
and his wife in it, glided swiftly past us, and this was
the first Indian, and the first of these slender craft, I had
seen.   Afterwards, I became more intimately acquainted
with them than was altogether agreeable.

In a short time we reached the wooden wharf, which
had rather an imposing look, and projected a long way

into the water; but our boat passed this and made for a
small slip, on which two or three gentlemen were waiting
to receive us. My voyage was ended. The boat's keel
grated harshly on the gravel, and the next moment my
feet once more pressed *terra firma*. I stood at last on
the shores of the New World, a stranger in a strange land.

I do not intend to give a minute description of York
factory here, as a full account of it will be found in a
succeeding chapter. I shall, therefore, confine myself
to a slight sketch of the establishment, and my proceedings there, during a stay of about three weeks.

York factory is the principal depôt of the Northern
department, from whence all the supplies for the trade
are issued, and where all the returns of the department
are collected and shipped for England. As may be supposed, then, the establishment is a large one. There are
always between thirty and forty men resident at the
post, summer and winter; generally four or five clerks,
a postmaster, and a skipper for the small schooners; and
the whole is under the direction and superintendence of
a chief factor, or chief trader.

As the winter is very long, nearly eight months, and
the summer consequently very short, all the transport of
goods to, and returns from, the interior, must necessarily
be effected as quickly as possible. The consequence
is, that great numbers of men and boats are constantly
arriving from inland, and departing again during the
summer; and, as each brigade is commanded by a chief
factor, trader, or clerk, there is a constant succession of

new faces, which, after a long and dreary winter, during which the inhabitants never see any stranger, renders the summer months at York factory the most agreeable part of the year. The arrival of the ship from England, too, delights them with letters from *home,* which can only be received twice a year.

The fort (as all establishments in the Indian country, whether small or great, are called) is a large square, I should think about six or seven acres, inclosed within high stockades, and built on the banks of Hayes River, nearly five miles from its mouth. The houses are all of wood, and of course, have no pretension to architectual beauty; but their clean white appearance, and regularity, have a very pleasing effect on the eye. Before the front gate stand four large brass field-pieces; but these warlike instruments are only used for the purpose of saluting the ship with blank cartridge, on her arrival and departure, the decayed state of the carriages rendering it dangerous to load the guns with a full charge.

The country, as I said before, is flat and swampy, and the only objects that rise very prominently above the rest, and catch the wandering eye, are a lofty "out-look" of wood, painted black, from which to look out for the arrival of the ship; and a flag-staff, from which on Sundays the snowy folds of St George's flag flutter in the breeze.

Such was York factory in 1841, and as this description is sufficient to give a general idea of the place, I shall conclude it, and proceed with my narrative.

Mr H——, the chief factor then in charge, received us very kindly, and introduced us to some of the gentlemen standing beside him on the wharf. Mr C——, being also a chief factor, was then taken by him to the commissioned gentlemen's house, while young W—— and I, being apprentice clerks, were shown the young gentlemen's house,—or as the young gentlemen themselves call it, Bachelor's Hall,—and were told to make ourselves at home. To Bachelor's Hall, then, we proceeded, and introduced ourselves. The persons assembled there were the accountant, some clerks, the postmaster, and one or two others. Some of them were smoking, and some talking, and a pretty considerable noise they made too. Bachelor's Hall, indeed, was worthy of its name, being a place that would have killed any woman, so full was it of smoke, noise, and confusion.

After having made ourselves acquainted with everybody, I thought it time to present my letter of introduction to Mrs H——, who received me very kindly. I was much indebted to this lady for supplying me with several pairs of moccasins for my further voyage, without which I should have been badly off indeed; and had it not been for her kindness, I should, in all probability, have been allowed to depart very ill provided for the journey to Red River, for which I was desired to hold myself in readiness. Young W——, on the other hand, learned that he was to remain at York factory that winter, and was placed in the office the day after our arrival, when he commenced work for the first time. We had a long and sage conversation upon the subject the same evening, and I well remember congratulating him, with an extremely grave face, upon his having now begun to *do for himself.* Poor fellow, his subsequent travels in the country were long and perilous.

As I have now landed the reader in a new country, it may be well, before describing my voyage to Red River, to make him acquainted with the peculiarities of the service, and the people with whom he will, in imagination, have to associate.

CHAPTER II.

DESCRIPTION OF THE HUDSON'S BAY COMPANY, ETC.

N the year 1669, a company was formed in London, under the direction of Prince Rupert, for the purpose of prosecuting the fur trade in the regions surrounding Hudson's Bay. This company obtained a charter from Charles II., granting to them and their successors, under the name of "The Governor and Company of Adventurers trading into Hudson's Bay," the sole right of trading in all the country watered by rivers flowing into Hudson's Bay. The charter also authorised them to build and fit out men-of-war, establish forts, prevent any other company from carrying on trade with the natives in their territories, and required that they should do all in their power to promote discovery.

Armed with these powers, then, the Hudson's Bay Company established a fort near the head of James' Bay, and soon after, several others were built in different parts of the country; and soon the company began to spread and grow wealthy, and extended their trade far beyond the chartered limits.

With the internal economy of the company under the

superintendence of Prince Rupert, however, I am not
acquainted; but as it will be necessary to the reader's
forming a correct idea of the peculiarities of the country
and service, that he should know something of its character under the direction of the present active governor,
I shall give a brief outline of its arrangements.

Reader, you will materially assist me in my description, if you will endeavour to draw the following landscape on the retina of your mind's eye.

Imagine an immense extent of country, many hundred
miles broad, and many hundred miles long, covered
with dense forests, expanded lakes, broad rivers, and
mighty mountains; and all in a state of primeval sim-
plicity—undefaced by the axe of civilized man, and un-
tenanted by aught save a few roving hordes of Red
Indians, and myriads of wild animals. Imagine, amid
this wilderness, a number of small squares, inclosing
half-a-dozen wooden houses, and about a dozen men,
and, between each of these establishments, a space of
forest varying from fifty to three hundred miles long,
and you will have a pretty correct idea of the Hudson's
Bay Company's territories, and the number of, and distance between, their forts. The idea, however, may be
still more correctly obtained, by imagining populous
Great Britain converted into a wilderness and planted
in the middle of Rupert's Land; the company would, in
that case, build *three* forts in it, one at the Land's-end,
one in Wales, and one in the Highlands; so that in
Britain there would be but three hamlets, with a po-

pulation of some thirty men, half-a-dozen women, and a
few children! The company's posts extend, with these
intervals between, from the Atlantic to the Pacific
Ocean, and from within the Arctic Circle to the northern boundaries of the United States.

Throughout this immense country there are probably
not more ladies than would suffice to form half-a-dozen
quadrilles; and these, poor banished creatures! are
chiefly the wives of the principal gentlemen connected
with the fur trade. The rest of the female population
consist chiefly of half-breeds and Indians; the latter
entirely devoid of education, and the former as much
enlightened as can be expected from those whose life
is spent in such a country. Even these are not very
numerous, and yet, without them, the men would be in
a sad condition, for they are the only tailors and washer-
women in the country, and make all the mittens, moccas-
sins, fur caps, deer-skin coats, &c. &c., worn in the land.

There are one or two favoured spots, however, into
which a missionary or two have penetrated; and in Red
River settlement, the only colony in the company's territories, there are several Protestant churches and
clergymen, besides others of Roman Catholics.

The country is divided into four large departments
The Northern department, which includes all the establishments in the far north and frozen regions; the
Southern department, including those to the south and
east of this, the posts at the head of James' Bay and
along the shores of Lake Superior; the Montreal de-

partment, including the country in the neighbourhood of Montreal, up the Ottawa river, and along the north shore of the Gulf of St Lawrence and Esquimaux Bay ; and the Columbia department, which comprehends an immense extent of country to the west of the Rocky Mountains, including the Oregon territory, which, although the Hudson's Bay Company still trade in it, now belongs, as every one is aware, to the Americans.

These departments are divided into a number of districts, each under the direction of an influential officer, and these again are subdivided into numerous establishments, forts, posts, and outposts.

The name of *fort*, as already remarked, is given to nearly all the posts in the country, but some of them certainly do not merit the name ; indeed, few of them do. The only two in the country that are real, *bonâ fide* forts, are Fort Garry and the Stone fort in the colony of Red River, which are surrounded by stone walls with bastions at the corners. The others are merely defended by wooden pickets or stockades; and a few, where the Indians are quiet and harmless, are entirely destitute of defence of any kind. Some of the chief posts have a complement of about thirty or forty men ; but the most of them have only ten, five, four, and even *two*, besides the gentleman in charge. As, in most instances, these posts are planted in a wilderness far from men, and the inhabitants have only the society of each other, some idea may be formed of the solitary life led by many of the Company's servants.

The following is a list of the forts in the four different departments, as correctly given as possible; but, owing to the great number in the country, the constant abandoning of old, and establishing of new forts, it is difficult to get at a perfectly correct knowledge of their number and names :—

NORTHERN DEPARTMENT.

York Fort (the depôt.)
Churchill.
Severn.
Oxford House.
Trout Lake House.
Norway House.
Nelson River House.
Berens River House.
Red River Colony.
Fort Garry.
Stone Fort.
Manitoba House.
Fort Pelly.
Cumberland House.
Carlton House.
Fort Pitt.
Edmonton.
Rocky Mountain House.
Fort Assinaboine.
Jasper's House.
Henry's House.
Fort Chipewyan.
Fort Vermilion.
Fort Dunvegan.
Fort Simpson.
Fort Norman.
Fort Good Hope.
Fort Halkett.
Fort Resolution.
Peel's River.
Fort Alexander.
Rat Portage House.
Fort Frances.
Isle à la Crosse.

SOUTHERN DEPARTMENT.

Moose Factory (the depôt.)
Rupert's House.
Fort George.
Michiskan.
Albany.
Lac Seul.
Kinogomousse.
Matawagamingue.
Kuckatoosh.
New Brunswick.
Abitibi.
Temiscamingue.
Grand Lac.
Trout Lake.
Matarva.
Catuasicomica.
Lacloche.
Sault de Ste Maria.
Fort William.
Pic House.
Michipicoton.
Bachiwino.

Nepigon.

Temagamy.

Washwonaby.

Green Lake.

Pike Lake.

Missisague.

MONTREAL DEPARTMENT.

Lachine (the depôt.)

Goodbout.

Rivière du Moine.

Trinity River.

Lac des Allumettes.

Seven Islands.

Fort Coulonge.

Mingan.

Rivière Desert.

Nabisippi.

Lac des Sables.

Natosquene.

Lake of Two Mountains.

Musquarro.

Kikandatch.

Fort Nascopie.

Weymontachingue.

Mainewan Lake.

Rat River.

Sandy Banks.

Ashabmoushwan.

Gull Islands.

Chicoutimie.

Northwest River.

Lake St John's.

Rigolet.

Tadousac.

Kiboksk.

Isle Jérémie.

Eyelick.

Port Neuf.

COLUMBIA DEPARTMENT.

Fort Vancouver (the depôt.)

Flat-head Post.

Fort George.

Nisqually.

Nez Percé.

Alexandria.

Ockanagan.

Fort Chilcotin.

Colvile.

Fort James.

Fort Hall.

Fort Fluz Cuz.

Thompson's River.

Babine Lake.

Fort Langley.

And an agency in the Sand-

Cootanies.

wich Islands.

There are seven different grades in the service. First, the labourer, who is ready to turn his hand to any thing; to become a trapper, fisherman, or rough carpenter, at the shortest notice. He is generally employed in cutting firewood, for the consumption of the establishment at which he is stationed, shovelling snow from before the

doors, mending all sorts of damages to all sorts of things ;
and, during the summer months, in transporting furs
and goods between his post and the nearest depôt. Next
in rank is the interpreter. He is generally an intelligent
labourer, of pretty long standing in the service, who
having picked up a smattering of Indian, is consequently
very useful in trading with the natives. After the interpreter comes the postmaster. He is generally a pro-
moted labourer, who, for good behaviour or valuable
services, has been put upon a footing with the gentlemen
of the service, in the same manner that a private soldier
in the army is sometimes raised to the rank of a commissioned officer. At whatever station a postmaster may
happen to be placed, he is generally the most useful and
active man there. He is often placed in charge of one
of the many small stations, or outposts, throughout the
country. Next are the apprentice clerks—raw lads, who
come out fresh from school at home, with their mouths
agape at the wonders they behold in Hudson's Bay.
They generally, for the purpose of appearing manly,
acquire all the bad habits of the country as quickly as
possible, and are stuffed full of what they call fun, with a
strong spice of mischief mixed through. They generally,
however, become more sensible and sedate ere they spend
the first five years of their apprenticeship, after which
they attain to the rank of clerks. The clerk, after a
number of years' service (averaging from thirteen to
twenty), becomes a chief trader (or half-share holder),
and in a few years more, he attains the highest rank to

which any one can rise in the service, that of chief factor
(or share-holder.)

It is a strange fact, that three-fourths of the Company's servants are Scotch Highlanders, and Orkneymen.   There are very few Irishmen, and still fewer
English.   A great number, however, are half-breeds, and
French Canadians, especially among the labourers and
voyageurs.

From the great extent, and variety of feature, in the
country occupied by the fur-traders, they subsist, as may
be supposed, on widely different kinds of food.   In the
prairie, or plain countries, animal food is chiefly used, as
there, thousands of deer and bisons wander about, while
the woods are stocked with game and wild-fowl.   In other
places, however, where deer are scarce, and game not so
abundant, fish of various kinds are caught in the rivers
and lakes; and in other parts of the country they live
partly upon fish and partly upon animal food.   Vegetables are very scarce in the more northern posts, owing
to the severity of the winter, and consequent shortness of summer.   As the Company's servants are liable,
on the shortest notice, to be sent from one end of the
continent to another, they are quite accustomed to
change of diet;—one year rejoicing in buffalo-humps
and marrow-bones, in the prairies of the Saskatchewan,
and the next devouring hung white-fish, and scarce venison, in the sterile regions of Mackenzie's River, or varying
the meal with a little of that delectable substance often
spoken of by Franklin, Back, and Richardson as their

only dish—namely, *tripe-de-roche*—a lichen or moss which grows on the most barren rocks, and is only used as food in the absence of all other provisions.

During the first years of the Company, they were much censured for not carrying out the provision contained in the royal charter, that they should prosecute discovery as much as possible ; and it was even alleged that they endeavoured to prevent adventurers, not connected with themselves, from advancing in their researches. There is every reason to believe, however, that this censure was undeserved. A new company, recently formed in a wild country, could not at first be expected to have time or funds to advance the arduous and expensive cause of discovery. With regard to their having impeded the attempts of others, it is doubtful whether any one in the service ever did so; but even had such been the case, the unauthorised and dishonourable conduct of one or two of their servants, does not sanction the condemnation of the whole Company. Besides, discoveries were made in former days by Herne, and in later years by Dease and Simpson; so that, whatever might have been the case at first, there can be no doubt that the Company are doing much for the cause now. At this moment there is an expedition on foot, under one of their most experienced and talented servants, to complete the survey of the northern coast of America, left unfinished by the last-named explorers.

The trade carried on by the Company is in peltries of all sorts, oil, dried and salted fish, feathers, quills, &c. ;

and a list of some of their principal articles of commerce is subjoined :—

Beaver-skins.
Bear-skins, Black.
Ditto, Brown.
Ditto, White or Polar.
Ditto, Grizly.
Badger-skins.
Buffalo or Bison Robes.*
Castorum.†
Deer-skins, Rein.
Ditto, Red.
Ditto, Moose or Elk.
Ditto, parchment.
Feathers of all kinds.
Fisher-skins.
Goose-skins.
Fox-skins, Black.
Ditto, Silver.

Fox-skins, Cross.
Ditto, Red.
Ditto, White.
Ditto, Blue.
Ivory (tusks of the Walrus.)
Lynx-skins.
Marten-skins.
Musquash-skins.
Otter-skins.
Oil, Seal.
Ditto, Whale.
Swan-skins.
Salmon, salted.
Seal-skins.
Wolf-skins.
Wolverine-skins.

The most valuable of the furs mentioned in the above list is that of the *black fox*. This beautiful animal resembles in shape the common fox of England, but it is much larger, and jet black, with the exception of one or two white hairs along the back bone, and a pure white tuft on the end of the tail. A single skin sometimes brings from twenty-five to thirty guineas in the British market; but unfortunately they are very scarce. The

* The hide of the bison—or, as it is called by the fur-traders, the buffalo—when dressed on one side and the hair left on the other, is called a robe. Great numbers are sent to Canada, where they are used for sleigh wrappers in winter. In the Indian country they are often used instead of blankets.

† A substance procured from the body of the beaver.

silver fox differs from the black fox only in the number of white hairs with which its fur is sprinkled; and the more numerous the white hairs, the less valuable does it become. The *cross fox* is a cross between the black or silver and the red fox. The *red fox* bears a much inferior fur to the other kinds; yet it is a good article of trade, as this species is very numerous. These four kinds of foxes are sometimes produced in the same litter, the mother being a red fox. The *white fox* bears about the same value as the red, and is also very numerous, particularly on the shores of Hudson's Bay. The variety termed the *blue fox* is neither numerous nor very valuable. It is of a dirty blueish-gray colour, and seldom makes its appearance at the Company's posts.

Beaver, in days of yore, was the staple fur of the country; but alas! the silk hat has given it its death-blow, and the star of the beaver has now probably set for ever—that is to say, with regard to men; probably the animals themselves fancy that their lucky star has just risen. The most profitable fur in the country is that of the marten. It somewhat resembles the Russian sable, and generally maintains a steady price. These animals, moreover, are very numerous throughout most part of the Company's territories, particularly in Mac-kenzie's River, from whence great numbers are annually sent to England.

All the above animals and a few others are caught in steel and wooden traps by the natives; while deer, buffaloes, &c., are run down, shot, and snared in various

ways, the details of which will be found in another part
of this volume.

Trade is carried on with the natives by means of
a standard valuation, called in some parts of the country
a *castor*. This is to obviate the necessity of circulating
money, of which there is little or none excepting in the
colony of Red River. Thus an Indian arrives at a fort
with a bundle of furs, with which he proceeds to the
Indian trading-room. There the trader separates the
furs into different lots, and, valuing each at the standard
valuation, adds the amount together, and tells the Indian
(who has been gazing all the time at the procedure with
great interest and anxiety) that he has got fifty or sixty
castors; at the same time he hands the Indian fifty or
sixty little bits of wood in lieu of cash, so that the latter
may know, by returning these in payment of the goods
for which he really exchanges his skins, how fast his
funds are decreasing. The Indian then proceeds to
look round upon the bales of cloth, powder-horns, guns,
blankets, knives, &c., with which the shop is filled,
and after a good while makes up his mind to have a
small blanket. This being given him, the trader tells
him that the price is six castors; the purchaser hands
back six of his little bits of wood, and proceeds to select
something else. In this way he goes on till all his
wooden cash is expended, and then, packing up his
goods, departs to show his treasures to his wife, and
another Indian takes his place. The value of a castor is
from one to two shillings. The natives generally visit

the establishments of the Company twice a-year—once in October, when they bring in the produce of their autumn hunts, and again in March, when they come in with that of the great winter hunt.

The number of castors that an Indian makes in a winter hunt varies from fifty to two hundred, according to his perseverance and activity, and the part of the country in which he hunts. The largest amount I ever heard of was made by a man called Piaquata-Kiscum, who brought in furs, on one occasion, to the value of two hundred and sixty castors. The poor fellow was soon afterwards poisoned by his relatives, who were jealous of his superior abilities as a hunter, and envied him for the favour shown him by the white men.

After the furs are collected in spring at all the different outposts, they are packed in conveniently sized bales, and forwarded, by means of boats and canoes, to the three chief depôts on the sea-coast—namely, Fort Vancouver at the mouth of the Columbia river, on the shores of the Pacific; York Fort on the shores of Hudson's Bay; and Moose Factory, on the shores of James's Bay—from whence they are transported in the Company's ships to England. The whole country, in summer, is consequently in commotion with the passing and re-passing of brigades of boats laden with bales of merchandise and furs; the still waters of the lakes and rivers are rippled by the paddle and the oar; and the long-silent echoes, which have been slumbering in the icy embrace of a dreary winter, are now once more awakened by the merry voice and tuneful song of the hardy voyageur.

This slight sketch of the Hudson's Bay Company, and of the territories occupied by them, may for the present serve to give a sufficiently correct idea of the nature of the service and the appearance of the country : we shall now proceed to write of the Indians inhabiting these wild regions.

CHAPTER III.

NORTH AMERICAN INDIANS.—THEIR MANNERS AND CUSTOMS, ETC.

HE aborigines of North America are divided into a great number of nations or tribes, differing not only in their outward appearance, but also in their customs, and modes of life, and in some instances entertaining for each other a bitter and implacable hatred.

To describe the leading peculiarities of some of these tribes, particularly those called Crees, will be my object in the present chapter.

Some of the tribes are known by the following names— Crees, Seauteaux, Stone Indians, Sioux, Blackfeet, Chipewyans, Slave Indians, Crows, Flatheads, &c. Of these, the Crees are the quietest and most inoffensive; they inhabit the woody country surrounding Hudson's Bay; dwell in tents; never go to war; and spend their time in trapping, shooting, and fishing. The Seauteaux are similar to the Crees in many respects, and inhabit the country farther in the interior. The Stone Indians, Sioux, Blackfeet, Slave Indians, Crows, and Flatheads, inhabit the vast plains and forests in the interior of America, on the east and west of the Rocky Mountains, and live chiefly by the produce of the chase. Their country swarms with bisons, and varieties of deer, bears, &c., which they hunt, shoot, snare, and kill in various ways. Some of these tribes are well supplied with horses, with which they hunt the buffalo. This is a wild inspiriting chase, and the natives are very fond of it. They use the gun a good deal, but prefer the bow and arrow (in the use of which they are very expert) for the chase, and reserve the gun for warfare, many of them being constantly engaged in skirmishing with their enemies. As the Crees were the Indians with whom I had the most intercourse, I shall endeavour to describe my old friends more at length.

The personal appearance of the men of this tribe is not bad. Although they have not the bold daring carriage of the wilder tribes, yet they have active-looking figures, fine intelligent countenances, and a peculiar brightness in their dark eyes, which, from a constant habit of looking around them while travelling through the woods, are seldom for a moment at rest. Their jet black hair generally hangs in straight matted locks over their shoulders, sometimes ornamented with beads and pieces of metal, and occasionally with a few partridge feathers; but they seldom wear a hat or cap of any kind, except in winter, when they make clumsy imitations of foraging caps with furs,—preferring, if the weather be warm, to go about without any head-dress at all, or, if it be cold, using the large hood of their capotes as a covering. They are thin, wiry men, not generally very muscular in their proportions, but yet capable of enduring

great fatigue. Their average height is about five feet
five inches; and one rarely meets with individuals varying much from this average, nor with deformed people,
among them. The step of a Cree Indian is much longer
than that of a European, owing, probably, to his being
so much accustomed to walking through swamps and
forests, where it is necessary to take long strides. This
peculiarity becomes apparent when an Indian arrives at
a fort and walks along the hard ground inside the walls
with the trader, whose short, bustling, active step contrasts oddly with the long, solemn, ostrich-like stride of
the savage; which, however appropriate in the woods,
is certainly strange and ungraceful on a good road.

The summer dress of the Indian is almost entirely
provided for him by the Hudson's Bay Company; it
consists chiefly of a blue or gray cloth, or else a blanket
capote reaching below the knee, made much too loose for
the figure, and strapped round the waist with a scarlet
or crimson worsted belt. A very coarse blue striped
cotton shirt is all the under-clothing
they wear, holding trowsers to be quite
superfluous; in lieu of which they make
leggins of various kinds of cloth, which
reach from a few inches above the knee
down to the ankle. These leggins are
sometimes very tastefully decorated
with bead-work, particularly those of

the women, and are provided with flaps or wings on either
side, which have a pretty and novel appearance.

This costume, however, is slightly varied in winter. The blanket or cloth capote is then laid aside for one of smoked red-deer-skin, which has very much the appearance of chamois leather. This is lined with flannel, or some other thick warm substance, and edged with fur (more for ornament, however, than warmth) of different kinds. Fingerless mittens, with a place for the thumb are also adopted; and shoes or moccasins, of the same soft material. The moccasins are very beautiful, fitting the feet as tightly as a glove, and are tastefully ornamented with dyed porcupine quills and silk thread of various colours; at which work the women are particularly *au-fait*. As the leather of the moccasin is very thin,*

 blanket and flannel socks are worn underneath,— one, two, or even four pairs, according to the degree of cold; and in proportion as these socks are increased in number, the moccasin, of course, loses its elegant appearance. The annexed figure represents the moccasin under its most favourable aspect, without any sock beneath it at all.

* Many people at home have asked me how such *thin things* can keep out the wet of the snow. The reader must bear in mind that the snow, for nearly seven months, is not even *damp* for five minutes, so constant is the frost. When it becomes wet in spring, Europeans adopt ordinary English shoes, and Indians do not mind the wet.

The Indian women are not so good-looking as the men. They have an awkward slouching gait, and a downcast look,—arising, probably, from the rude treatment they experience from their husbands; for the North American Indians, like all other savages, make complete drudges of their women, obliging them to do all the laborious and dirty work, while they reserve the pleasures of the chase for themselves. Their features are sometimes good, but I never saw a really pretty woman among the Crees. Their colour, as well as that of the men, is a dingy brown, which, together with their extreme filthiness, renders them any thing but attractive. They are, however, quiet, sweet-tempered, and inoffensive creatures, destitute as well of artificial manners as of *stays*. Their dress is a gown, made without sleeves, and very scanty in the skirt, of coarse blue or green cloth; it reaches down to a little below the knee, below which their limbs are cased in leggins beautifully ornamented. Their whole costume, however, like that of the men, is almost always hid from sight by a thick blanket, without which the Indian seldom ventures abroad. The women usually make the top of the blanket answer the purpose of a head-dress; but when they wish to appear very much to advantage, they put on the cap represented in the accompanying illustration. It is a square piece of blue cloth, profusely decorated with different coloured beads, and merely sewed up at the top. They wear their hair in long straggling locks, which have not the slightest tendency to curl, and occasionally in queues or pigtails behind; but in this respect, as in every other, they are very careless of their personal appearance.

These primitive children of the forest live in tents of deer-skin or bark; and, sometimes, where these are scarce, of branches of trees. They are conically shaped, and are constructed thus:—the Indian and his family, (probably two wives and three or four children) arrive in their bark canoe at a pretty level spot, sheltered from the north wind, and conveniently situated on the banks of a small steam, where fish are plentiful, and pine branches (or brush), for the floor of his tent, abundant. Here he runs his canoe ashore, and carries his goods and chattels up the bank. His first business is to cut a number of long poles, and tie three of them at the top, spreading them out in the form of a tripod. He then piles all the other poles round these, at half-a-foot distance from each other, and thus incloses a circle of nearly fifteen or twenty feet in diameter. Over the poles (if he is a good hunter, and has plenty of deer-skins), he spreads the skin tent, leaving an opening at the top for the egress of the smoke. If the tent be a birch-bark one, he has it in separate rolls, which are spread over the poles, till the whole is covered. A small opening is left facing the river or lake, which serves for a doorway; and this is covered with an old blanket, a piece of deer-skin, or, in some instances, by a bison-skin or buffalo robe. The floor is covered with a layer of small pine branches, which serve for carpet and mattress; and in the centre is placed the wood fire, which, when blazing brightly, gives a warmth and comfort to the slight habitation that could scarcely be believed. Here the Indian spends a few days or weeks, according to the amount of game in the vicinity; and then removes to some other place, carrying with him the covering of the tent, but leaving the poles standing, as they would be cumbrous to carry in his small canoe, and thousands can be had at every place where he may wish to land.

The Indian canoe is an exceedingly light and graceful little craft, and well adapted for travelling in through a wild country, where the rivers are obstructed by long rapids, waterfalls, and shallows. It is so light that one man can easily carry it on his shoulders over the land, when a waterfall obstructs his progress; and as it only

sinks about four or six inches in the water, few places
are too shallow to float it.   The birch bark of which it
is made is about a quarter of an inch thick, and the
inside is lined with extremely thin flakes of wood, over
which a number of light timbers are driven, to give
strength and tightness to the machine.   In this frail

bark, which generally measures about twelve or fifteen
feet long, and from two to three feet broad in the middle, a whole Indian family of eight or ten souls will travel
hundreds of miles over rivers and lakes innumerable ;
now floating swiftly down a foaming rapid, and anon
gliding over the surface of a quiet lake, or *making a
portage* over-land when a rapid is too dangerous to
descend ; and, while the elders of the family assist in
carrying the canoe, the youngsters run about plucking
berries, and the shaggy little curs (one or two of which
are possessed by every Indian family) search for food, or

bask in the sun at the foot of the baby's cradle, which stands bolt upright against a tree, while the child gazes upon all these operations with serene indifference.

Not less elegant and useful than the canoe, is the snow-shoe, without which the Indian would be badly off indeed. It is not, as many suppose, used as a kind of *skate*, with which to *slide* over the snow, but as a machine to prevent, by its size and breadth, the wearer from sinking into the snow, which is so deep that, without the assistance of the snow-shoe, no one could walk a quarter of a mile through the woods in winter without being utterly exhausted.

It is formed of two thin pieces of light wood, which are tied at both ends, and spread out near the middle; thus making a kind of long oval, the interior of which is filled up with net-work of deer-skin threads. Strength is given to the frame by placing wooden bars across ; and it is fastened *loosely* to the foot by a slight line going over the toe.   In case, however, it may be supposed that by a shoe I mean an article something the size of a man's foot, it may be as well to state, that snow-shoes measure from *four* to *six feet* long, and from thirteen to twenty inches wide.   Notwithstanding their great size yet, from the extreme lightness of the material with which they are made, they are not at all

cumbrous; and, after a little practice, a traveller forgets
that he has them on, if the weather be good for such
walking.   Frosty weather is the best for snow-shoe travelling, as the snow is fine and dust-like, and falls through
the net-work.   If the weather is warm, the wet snow

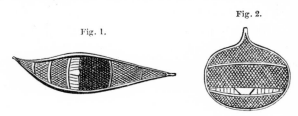

Fig. 1.   Fig. 2.

renders the shoe heavy, and the lines soon begin to gall
the feet.   The engraving above (fig. 1), represents the
kind most commonly used by the Crees, but they vary
in shape in different parts of the country, some times
taking the form represented in fig. 2.   On these shoes
an Indian will travel between twenty and thirty miles
a-day, and they often accomplish from thirty to forty,
when hard pressed.

   The food of the Indian varies according to circumstances.   Sometimes he luxuriates on deer, partridges,
and fat beaver; while at other times he is obliged to live
almost entirely on fish, and not unfrequently on *tripe-de-
roche*.   This substance, however, does no more than re-
tard his ultimate destruction by starvation; and, unless
he meets with something more nourishing, it cannot prevent it.   When starving, the Indian will not hesitate to
appease the cravings of hunger by resorting to canni-

balism ; and there were some old dames with whom I was myself acquainted, who had at different periods eaten several of their children. Indeed, some of them, it was said, had also eaten their husbands.

The following anecdote, related to me by a friend who spent many years of his life among the North American Indians, depicts one of the worst of these cases of cannibalism.

It was in the spring of —— that my friend, Mr C—— stood in the Indian Hall of one of the far-distant posts in Athabasca, conversing with a party of Chipewyan Indians, who had just arrived with furs from their winter hunting grounds. The large fires of wood, which sparkled and blazed cheerfully up the wide chimney, cast a bright light round the room, and shone upon the dusky countenances of the Chipewyans, as they sat gravely on the floor, smoking their spwagans in silence. A dark shade lowered upon every face, as if thoughts of an unpleasant nature disturbed their minds ; and so it was. A deed of the most revolting description had been perpetrated by an Indian of the Cree tribe, and they were preparing to relate the story to Mr C——.

After a short silence, an old Indian removed his pipe : and, looking round upon the others, as if to ask their consent to his becoming spokesman, related the particulars of the story, the substance of which I now give.

Towards the middle of winter, Wisagun, a Cree Indian, removed his encampment to another part of the country, as game was scarce in the place where he had been

residing. His family consisted of a wife, a son of eight
or nine years of age, and two or three children, besides
several of his relations ; in all, ten souls, including himself. In a few days they arrived at their new encamping
ground, after having suffered a great deal of misery by
the way, from starvation. They were all much exhausted
and worn out, but hoped, having heard that buffaloes
were in the vicinity, that their sufferings would soon be
relieved.

Here they remained several days without finding any
game, and they were reduced to the necessity of devouring their moccasins and leather coats, which were
rendered eatable by being singed over the fire. Soon
this wretched resource was also gone, and they were reduced to the greatest extremity, when a band of buffaloes
were descried, far away in the prairie, on the edge of
which they were encamped. All were instantly on the
qui vive. Guns were loaded, snow-shoes put on, and, in
ten minutes, the males of the hungry party set off after
the herd, leaving Wisagun's wife and children with
another girl in the tent. It was not long, however, before the famished party began to grow tired. Some of
the weakest dropped behind; while Wisagun, with his son
Natappe, gave up the chase, and returned to the encampment. They soon arrived at it, and Wisagun, peeping
in between the chinks of the tent, to see what the women
were doing, saw his wife engaged in cutting up one of
her own children, preparatory to cooking it. In a transport of passion, the Indian rushed forward and stabbed

her, and also the other woman; and then, fearing the
wrath of the other Indians, he fled to the woods. It may
be conceived what were the feelings of the remainder
of the party, when they returned, and found their relatives murdered. They were so much exhausted, however, by previous suffering, that they could only sit down
and gaze on the mutilated bodies in despair. During
the night, Wisagun and Natappe returned stealthily to
the tent; and, under cover of the darkness, murdered
the whole party, as they lay asleep. Soon after this, the
two Indians were met, by another party of savages, in
good condition; although, from the scarcity of game, the
others were starving. The former accounted for this,
however, by saying that they had fallen in with a deer
not long ago; but that, before this had happened, all the
rest of the family had died of starvation.

It was the party who had met the two Indians wandering in the plains, that now sat round the fire, relating
the story to Mr C——.

While they were yet speaking, the hall door slowly
opened, and Wisagun, gaunt and cadaverous, the very
impersonation of famine, slunk into the room, with Natappe, and seated himself in a corner near the fire. Mr
C—— soon learned the truth of the foregoing story from
his own lips; but he excused his horrible deed by saying,
that the *most* of his relations had died before he ate them.

In a few days after this the party of Indians took their
departure from the house, to proceed to their village in
the forest: and, shortly after, Wisagun and Natappe also

left, to rejoin their tribe. The news of their deeds, however, had gone before them, so they were received very coldly; and soon after Wisagun pitched his tent, they all, with one accord, removed to another place, as though it were impossible to live happily under the shadow of the same trees. This exasperated Wisagun so much, that he packed up his tent and goods, launched his canoe, and then, before going off, went up to the village, and told them that it was true he had killed all his relatives, and that he was a conjuror, and had both power and inclination to conjure them to death too. He then strode down to the banks of the river, and, embarking with his son, shot out into the stream. The unhappy man had acted rashly in his anger. There is nothing more dangerous than to threaten to kill a savage, as he will certainly endeavour to kill the person who threatens him, in order to render the execution of his purpose impossible. Wisagun and his son had no sooner departed, than two men coolly took up their guns, and embarking in an empty canoe, followed after them. Upon arriving at a secluded spot, one of them raised his gun, and fired at Wisagun, who fell over the side of the canoe, and sank to rise no more. With the rapidity of thought, Natappe seized his father's gun, sprang ashore, and bounded up the bank; a shot was fired, which went through the fleshy part of his arm, and the next moment he was behind a tree. Here he called out to the Indians, who were reloading their guns, not to kill him, and he would tell them all. After a little consideration, they agreed to spare him: he embarked with them, and was taken afterwards to the fort, where he remained many years in the Company's service.

Instances of cannibalism are not unusual among the Indian tribes; but they do not resort to it from choice, and, indeed, never but when urged to it by the irrepressible cravings of hunger.

All the tribes of Indians are fond of spirits; and in former times, when the distribution of rum and whisky to the natives was found necessary to compete with other companies, the use of the " fire-water " was carried to a fearful extent. Since Sir George Simpson has been governor, however, the distribution of spirits has been almost entirely given up ; and this has proved a most beneficial measure for the poor Indians.

Tobacco also is consumed by them in great quantities; indeed, the pipe is seldom out of the Indian's mouth. If he is not hunting, sleeping, or eating, he is sure to be smoking. A peculiar kind of shrub is much used by them, mixed with tobacco, partly for the purpose of making it go far, and partly because they can smoke more of it at a time with impunity.

The Indian is generally very lazy, but can endure great fatigue and much privation when necessary. He can go longer without eating than a European, and from the frequent fasts he has to sustain, he becomes accustomed, without injury, to eat more at a meal than would kill a white man. The Indian children exhibit this power in a very extraordinary degree, looking sometimes wretchedly thin and miserable, and an hour

or two afterwards waddling about with their little
stomachs swollen almost to bursting!

When an Indian wants a wife, he goes to the *fair* one's
father and asks his consent. This being obtained, he
informs the young lady of the circumstance, and then
returns to his wigwam, whither the bride follows him, and
installs herself as mistress of the house without further
ceremony. Generally speaking, Indians content themselves with one wife, but it is neither looked upon as
unusual nor improper should he take two, or even three
wives. The great point to settle is his ability to support
them. Thus, a bad hunter can only afford one wife, while
a good one may have three or four.

If an old man or woman of the tribe becomes infirm,
and unable to proceed with the rest when travelling, he
or she, as the case may be, is left behind in a small tent
made of willows, in which are placed a little firewood,
some provisions, and a vessel of water. Here the unhappy wretch remains in solitude till the fuel and provisions are exhausted, and then dies. Should the tribe
be in their encampment when an Indian dies, the deceased is buried sometimes in the ground and sometimes
in a rough wooden coffin raised a few feet from the ground.
They do not now bury guns, knives, &c., with their dead
as they once did, probably owing to their intercourse
with white men.

The Supreme Being among the Indians is called
Manitow; but he can scarcely be said to be worshipped
by them, and the few ideas they have of his attributes

are imperfect and erroneous. Indeed, no religious rites exist among them, unless the unmeaning mummery of the medicine tent can be looked upon as such. Of late years, however, missionaries, both of the church of England and the Wesleyans, have been exerting themselves to spread the Christian religion among these tribes, than whom few savages can be more unenlightened or morally degraded; and there is reason to believe that the light of the gospel is now beginning to shine upon them with beneficial influence.

There is no music in the soul of a Cree, and the only time they attempt it is when gambling, of which they are passionately fond, when they sing a kind of monotonous chant accompanied with a noisy rattling on a tin kettle. The celebrated war-dance is now no longer in existence among this tribe. They have wisely renounced both war and its accompaniments long ago. Among the wilder inhabitants of the prairies, however, they are still in vogue, with all the dismal accompaniments of killing, scalping, roasting, and torturing, that distinguished American warfare a hundred years ago.

The different methods by which the Indian succeeds in snaring and trapping animals are numerous. A good idea of these may be had by following an Indian in his rounds.

Suppose yourself, gentle reader, standing at the gate of one of the forts in Hudson's Bay, watching a savage arranging his snow-shoes preparatory to entering the gloomy forest. Let us walk with this Indian while he visits his traps.

The night is very dark, as the moon is hid by thick
clouds, yet it occasionally breaks out sufficiently to
illumine our path to Stemaw's wigwam, and to throw
the shadows of the neighbouring trees upon the pale
snow, which *crunches* under our feet as we advance,
owing to the intense cold. No wind breaks the stillness
of the night, or shakes the lumps of snow off the branches
of the neighbouring pines or willows; and nothing is
heard save the occasional crackling of the trees as the
severe frost acts upon their branches. The tent at
which we soon arrive is pitched at the foot of an immense tree, which stands in a little hollow where the
willows and pines are luxuriant enough to afford a
shelter from the north wind. Just in front, a small path
leads to the river, of which an extensive view is had
through the opening, showing the long fantastic shadows
of huge blocks and mounds of ice cast upon the white
snow by the flickering moonlight. A huge chasm, filled
with fallen trees and mounds of snow, yawns on the left
of the tent, and the ruddy sparks of fire which issue
from a hole in its top throw this and the surrounding
forest into deeper gloom. The effect of this wintry
scene upon the mind is melancholy in the extreme—
causing it to fly over the bleak and frozen plains, and
visit again the warm fireside and happy faces in a far
distant home; and yet there is a strange romantic
attraction for the wild woods mingled with this feeling
that gradually brings the mind back again, and makes
us impatient to begin our walk with the Indian. Sud-

denly the deer-skin robe that covers the aperture of the
wigwam is raised, and a bright stream of warm light
gushes out, tipping the dark green points of the opposite
trees, and mingling strangely with the paler light of the
moon—and Stemaw stands erect in the front of his solitary home, to gaze a few moments on the sky and judge
of the weather, as he intends to take a long walk before
laying his head upon his capote for the night. He is
dressed in the usual costume of the Cree Indians: a
large leathern coat, very much overlapped in front, and
fastened round his waist with a scarlet belt, protects his
body from the cold. A small rat-skin cap covers his
head, and his legs are cased in the ordinary blue cloth
leggins. Large moccasins, with two or three pair of
blanket socks, cover his feet, and a pair of fingerless
mittens, made of deer-skin, completes his costume. After
having stood for a few minutes wrapped in contemplation
of the heavens, the Indian proceeds to prepare himself
for the walk. First he sticks a small axe in his belt,
which serves as a counterpoise to a large hunting-knife
and fire-bag which depend from the other side. He
then slips his feet through the lines of his snow-shoes,
and throws the line of a small hand-sledge over his
shoulder. The hand-sledge is a thin flat slip or plank
of wood, from five to six feet long by one foot broad,
and is turned up at one end. It is extremely light, and
Indians invariably use it while visiting their traps, for
the purpose of dragging home the animals or game they
may have caught. Having attached this, then, to his

back, he stoops to receive his gun from his faithful *squaw*,* who has been watching his operations through a hole in the tent; and throwing it on his shoulder, strides off, without uttering a word, across the moonlit space in front of the tent, and turning into a small narrow track, that leads down the darkravine before mentioned, disappears in the dark shades of the forest. Soon he reaches the termination of the track (which had been made for the purpose of reaching some good dry trees for firewood), and, stepping into the deep snow with the long, regular, firm tread of one accustomed to snow-shoe walking, he winds his way rapidly through the thick stems of the surrounding trees, and turns aside the smaller branches of the bushes.

The forest is now almost quite dark, as the foliage over head has become so dense that the moon only penetrates through it in a few places, causing the spots on which it falls to shine with a strange phosphoric light, and rendering the surrounding masses more dark by contrast. The faint outline of an old snow-shoe track, which was at first discernible, is now quite invisible; but still Stemaw moves forward with rapid, noiseless step, as sure of his way as if he saw a broad beaten track before him. In this manner he moves on for nearly two miles, sometimes stooping to examine closely the newly made track of some wild animal, and occasionally giving a glance at

---

* *Squeiaw* is the Indian for a woman. *Squaw* is the English corruption of the word, and is used to signify a wife.

the sky through the openings in the leafy canopy above him, when a faint sound among the bushes ahead brings him to a full stop. He listens attentively, and a faint sound, like the rattling of a chain, is heard proceeding from the recesses of a dark wild-looking hollow a few paces in front. Another moment, and the rattle is again distinctly heard: a slight smile of satisfaction crosses Stemaw's dark visage, for one of his traps had been set in that place, and he knows that something has been caught. Quickly descending the slope, he enters the bushes from whence the sound proceeds, and pauses when within a yard or two of his trap to peer through the gloom. A cloud passes off the moon, and a faint ray reveals, it may be, a beautiful black fox caught in the snare. A slight blow on the snout from Stemaw's axe-handle kills the unfortunate animal; in ten minutes more it is tied to his sledge, the trap re-set and again

covered over with snow, so that it is almost impossible to tell that any thing is there; and the Indian pursues his way.

The steel trap used by the Indians is almost similar to the ordinary rat-trap of England, with this difference, that it is a little larger, is destitute of teeth, and has two springs in place of one. A chain is attached to one spring for the purpose of fixing a weight to the trap, so that the animal caught may not be able to drag it far from the place where it was set. The track in the snow enables the hunter to find his trap again. It is generally set so that the jaws, when spread out flat, are exactly on a level with the snow. The chain and weight are both hid, and a thin layer of snow spread on top of the trap. The bait (which generally consists of chips of a frozen partridge, rabbit, or fish) is then scattered around in every direction; and, with the exception of this, nothing distinguishes the spot. Foxes, beavers, wolves, lynx, and other animals are caught in this way, sometimes by a fore-leg, sometimes by a hind-leg, and sometimes by two legs at once, and occasionally by the nose. Of all these ways the Indians prefer catching by two legs, as there is then not the slightest possibility of the animal escaping. When foxes are caught by one leg, they often *eat it off* close to the trap, and escape on the other three. I have frequently seen this happen; and I once saw a fox caught which had evidently escaped in this way, as one of its legs was gone, and the stump healed up and covered again with hair. When they are caught by the nose they are almost sure to escape, unless taken out of the trap very soon after being caught, as their snouts are so sharp or wedge-like that they can pull them from between the jaws of the trap with the greatest ease.

Having now described the way of using this machine, we will rejoin Stemaw, whom we left on his way to the next trap. There he goes, moving swiftly over the snow mile after mile as if he could not feel fatigue, turning aside now and then to visit a trap, and giving a short grunt when nothing is in it, or killing the animal when caught, and tying it on the sledge. Towards midnight, however, he begins to walk more cautiously, examines the priming of his gun, and moves the axe in his belt as if he expected to meet some enemy suddenly. The fact is, that close to where he now stands are two traps which he set in the morning close to each other for the purpose of catching one of the formidable coast wolves. These animals are so sagacious that they will scrape all round a trap, let it be ever so well set, and, after eating all the bait, leave it. Indians consequently endeavour in every possible way to catch them, and, among others, by setting *two* traps close together; so that, while the wolf is scraping at one, he may perhaps put his foot in the other. It is in this way that Stemaw's traps are set; and he now advances cautiously towards them with the gun in the hollow of his left arm. Slowly he advances peering through the bushes, but nothing is visible: suddenly a branch crashes under his snow-shoe, and a large wolf bounds from the snow towards him with a savage growl landing almost at his feet. A single glance, however, shows the Indian that both traps are on his legs, and that the chains prevent him from advancing farther. He therefore, placing his gun against a tree, draws his axe from the belt, and advances to kill the animal. It is an undertaking, however, of some difficulty. The fierce brute, which is larger than a Newfoundland dog, strains every nerve and sinew to break its chains ; while its eyes glisten in the uncertain light, and foam curls from its blood-red mouth. Now it retreats as the Indian advances, grinning horribly as it goes ; and anon, as the chains check its farther retreat, it springs with fearful growl towards Stemaw, who slightly wounds it with his axe, as he jumps backward just in time to save himself from the infuriated animal, which catches in its fangs the flap of his leggin, and tears it from his limb. Again Stemaw advances, and the wolf retreats and again springs on him, but without success. At last, as the wolf glances for a moment to one side—apparently to see if there is no way of escape—quick as lightning the axe flashes in the air, and descends with stunning violence on its head : another blow follows, and in five minutes more the animal is fastened to the sledge.

This, however, has turned out a more exhausting business than Stemaw expected ; so he determines to encamp and rest for a few hours. Selecting a large pine, whose spreading branches cover a tolerably large space of ground free from underwood, he proceeds to scrape away the snow with his snow-shoe. Silently but busily he labours for a quarter of an hour ; and then, after having cleared a space about seven or eight feet in

diameter, and nearly four feet deep, he cuts down a
number of small branches, which he strews on the bottom
of the encampment, till all the snow is covered. This
done, he fells two or three of the nearest trees, cuts them
up into lengths of about five feet long, and piles them at
the root of the tree. A light is soon applied to the pile,
and up glances the ruddy flame, crackling among the
branches overhead, and sending thousands of bright
sparks into the air. No one who has not seen it can have
the least idea of the change that takes place in the
appearance of the woods at night, when a large fire is
suddenly lighted. Before, all was cold, silent, chilling,
gloomy, and desolate, and the pale snow looked unearthly
in the dark. Now, a bright ruddy glow falls upon the
thick stems of the trees, and penetrates through the
branches overhead, tipping those nearest the fire with a
ruby tinge, that actually warms one to look at. The
white snow changes to a beautiful pink, while the stems
of the trees, bright and clearly visible near at hand,
become more and more indistinct in the distance, till they
are lost in the black background. The darkness, however, need not be seen from the encampment, for, when
the Indian lies down, he will be surrounded by the snow
walls, which sparkle in the firelight as if set with diamonds. It does not melt either, as might be expected.
The frost is much too intense for that, and nothing melts
except the snow quite close to the fire. Stemaw has
now concluded his arrangements : a small piece of dried
deer's meat, which he brought with him, warms before the

blaze ; and while this is preparing, he spreads his green blanket on the ground, and proceeds to fill a stone callumet (or pipe with a wooden stem) with tobacco, mixed with a kind of weed prepared by himself. The white smoke from this soon mingles with the thicker volumes from the fire, which curl up through the branches into the sky, now shrouding him in their wreaths, and then, as the bright flame obtains the mastery, leaving his dark face and coal-black eyes shining in the warm light. No one enjoys a pipe more than an Indian ; and Stemaw's tranquil visage, wreathed in tobacco smoke, as he reclines at full length under the spreading branches of the pine, and allows the white vapour to pass slowly out of his mouth *and nose*, certainly gives one an excellent idea of savage enjoyment.

Leaving him here, then, to solace himself with a pipe, preparatory to resting his wearied limbs for the night, we will change the hour, and conduct the reader to a different scene.

It is now day. The upper edge of the sun has just risen, red and frosty-looking, in the east, and countless myriads of icy particles glitter on every tree and bush, in its red rays ; while the white tops of the snow-drifts, which dot the surface of the small lake at which we have just arrived, are tipped with the same rosy hue. The ake is of considerable breadth, and the woods on its opposite shore are barely visible. An unbroken coat of pure white snow covers its entire surface, while here and there a small islet, covered with luxuriant evergreens, attracts the eye, and breaks the sameness of the scene. At the extreme left of the lake, where the points of a few bullrushes and sedgy plants appear above the snow, are seen a number of small earthy mounds, in the immediate vicinity of which the trees and bushes are cut and barked in many places, while some of them are nearly cut down. This is a colony of beaver. In the warm months of summer and autumn, this spot is a lively stirring place, as the beavers are then employed *nibbling* down trees and bushes, for the purpose of repairing their dams, and supplying their store-houses with food. The bark of willows is their chief food, and all the bushes in the vicinity are more or less cut through by these persevering little animals. Their dams, however, (which are made for the purpose of securing to themselves a constant sufficiency of water) are made with large trees ; and stumps will be found, if you choose to look for them, as thick as a man's leg, which the beavers have entirely nibbled through, and dragged by their united efforts many yards from where they grew.

Now, however, no sign of animal life is to be seen, as the beaver keep within doors all winter ; yet I venture to state that there are many now asleep under the snow before us. It is not, reader, merely for the purpose of showing you the outside of a beaver-lodge that I have brought you such a distance from human habitations. Be patient and you shall soon see more. Do you observe that small black speck moving over the white surface of the lake, far away on the horizon ? It looks like a

crow, but the forward motion is much too steady and
constant for that.   As it approaches it assumes the form
of a man, and at last the figure of Stemaw, dragging his
empty sleigh behind him, (for he has left his wolf and
foxes in the last night's encampment, to be taken up
when returning home,) becomes clearly distinguishable
through the dreamy haze of the cold wintry morning.
He arrives at the beaver-lodges, and, I warrant, will
soon create some havoc among the inmates.

His first proceeding is to cut down several stakes,
which he points at the ends.   These are driven, after he
has cut away a good deal of ice from around the beaver-
lodge, into the ground between it and the shore.   The
reason of this is to prevent the beaver from running
along the passage which they always have from their
lodges to the shore, where their store-house is kept,
which would make it necessary to excavate the whole
passage.   The beaver, if there are any, being thus im-
prisoned in the lodge, the hunter next proceeds to stake
up the opening into the store-house on shore, and so im-
prison those that may have fled there for shelter, on
hearing the noise of his axe at the other house.   Things
being thus arranged to his entire satisfaction, he takes
an instrument called an ice-chisel, which is a bit of steel
about a foot long, by one inch broad, fastened to the end
of a stout pole, wherewith he proceeds to dig through
the lodge.   This is by no means an easy operation ; and
although he has covered the snow around him with great
quantities of mud and sticks, yet his work is not half

finished. In process of time, however, the interior of
the hut is laid bare, and the Indian, stooping down, gives
a great pull, when out comes a large, fat, sleepy beaver,
which he flings sprawling on the snow. Being thus
unceremoniously awakened from its winter nap, the
shivering animal looks languidly round, and even goes
the length of making a face at Stemaw, by way of
showing its teeth, for which it is rewarded with a blow
on the head from the pole of the ice-chisel, which puts
an end to it. In this way several more are killed, and
packed on the sleigh. Stemaw then turns his face towards his encampment, where he collects the game previously left there; and away he goes at a tremendous
pace, dashing the snow in clouds from his snow-shoes,
as he hurries over the trackless wilderness to his forest
home.

Near his tent, he makes a detour to visit a marten
trap; where, however, he finds nothing. This trap is of
the simplest construction, being composed of two logs,
the one of which is supported over the other by means
of a small stick, in such a manner that when the marten
creeps between the two and pulls the bait, the support
is removed and the upper log falls on and crushes it
to death.

In half-an-hour the Indian arrives at his tent, where
the dark eyes of his wife are seen gazing through a
chink in the covering, with an expression that denotes
immense joy at the prospect of gorging for many days
on fat beaver, and having wherewithal to purchase beads

and a variety of ornaments from the white men, upon the occasion of her husband and herself visiting the posts of the fur-traders, in the following spring.

I must now crave the reader's pardon for this long digression, and beg him to recollect, that at the end of the first chapter, I left myself awaiting orders to depart for Red River, to which settlement we will now proceed.

CHAPTER IV.

VOYAGE FROM YORK FACTORY TO RED RIVER.

OMEWHERE about the beginning of September, Mr C——, Mr and Mrs G——, Mr R——, and myself, set out with the *Portage la Loche* brigade, for the distant colony of Red River. The Portage la Loche brigade usually numbers six or seven boats, adapted for inland travelling, where the navigation is obstructed by rapids, waterfalls, and cataracts, to surmount which, boats and cargo are carried overland by the crews. These carrying places are called *portages,* and between York Factory and Red River there are upwards of thirty-six, of various lengths. Besides these, there are innumerable rapids, up which the boats have to be pushed, inch by inch, with poles, for miles together; so that we had to look forward to a long and tedious voyage.

The brigade with which we left York Factory usually leaves Red River about the end of May, and proceeds to Norway House, where it receives Athabasca and M'Kenzie's River outfits. It then sets out for the interior, and upon arriving at Portage la Loche, the different boats land their cargoes, while the M'Kenzie's River boats, which came to meet them, exchange their furs for the outfits. The brigade then begins to retrace its way, and returns to Norway House, whence it proceeds to York Factory, where it arrives about the commencement of September, lands the furs, and receives part of the Red River outfit, with which it sets out for that place as soon as possible.

With this brigade, then, we started from York Factory, with a cheering song from the men in full chorus. They were in good spirits, being about to finish the long voyage, and return to their families at Red River, after an absence of nearly five months, during which time they had encountered and overcome difficulties that would have cooled the most sanguine temperament; but these hardy Canadians and half-breeds are accustomed to such voyages from the age of fifteen or sixteen, and think no more of them than other men do of ordinary work.

Mr C—— and I travelled together in the guide's boat; Mr and Mrs G—— in another, and Mr R—— in a third by himself. We took the lead, and the others followed as they best could. Such was the order of march in which we commenced the ascent of Hayes River.

It may not be uninteresting here to describe the *matériel* of our voyage.

Our boat, which was the counterpart of the rest, was built in a manner adapted to the travelling in the country. It was long, broad, and shallow, capable of carrying forty hundredweight, and nine men, besides three or four passengers, with provisions for themselves and the crew. It did not, I suppose, draw more than three feet of water when loaded, perhaps less, and was moreover very light for its size. The cargo consisted of bales, being the goods intended for the Red River sale-room and trading-shop. A rude mast and tattered sail lay along the seats, ready for use, should a favourable breeze spring up; but this seldom occurred, the oars being our chief dependence during the greater part of the voyage.

The provisions of the men consisted of pemican and flour; while the passengers revelled in the enjoyment of a ham, several cured buffalo tongues, tea, sugar, butter, and biscuit, and a little brandy and wine, wherewith to warm us in cold weather, and to cheer the crew with a dram after a day of unusual exertion. All our provisions were snugly packed in a case and basket, made expressly for the purpose.

Pemican being a kind of food with which people in the civilised world are not generally acquainted, I may as well describe it here.

It is made by the buffalo hunters of the Red River, Swan River, and Saskatchewan prairies; more particularly by those of Red River, where many of the colonists spend a great part of the year in pursuit of the buffalo. They make it thus: having shot a buffalo (or bison), they cut off lumps of his flesh, and slitting it up into flakes or layers, hang it up in the sun to dry. In this state it is often made up into packs, and sent about the country to be consumed as dried meat; but when *vemican* is wanted it has to go through another process.　When dry, the meat is pounded between two stones till it is broken into small pieces; these are put into a bag made of the animal's hide, with the hair on the outside, and well mixed with melted grease; the top of the bag is then sewed up and the pemican allowed to cool.　In this state it may be eaten without being cooked; but the voyageurs, who subsist on it when travelling, mix it with a little flour and water and then boil it; in which state it is known throughout the country by the elegant name of *robbiboo*.　Pemican is good wholesome food, will keep fresh for a great length of time, and were it not for its unprepossessing appearance, and a good many buffalo hairs mixed with it, through the carelessness of the hunters, would be very palatable.　After a time, however, one becomes accustomed to those little peculiarities.

It was late in the afternoon when we left York Factory; and, after travelling a few miles up Hayes River, put ashore for the night.

We encamped upon a rough gravelly piece of ground, as there was no better in the neighbourhood; so that my first night in the woods did not hold out the prospect of being a very agreeable one.　The huge log fires, however, soon blazed cheerily up, casting a ruddy glow upon the surrounding foliage and the wild uncouth figures of the voyageurs, who, with their long dark hair hanging in luxuriant masses over their bronzed faces, sat or reclined round the fires, smoking their pipes and chatting with as much carelessness and good-humour, as if the long and

arduous journey before them never once entered their
minds. Our tent, and those of our travelling companions,
were pitched on the most convenient spot we could find;
and when supper was spread out, and a candle lighted,
(which, by the way, the strong blaze of our camp-fire
rendered quite unnecessary,) and Mr C——, seating
himself upon a pile of cloaks, blankets, and cushions,
looked up with a broad grin on his cheerful, good-
humoured countenance, and called me to supper, I
began to think, that if all travelling in Hudson's Bay
were like this, a voyage of discovery to the North
Pole would be a mere pleasure trip! Alas! in after
years I found it was not always thus.

Supper was soon disposed of, and having warmed ourselves at the fire, and ventured on a few rash prophecies
on the probable weather of the morrow, we spread our
blankets over an oiled cloth, and lay lovingly down together; Mr C—— to snore vociferously, and I to dream
of home.

At the first blush of day I was awakened by the loud
halloo of the guide, who with the voice of a Stentor gave
vent to a "*Lève! lève! lève!*" that roused the whole
camp in less than two minutes. Five minutes more suf-
ficed to finish our toilet, (for, be it known, Mr C—— and
I had only taken off our coats,) tie up our blankets, and
embark. In ten minutes we were once more pulling
slowly up the current of Hayes River.

The missionaries turned out to be capital travellers,
and never delayed the boats a moment; which is saying

a good deal for them, considering the short space of time allowed for dressing. As for the hardy voyageurs, they slept in the same clothes in which they had wrought during the day, each with a single blanket round him, in the most convenient spot he could find. A few slept in pairs, but all reposed under the wide canopy of heaven.

Morning is always the most disagreeable part of the traveller's day. The cold dews of the past night render the air chilly, and the gloom tends greatly to depress the spirits. As I became acquainted with this mode of travelling, I became more knowing, and when there was not much probability of being interrupted by portages, I used to spread out my blanket in the stern of the boat, and snooze till breakfast time. The hour for breakfast used to vary, according as we arrived late or early at an eligible spot. It was seldom earlier than seven, or later than nine o'clock.

Upon the occasion of our first breakfast in the woods, we were fortunate. The sun shone brightly on the surrounding trees and bushes; the fires blazed and crackled; the pots boiled, and cooks worked busily on a green spot, at the side of a small bay or creek, in which the boats floated quietly, scarce rippling the surface of the limpid water. A little apart from the men, two white napkins marked the spot where we were to breakfast, and the busy appearance of our cook gave hopes that we should not have to fast much longer. The whole scene was indescribably romantic and picturesque, and worthy of delineation by a more experienced pencil than mine.

Breakfast was a repetition of the supper of the night before; the only difference being that we ate it by daylight, in the open air, instead of by candle-light, under the folds of our canvass tent. After it was over, we again embarked, and proceeded on our way.

The men used to row for a space of time, denominated a *pipe*, so called from the circumstance of their taking a smoke at the end of it. Each *spell* lasted for nearly two hours, during which time they rowed without intermission. The *smoke* usually occupied five or ten minutes, after which they pulled again for two hours more, and so on. While travelling in boats, it is only allowable to put ashore for breakfast; so, about noon, we had a cold dinner in the boat; and, as our appetites began to be sharpened by exposure to the fresh air, we enjoyed it pretty well.

In a couple of days we branched off into Steel River, and began to ascend it. The current here was more rapid than that of Hayes River; so much so, indeed, that our oars being useless, we were obliged to send the men ashore with the tracking line. Tracking, as it is called, is dreadfully harassing work. Half of the crew go ashore, and drag the boat slowly along, while the other half go to sleep. After an hour's walk, the others then take their turn; and so on, alternately, during the whole day.

The banks of the river were high, and very precipitous; so that the poor fellows had to scramble along, sometimes close to the water's edge, and sometimes high up the

bank, on ledges so narrow that they could scarcely find a
footing, and where they looked like flies on a wall. The
banks, too, being composed of clay or mud, were very soft,
rendering the work disagreeable and tiresome ; but the
light-hearted voyageurs seemed to be quite in their element, and laughed and joked, while they toiled along,
playing tricks with each other, and plunging occasionally
up to the middle in mud, or the neck in water, with as
much nonchalance as if they were jumping into bed.

On the fifth day after leaving York Factory, we arrived at the Rock Portage. This is the first on the route,
and it is a very short one.   A perpendicular water-fall,
eight or ten feet high, forms an effectual barrier to the
upward progress of the boats by water ; so that the only
way to overcome the difficulty, is to carry every thing
across the flat rock, from which the portage derives its
name, and reload at the upper end.

Upon arriving, a novel and animating scene took place.
Some of the men, jumping ashore, ran briskly to and fro,
with enormous burdens on their backs ; while others
hauled and pulled the heavy boats slowly up the cataract,
hallooing and shouting all the time, as if they wished to
drown the thundering noise of the water, which boiled
and hissed furiously around the rocks on which we stood.
In about half an hour our boat, and one or two others,
had passed the falls ; and we proceeded merrily on our
way, with spirits elevated in proportion to the elevation
of our bodies.

It was here that I killed my first duck ; and well do I

remember the feeling of pride with which I contemplated
the achievement. That I had shot her sitting about
five yards from the muzzle of my gun, which was loaded
with an enormous charge of shot, is undeniable; but this
did not lessen my exultation a whit. The sparrows I used
to kill in days of yore, with inexpressible delight, grew
" small by degrees," and comically less, before the plump
inhabitant of the marshes, till they dwindled into nothing; and, in short, the joy and fuss with which I
hailed the destruction of the unfortunate bird can only
be compared to, and equalled by, the crowing and flurry
with which a hen is accustomed to announce the produc-
tion of her first egg.

During the voyage, we often disturbed large flocks of
geese, and sometimes shot a few. When we chanced to
come within sight of one before they saw us, the boats all
put ashore; and L'Esperance, our guide, went round
through the bushes, to the place where they were, and
seldom failed in rendering at least one of the flock *hors
de combat*. At first I would as soon have volunteered to
shoot a lion in Africa, with a Bushman beside me, as have
presumed to attempt to kill geese, while L'Esperance
was present,—so poor an opinion had I of my skill as a
marksman; but, as I became more accustomed to seeing
them killed, I waxed bolder, and at last, one day, having
come in sight of a flock, I begged to be allowed to try
my hand. The request was granted; L'Esperance lent
me his gun, and away I went cautiously through the
bushes. After a short walk, I came close to where they

were swimming about in the water; and cocking my gun, I rushed furiously down the bank, breaking every thing before me, and tumbling over half a dozen fallen trees in my haste, till I cleared the bushes; and then, scarcely taking time to raise the gun to my shoulder, banged right into the middle of the flock, just as they were taking wing. All rose; but they had not gone far when one began to waver a little, and finally sat down in the water again— a sure sign of being badly wounded. Before the boats came up, however, he had swam to the opposite bank, and hid himself among the bushes; so that, much to my disappointment, I had not the pleasure of handling this new trophy of my prowess.

Upon one occasion, while sauntering along the banks of the river, in search of ducks and geese, while the boats were slowly ascending against the strong current, I happened to cast my eyes across the stream, and there, to my amazement, beheld a large black bear bounding over the rocks with the ease and agility of a cat. He was not within shot, however, and I was obliged to content myself with seeing him run before me for a quarter of a mile, and then turn off into the forest.

This was truly the happiest time I ever spent in the Nor'-west. Every thing was full of novelty and excitement. Rapid succeeded rapid, and portage followed portage, in endless succession—giving me abundance of opportunities to range about in search of ducks and geese, which were very numerous, while the men were dragging the boats, and carrying the goods over the

portages. The weather was beautiful, and just the season of the year when the slight frost in the mornings
and evenings renders the blazing camp-fire agreeable,
and destroys those little wretches—the musquitoes. My
friend, Mr C——, was a kind and indulgent companion,
bearing good-naturedly with my boyish pranks, and
cautioning me against running into danger. I had just
left home and the restraint of school, and was now entering upon a wild and romantic career. In short, every
thing combined to render this a most agreeable and
interesting voyage. I have spent many a day of amusement and excitement in the country, but on none can I
look back with so much pleasure as on the time spent
in this journey to Red River.

The scenery through which we passed was pretty and
romantic, but there was nothing grand about it. The
country generally was low and swampy ; the highest
ground being the banks of the river, which sometimes
rose to from sixty to seventy feet. Our progress in
Hill River was slow and tedious, owing to the number of
rapids encountered on the way. The hill from which
the river derives its name, is a small insignificant mound,
and owes its importance to the flatness of the surrounding
country.

Besides the larger wild-fowl, small birds of many kinds
were very numerous. The most curious, and at the
same time the most impudent, among the latter, were
the whisky-jacks ; they always hovered round us while
we were at breakfast, ready to snap up any thing that

came within their reach, advancing sometimes to within
a yard or two of our feet, and looking at us with a very
comical expression of countenance.   One of the men told
me that he had often caught them in his hand, with a
piece of pemican for a bait; so, one morning after breakfast, I went a little to one side of our camp, and covering
my face with leaves, extended my hand with a few crumbs
in the open palm.   In five minutes a whisky-jack jumped
upon a branch over my head, and after reconnoitring a
minute or so, lit upon my hand and began to breakfast
forthwith.   You may be sure the *trap* was not long in
going off, and the screeching Mr Jack set up, on finding my fingers firmly closed upon his toes, was tremendous.   I never saw a more passionate little creature in
my life: it screamed, struggled, and bit unceasingly,
until I let it go, and even then, it lighted on a tree close
by, and looked at me as impudently as ever.   The same
day I observed that when the men were ashore, the
whisky-jacks used to eat out of the pemican bags left in
the boats; so I lay down close to one, under cover of a
buffalo skin, and in three minutes had made prisoner of
another of these little inhabitants of the forest.   They are
of a blueish gray colour, and nearly the size of a black-
bird, but they are such a bundle of feathers, that when
plucked they do not look much larger than a sparrow.
They live apparently on animal food, (at least, they are very
fond of it,) and are not considered very agreeable eating.

We advanced very slowly up Hill River.   Sometimes,
after a day of the most toilsome exertions, during which

the men were constantly pushing the boats up long
rapids, with poles, at a very slow pace, we found ourselves only four or five miles a-head of the last night's
encampment.   As we ascended higher up the country,
however, travelling became more easy.   Sometimes small
lakes and tranquil rivers allowed us to use the oars,
and even occasionally the sails, when a puff of fair wind
arose.   Occasionally we were sweeping rapidly across
the placid water; anon, buffeting with, and advancing
against, the foaming current of a powerful river, whose
raging torrent seemed to bid defiance to our farther
progress: now dragging boats and cargoes over rocks,
and through the deep shades of the forest, when a waterfall checked us on our way; and again, dashing across
a lake, with favouring breeze, and sometimes, though
rarely, were wind-bound on a small islet, or point of land.

Our progress was slow, but full of interest, novelty,
and amusement.   My fellow travellers seemed to enjoy
the voyage very much, and even poor Mrs G——, to
whom hardships were new, liked it exceedingly.

On our way we passed Oxford House, a small outpost
of York Factory district.   It is built on the brow of a
grassy hill, which rises gradually from the margin of
Oxford Lake.   Like most of the posts in the country, it
is composed of a collection of wooden houses, built in
the form of a square, and surrounded by tall stockades,
pointed at the tops.   These, however, are more for
ornament than defence.   A small flag-staff towers above
the buildings, from which, upon the occasion of an arri-

val, a little red Hudson's Bay Company's flag waves its
tiny folds in the gentle current of an evening breeze.
There were only two or three men at the place; and not
a human being, save one or two wandering Indians, was
to be found within hundreds of miles of this desolate
spot.

After a stay here of about half-an-hour, we proceeded
on our way.

There is scarcely any thing more beautiful or delightful than crossing a lake in the woods, on a lovely morning
at sunrise.   The brilliant sun, rising in a flood of light,
pierces through the thin haze of the morning, converting
the countless myriads of dew-drops that hang on the
trees and bushes into sparkling diamonds, and burnish-
ing the motionless flood of water, till a new and mighty
firmament is reflected in the wave—as if nature, rising
early from her couch, paused to gaze with admiration on
her own resplendent image, reflected in the depths of her
own matchless mirror.   The profound stillness, too, of
all around, broken only by the measured sweep of the
oars, fills the soul with awe; at the same time that a
tranquil but unbounded happiness steals over the heart
of the traveller, as he gazes out upon the distant horizon,
broken here and there by small verdant islets, floating
as it were in air.   He wanders back, in thought, to
scenes in far distant climes, or wishes, mayhap, that it
were possible, in scenes like this, to dwell with those he
loves, for ever.

As the day advances, the scene, though slightly

changed, is still most beautiful. The increasing heat dispelling the mists, reveals, in all its beauty, the deep blue sky speckled with thin fleecy clouds ; and, spreading a genial warmth over the body, creates a sympathetic warmth in the soul. Flocks of snow-white gulls sail in graceful evolutions round the boats, dipping lightly in the water as if to kiss their reflected images, and, rising suddenly in long rapid flights, mount in circles up high above the tranquil world into the azure sky, till small white specks alone are visible in the distance. Up, up, they rise, on sportive wing, till the straining eye can no longer distinguish them, and they are gone !

Ducks, too, whirr past in rapid flight, steering wide of the boats, and bending in a long graceful curve into their course again. The sweet, plaintive cry of a whip-poor-will, or some bird of the same description, rings along the shore, and the faint answer of his mate floats over the lake, mellowed by distance to a long tiny note. The air is motionless as the water, and the enraptured eye gazes on all that is lovely and peaceful in nature, in dreamy enjoyment.

These are the *pleasures* of travelling in the wilderness. Let us change the picture.

The sun no longer shines upon the tranquil scene. Dark, heavy clouds obscure the sky ; a suffocating heat depresses the spirits and enervates the frame ; sharp, short gusts of wind now ruffle the inky waters, and the floating islands sink into insignificance, as the deceptive haze which elevated them flies before the approaching

storm.   The ducks are gone, and the plaintive notes of
the whip-poor-will are hushed as the increasing breeze
rustles the leafy drapery of the forest.   The gulls wheel
round still, but in more rapid and uncertain flight, accompanying their motions with shrill and mournful cries, like
the dismal wailings of the spirit of the storm.   A few
drops of rain patter on the boats, or plump like stones
into the water, and the distant melancholy growl of
thunder swells upon the coming gale.   Uneasy glances
are cast, ever and anon, towards the black clouds and
the shore, and grumbling sentences are uttered by the
men.   Suddenly a hissing sound is heard; a loud clap of
thunder growls over head, and the gale, dashing the
white spray wildly before it, rushes down upon the
boats.

   " *A terre ! à terre !*" shout the men.   The boats are
turned towards the shore, and the bending oars creak
and groan as they pull swiftly on.   Hiss ! whirr ! the
gale bursts forth, dashing clouds of spray into the air ;
twisting and curling the foaming water in its fury.   The
thunder crashes with fearful noise, and the lightning
gleams in fitful lurid streaks across the inky sky.   Presently the shore is gained, amid a deluge of rain which
saturates every thing with water in a few minutes.   The
tents are pitched, but the fires will scarcely burn, and
are at last allowed to go out.   The men seek shelter
under the oiled cloths of the boats ; while the travellers,
rolled up in damp blankets, with the rain oozing through
the tents upon their couches, gaze mournfully upon the

dismal scene, and reflect sadly on the shortness of the step in human life between happiness and misery.

Nearly eighteen days after we left York Factory, we arrived in safety at the depôt of Norway House.

This fort is built at the mouth of a small and sluggish stream, known by the name of Jack River. The houses are ranged in the form of a square; none of them exceed one storey in height, and most of them are whitewashed. The ground on which it stands is rocky, and a small garden, composed chiefly of sand, juts out from the stockades like a strange excrescence. A large, rugged mass of rocks rises up between the fort and Playgreen Lake, which stretches out to the horizon on the other side of them. On the top of these rocks stands a flag-staff as a beacon to guide the traveller; for Norway House is so ingeniously hid in a hollow that it cannot be seen from the lake till the boat almost touches the wharf.

On the left side of the building extends a flat, grassy park, or green, upon which, during the summer months, there is often a picturesque and interesting scene. Spread out to dry in the sun, may be seen the snowy tent of the chief factor, lately arrived; a little farther off, on the rising ground, stands a dark and almost imperceptible wigwam, the small wreath of white smoke issuing from the top proving that it is inhabited; on the river bank, three or four boats and a north canoe are hauled up; and just above them a number of sunburnt voyageurs and a few Indians amuse themselves with

various games, or recline upon the grass, basking in the
sunshine.

Behind the fort stretches the thick forest, its outline
broken here and there by cuttings of firewood or small
clearings for farming.

Such was Norway House in 1841. The rocks were
crowded when we arrived, and we received a hearty
welcome from Mr R——, (the chief factor in charge,)
and his amiable family. As it was too late to proceed
any farther that day, we determined to remain here
all night.

From the rocks before mentioned, on which the flag-
staff stands, we had a fine view of Playgreen Lake.
There was nothing striking or bold in the scene, the
country being low and swampy, and no hills rose on the
horizon, or cast their shadows on the lake; but it was
pleasing and tranquil, and enlivened by one or two boats
sailing about on the water.

We spent an agreeable evening, and early on the
following morning started again on our journey, having
received an agreeable addition to our party in the person
of Miss Jessie R——, second daughter of Mr R——,
from whom we had just parted.

On the evening of the first day after our departure
from Norway House, we encamped on the shores of
Lake Winipeg. This immense body of fresh water is
about three hundred miles long by about fifty broad.
The shores are generally flat and uninteresting, and the
water shallow; yet here and there a few pretty spots

may be seen at the head of a small bay or inlet, where the ground is a little more elevated aud fertile.

Nothing particular occurred during our voyage along the shores of the lake, except that we hoisted our sails oftener to a favourable breeze, and had a good deal more night travelling than heretofore. In about five days after leaving Norway House we arrived at the mouth of Red River; and a very swampy, sedgy, flat-looking mouth it was, covered with tall bullrushes and swarming with waterfowl. The banks, too, were low and swampy; but, as we ascended, they gradually became more woody and elevated, till we arrived at the Stone fort—twenty miles up the river—where they were tolerably high.

A few miles below this we passed an Indian settlement, the cultivated fields and white houses of which, with the church spire in the midst, quite refreshed our eyes, after being so long accustomed to the gloomy shades of the primeval forest.

The Stone fort is a substantial fortification, surrounded by high walls and flanked with bastions, and has a fine appearance from the river. It was not garrisoned, however, but we found it under the charge of Mr B——, the Hudson's Bay Company's agent.

Here my friend and fellow-traveller, Mr C——, hearing of his wife's illness, left us and proceeded up the settlement on horseback. The missionaries also left the boats a little farther up, and I was left alone to be rowed slowly to Fort Garry, nearly twenty miles farther up the river.

The banks of the river were lined all the way along
with the houses and farms of the colonists, which had a
thriving, cleanly appearance; and, from the quantity of
live stock in the farm-yards, the number of pigs along
the banks, and the healthy appearance of the children
who came running out of the cottages to gaze upon us
as we passed, I inferred that the settlers generally were
well to do in the world.

The houses of some of the more wealthy inhabitants
were very handsome-looking buildings, particularly that
of Mr M‘Allum, where, in a few hours, I landed. This
gentleman is the superintendent of the Red River Aca-
demy, where the children of the wealthier colonists,
and those of the gentlemen belonging to the Hudson's
Bay Company, are instructed in the various branches of
English literature, and made to comprehend how the
world was convulsed in days of yore by the mighty
deeds of the heroes of ancient Greece and Rome.

Here I was hospitably treated to an excellent and
most classical breakfast, and then proceeded on foot
with Mr C—— (who rejoined me here) to Fort Garry,
which lay about two miles distant. Upon arriving, I was
introduced to Mr Finlayson, the chief factor in charge,
who received me very kindly, and introduced me to my
fellow-clerks in the office. Thus terminated my first
inland journey.

CHAPTER V.

RED RIVER SETTLEMENT.

ED RIVER settlement is, to use a high-flown expression, an oasis in the desert; and may be likened to a spot upon the moon, or a solitary ship upon the ocean. In plain English, it is an isolated settlement on the borders of one of the vast prairies of North America.

It is situated partly on the banks of Red River, and partly on the banks of a smaller stream called the Assinaboine, in latitude 50°, and extends upwards of fifty miles along the banks of these two streams.

The country around it is a vast treeless prairie, upon which scarcely a shrub is to be seen; but a thick coat of grass covers it throughout its entire extent, with the exception of a few spots, where the hollowness of the ground has collected a little moisture, or the meandering of some small stream or rivulet enriches the soil, and covers its banks with verdant shrubs and trees.

The banks of the Red and Assinaboine rivers, are covered with a thick belt of woodland, which, however, does not extend far back into the plains. It is composed of oak, poplar, willows, &c., the first of which is much used for firewood by the settlers. The larger timber in the adjacent woods is thus being rapidly thinned, and, ere long, the inhabitants will have to raft their firewood down the rivers from a considerable distance.

The settlers are a mixture of French Canadians, Scotchmen, and Indians. The first of these occupy the upper part of the settlement; the second live near the middle: and the Indians inhabit a village at its lower extremity.

There are four Protestant churches; the upper, middle, and lower churches, and one at the Indian settlement. The upper and middle churches were, in 1841, under the superintendence of the Rev. Mr Cockran and the Rev. Mr Cowley; while the lower and Indian churches were intrusted to the care of the Rev. Mr Smithurst, who had also the entire management of the Indian village, where he discharged his duties zealously, and was looked upon by the poor natives as a father. Mr Cockran was universally respected by all classes, for the exemplary manner in which he discharged his arduous duties, and for his boundless generosity. There are also two Roman Catholic chapels, some priests, and a Roman Catholic bishop, resident in the colony. There are one or two schools, the principal being, as before mentioned, under the superintendence of Mr M'Allum, who has since been ordained by the Bishop of Montreal, during that prelate's visit to Red River.

For the preservation of the peace, and the punishment of evil-doers, a Recorder and body of magistrates are provided, who assemble every quarter at Fort Garry, the seat of the court-house, for the purpose of redressing wrongs, punishing crimes, giving good advice, and eating an excellent dinner at the Company's table. There was once, also, a body of policemen; but, strange to say, they were chosen from among the most turbulent of the settlers, and were never expected to be on duty except when a riot took place: the policemen themselves generally being the ringleaders on those occasions, it may be supposed they did not materially assist in quelling disturbances. Since I left the colony, however, troops have been sent out from Britain, so that the law will now be inforced, and, consequently, respected.

The Scotch and Indian settlers cultivate wheat, barley, and Indian corn, in abundance, for which the only market is that afforded by the Company, the more wealthy settlers, and retired chief factors. This market, however, is a poor one, and in years of plenty, the settlers find it difficult to dispose of their surplus produce. Wild fruits of various descriptions are abundant, and the gardens are well stocked with vegetables. The settlers have plenty of sheep, pigs, poultry, and horned cattle; and there is scarcely a man in the place who does not drive to church on Sundays in his own cariole—a vehicle depicted below in a *vigorous* manner.

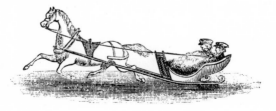

Red River is rather a populous place; the census taken in 1843 proved it to contain upwards of 5000 souls, and since then it has been rapidly increasing.

There is a paper currency in the settlement, which obviates the necessity of having coin afloat. English pence and half-pence, however, are plentiful. The lowest paper note is one shilling sterling, the next five shillings, and the highest twenty shillings. The Canadian settlers and half-breeds are employed, during the greater part of the year, in travelling with the Company's boats, and in buffalo hunting. The Scotch settlers are chiefly farmers, tradesmen, and merchants.

The rivers, which are crossed in wooden canoes, in the absence of bridges, are well stocked with fish. The principal kinds are goldeyes, sturgeon, and catfish. Of these I think the goldeyes the best, at any rate they are the most numerous. The wild animals inhabiting the woods and prairies are much the same as in the other parts of North America, viz.—wolves, foxes, brown and black bears, martens, minx, musquash, rabbits, &c.; while the woods are filled with game, the marshes and ponds with ducks, geese, swans, cranes, and a host of other water-fowl.

Red River was first settled upon by the fur-traders, who established a trading post many years ago on its banks; but it did not assume the character of a colony till 1811, when Lord Selkirk sent out a number of emigrants to form a settlement in the wild regions of the North West. Norwegians, Danes, Scotch, and Irish,

composed the motley crew ; but the great bulk of the
colonists then, as at the present time, consisted of Scotchmen and Canadians. Unlike other settlements in a wild
country inhabited by Indians, the infant colony had few
difficulties to contend with at the outset. The Indians
were friendly, and had become accustomed to white men
from their previous contact, for many years, with the
servants of the Hudson's Bay Company; so, with the exception of one or two broils among themselves and other
fur-traders, the colonist plodded peacefully along. On
one occasion, however, the Hudson's Bay Company and
the North-West Company, who were long at enmity with
each other, had a sharp skirmish ; in which Mr Semple,
then Governor of the Hudson's Bay Company, was killed,
and a number of his men killed and wounded. The whole
affair originated very foolishly. A body of men had been
observed from the walls of Fort Garry, travelling past
the fort, and, as Governor Semple was not sure of their
intentions, he sallied forth with a few men to intercept
them, and demand their object. The North-West party,
on seeing a body of men coming towards them from the
fort, halted till they came up ; and Cuthbert Grant, who
was in command, asked what they wanted. Governor
Semple required to know where they were going to ;
being answered in a surly manner, an altercation took
place between the two parties, (of which the North-West
was by far the stronger,) in the middle of which, a shot
was unfortunately fired by one of the Hudson's Bay
party. It was never known who fired this shot, and many

believe that it was discharged accidentally ; at any rate, no one was injured by it.   The moment the report was heard, a volley was fired by the North-Westers upon the Hudson's Bay party, which killed a few, and wounded many ; among the latter was Governor Semple.   Cuthbert Grant did his utmost to keep back the fierce half-casts under his command, but without avail ; and at last, seeing that this was impossible, he stood over the wounded Semple, and endeavoured to defend him.   In this he succeeded for some time, but a shot from behind at last took effect in the unfortunate Governor's body, and killed him.   After this, the remainder of his party fled to the fort, and the victorious half-breeds pursued their way.

During the time that these two companies opposed each other, the country was in a state of constant turmoil and excitement.   Personal conflicts with fists, between the men—and, not unfrequently, the gentlemen—of the opposing parties, were of the commonest occurrence, and frequently more deadly weapons were resorted to.   Spirits were distributed among the wretched natives to a dreadful extent, and the scenes that sometimes ensued were disgusting in the extreme. Amid all this, however, stratagem was more frequently resorted to than open violence, by the two Companies, in their endeavours to prevent each other from procuring furs from the Indians.   Men were constantly kept on the look-out for parties of natives returning from hunting expeditions ; and those who could arrive first at the en-

campment, always carried off the furs. The Indians did
not care which company got them; "first come, first
served," was the order of the day; and both were equally
welcome, provided they brought plenty of *fire-water*.

Although the individuals of the two companies were
thus almost always at enmity, strange to say, at the forts
they often acted in the most friendly manner to each
other, and (except when furs were in question) more
agreeable or friendly neighbours seldom came together
than the Hudson's Bay and North-West Companies, when
they planted their forts (which they often did) within
two hundred yards of each other, in the wilds of North
America. The clerks and labourers of the opposing
establishments constantly visited each other, and during
the Christmas and New-Year's holidays, parties and balls
were given without number. Dances, however, were not
confined entirely to the holidays; but whenever one was
given at an unusual time, it was generally for the purpose
of drawing the attention of the entertained party from
some movement of their entertainers.

Thus, upon one occasion the Hudson's Bay Company's
look-out reported that he had discovered the tracks of
Indians in the snow, and that he thought they had just
returned from a hunting expedition. No sooner was this
heard, than a grand ball was given to the North-West
Company. Great preparations were made; the men,
dressed in their newest capôtes and gaudiest hat-cords,
visited each other, and nothing was thought of or talked
of but the ball. The evening came, and with it the

guests; and soon might be heard within the fort sounds
of merriment and revelry, as they danced, in lively
measures, to a Scottish reel, played by some native
fiddler upon a violin of his own construction. Without
the gates, however, a very different scene met the eye.
Down in a hollow, where the lofty trees and dense
underwood threw a shadow on the ground, a knot of
men might be seen, muffled up in their leathern coats
and fur caps, hurrying to and fro with bundles on their
backs and snow-shoes under their arms; packing and
tying them firmly on trains of dog-sledges, which
stood, with the dogs ready harnessed, in the shadow of
the bushes. The men whispered eagerly and hurriedly
to each other, as they packed their goods, while others
held the dogs, and patted them to keep them quiet;
evidently showing, that whatever was their object, expedition and secrecy were necessary. Soon all was in
readiness: the bells, which usually tinkled on the dogs'
necks, were unhooked and packed in the sledges—an
active-looking man sprang forward and set off at a round
trot over the snow, and a single crack of the whip sent
four sledges, each with a train of four or five dogs, after
him, while two other men brought up the rear. For a
time the muffled sound of the sledges was heard as they
slid over the snow, while now and then the whine of a
dog broke upon the ear, as the impatient drivers urged
them along. Gradually these sounds died away, and
nothing was heard but the faint echoes of music and
mirth, which floated on the frosty night-wind, giving

token that the revellers still kept up the dance, and were ignorant of the departure of the trains.

Late on the following day the Nor'-West scouts reported the party of Indians, and soon a set of sleighs departed from the fort with loudly ringing bells. After a long day's march of forty miles, they reached the encampment, where they found all the Indians dead drunk, and not a skin, not even the remnant of a musquash, left to repay them for their trouble! Then it was that they discovered the ruse of the ball, and vowed to have their revenge.

Opportunity was not long wanting. Soon after this occurrence one of their parties met a Hudson's Bay train on its way to trade with the Indians, of whom they also were in search. They exchanged compliments with each other; and as the day was very cold, proposed lighting a fire and taking a dram together. Soon five or six goodly trees yielded to their vigorous blows, and fell crashing to the ground; and in a few minutes one of the party, lighting a sulphur match with his flint and steel, set fire to a huge pile of logs, which soon crackled and burned furiously, sending up clouds of sparks into the wintry sky, and casting a warm tinge upon the snow and the surrounding trees. The canteen was quickly produced, and they began to tell their stories and adventures, while the liquor mounted to their brains. The Nor'-Westers, however, after a little time, began to spill their grog on the snow, unperceived by the others, so that they kept tolerably sober, while their

rivals became very much elevated; and at last they
began boasting of their superior powers of drinking,
and, as a proof, each of them swallowed a large bumper.   The Hudson's Bay party, who were nearly dead
drunk by this time, of course followed their example,
and almost instantly fell in a heavy sleep on the snow.
In ten minutes more they were tied firmly upon their
sledges, and the dogs being turned homewards, away
they went straight for the Hudson's Bay fort, where
they soon after arrived, the men still sound asleep; while
the Nor'-Westers started for the Indian camp, and,
this time at least, had the furs all to themselves.

Such were the scenes that took place thirty years ago
in the northern wildernesses of America.   Since then, the
two companies have joined, retaining the name of the
richer and more powerful of the two, the "Hudson's
Bay Company."   Spirits were still imported after the
junction; but of late years they have been dispensed
with throughout the country, except at the colony of
Red River, and the few posts where opposition is carried
on by the American fur companies; so that now the poor
savage no longer grovels in the dust of his native wilderness under the influence of the white man's fire-water;
and the stranger who travels through those wild romantic regions no longer beholds the humiliating scenes, or
hears of the frightful crimes, which were seen and heard
of too often in former days, and which have always been,
and always must be prevalent wherever spirituous liquors,
the great curse of mankind, are plentiful; and particularly

where, as in that country, the wild inhabitants fear no laws, human or divine.

In the year 1826, Red River overflowed its banks and flooded the whole settlement, obliging the settlers to forsake their houses, and drive their horses and cattle to the trifling eminences in the immediate vicinity. These eminences were few and very small, so that during the flood they presented a curious appearance, being crowded with men, women, and children, horses, cattle, sheep, and poultry. The houses being made of wood, and only built on the ground, not sunk into it, were carried away by dozens, and great numbers of horses and cattle were drowned. During the time it lasted, the settlers sailed and paddled among their houses in boats and canoes; and often lately, while ranging about the prairies, has the settler pointed out to me, among the waving grass and verdant bushes, the spot where he dwelt in his tent, and paddled about the deep waters in his canoe in the " year of the flood." This way of speaking has a strangely antediluvian sound ; the hale, middle-aged colonist will tell you, with a ludicrously grave countenance, that his house stood on such a spot, or such and such an event happened, " *a year before the flood.*"

Fort Garry, the principal establishment of the Hudson's Bay Company, stands on the banks of the Assinaboine river, about two hundred yards from its junction with Red River. It is a square stone building, with bastions pierced for cannon at the corners. The principal dwelling-houses, stores, and offices, are built within the walls, and the stables at a small distance from the fort. The situation is pretty and quiet; but there is too much flatness in the surrounding country for the lover of the grand and picturesque. Just in front of the gate runs or rather glides the peaceful Assinaboine, where, on a fine day in autumn, may be seen thousands of gold-eyes playing in its limpid waters, and glittering in the sunshine.

On the left extends the woodland fringing the river, with here and there a clump of smaller trees and willows surrounding the swamps formed by the melting snows of spring, where flocks of wild-ducks and noisy plover give animation to the scene, while, through the openings in the forest, are seen glimpses of the rolling prairie. Down in the hollow, where the stables stand, are always to be seen a few horses and cows, feeding or lazily chewing their cud in the rich pasturage, giving an air of repose to the scene, which contrasts forcibly with the view of the wide plains which roll out like a vast green sea from the back of the fort, studded here and there with little islets and hillocks, around which may be seen hovering a watchful hawk or solitary raven.

The climate of Red River is salubrious and agreeable. Winter commences about the month of November, and spring generally begins in April. Although the winter is very long and extremely cold, (the thermometer usually varying between ten and thirty degrees below zero,) yet, from its being always *dry* frost, it is much more agreeable than people, accustomed to the damp thawy weather of Great Britain, might suppose.

Winter is here the liveliest season of the year. It is then that the wild, demi-savage colonist leads the blushing half-breed girl to the altar, and the country about his house rings with the music of the sleigh bells, as his friends assemble to congratulate the happy pair, and dance for three successive days. It is in this season that the hardy voyageurs rest from their toils, and, circling round the blazing fire, recount many a tale of danger, and paint many a wild romantic scene of their long and tedious voyages among the lakes and rapids of the interior; while their wives and children gaze with breathless interest upon their swarthy sun-burnt faces, lighted up with animation as they recall the scenes of other days, or, with low and solemn voice, relate the death of a friend and fellow voyageur who perished among the foaming cataracts of the wilderness.

During the summer months there are often very severe thunder-storms, accompanied with tremendous showers of hail, which do a great deal of mischief to the crops and houses. The hailstones are of an enormous size, upwards of an inch in diameter; and on two or three occasions they broke all the windows in Fort Garry that were exposed to the storm.

Generally speaking, however, the weather is serene and calm, particularly in autumn, and during the delicious season, peculiar to America, called the Indian summer, which precedes the commencement of winter.

The scenery of Red River, as I said before, is neither grand nor picturesque, yet, when the sun shines brightly on the waving grass, and glitters on the silver stream, and when the distant and varied cries of wild-fowl break in plaintive cadence on the ear, one experiences a sweet exulting happiness, akin to the feelings of the sailor when he gazes forth at early morn upon the polished surface of the sleeping sea.

Such is Red River, and such the scenes on which I gazed in wonder, as I rode by the side of my friend and fellow clerk, M'K——, on the evening of my arrival at my new home. Mr M'K—— was mounted on his handsome horse "Colonel," while I cantered by his side on a horse that afterwards bore me over many a mile of prairie land. It is not every day that one has an opportunity of describing a horse like the one I then rode, so the reader will be pleased to have a little patience while I draw his portrait. In the first place, then, he revelled in the name of "Touron," which, being interpreted, means *pemican;* wherein, however, consisted his resemblance to pemican, I know not, unless indeed in this, that his good qualities did not become visible at first sight. He was of a moderate height, of a brown colour, and had the general outlines of a horse, when viewed as that animal might be supposed to appear if reflected from the depths of a bad looking-glass. His chief peculiarity, however, was the great height of his hind-quarters. In youth they had outgrown the fore-quarters, so that, upon a level road, you had all the advantages of riding downhill. He cantered delightfully, trotted badly, walked slowly, and, upon all and every occasion, evinced a reso-

lute pig-headedness, and disinclination to accommodate
his will to that of his rider. He was decidedly porcine
in his disposition, very plebeian in his manners, and
doubtless also in his sentiments.

Such was the Bucephalus upon which I took my first
ride over the Red River prairie; now swaying to and
fro on his back as we gallopped over the ground, anon
stotting, in the manner of a recruit in a cavalry regi-
ment as yet unaccustomed to the saddle, when he trotted
on the beaten track; and occasionally, to the immense
delight of M'K——, seizing tight hold of the saddle, as
an uncertain waver in my body reminded me of Sir
Isaac Newton's law of gravitation, and that any rash
departure on my part from my *understanding*, would
infallibly lay me prostrate on the ground.

Soon after my arrival, I underwent the operation
which my horse had undergone before me, viz. that of
being broken in; the only difference being, that he was
broken in to the saddle and I to the desk. It is needless
to describe the agonies I endured while sitting, hour
after hour, on a long-legged stool, my limbs quivering
for want of their accustomed exercise, while the twitter-
ing of birds, barking of dogs, lowing of cows, and
neighing of horses, seemed now to invite me to join them
in the woods; and anon, as my weary pen scratched
slowly over the paper, their voices seemed to change to
hoarse derisive laughter, as if they thought that the
little mis-shapen frogs croaking and whistling in the
marshes were freer far than their proud masters, who

coop themselves up in smoky houses during the live-long day, and call themselves the free, unshackled "lords of the creation!"

I soon became accustomed to these minor miseries of human life, and ere long could sit

> From morn till night
> To scratch and write
>   Upon a three-legg'd stool ;
> Nor mourn the joys
> Of truant boys
>   Who stay away from school.

There is a proverb which says, "It is a poor heart that never rejoices." Now, taking it for granted that the proverb speaks truth, and not wishing by our disregard of it to be thought poor-hearted, we, that is M'K——— and I, were in the habit of rejoicing our spirits occasionally—not in the usual way, by drinking brandy and water, (though we did sometimes, when nobody knew it, indulge in a glass of beer, with the red-hot poker thrust into it to make it fizzy), but by shouldering our guns and sallying forth to shoot the partridges, or rather grouse, which abound in the woods of Red River.   On these occasions M'K——— and I used to range the forest in company, enlivening our walk by chatting upon every sort of subject, and not unfrequently talking of our happy homes in " bonnie Scotland," and thinking of the "light of other days."   We seldom went out without bringing home a few brace of gray grouse, which were exceedingly tame ; so tame, indeed, that sometimes they

did not take wing until two or three shots had been
fired. On one occasion, after walking about for half an
hour without getting a shot, we started a covey of seven,
which alighted upon a tree close at hand; we instantly
fired at the two lowest, and brought them down, while
the others only stretched out their long necks, as if to
see what had happened to their comrades, but did not
fly away. Two more were soon shot; and while we were
reloading our guns, the other three flew off to a neighbouring tree. In a few minutes more, they followed
their companions, and we had bagged the whole seven.
This is by no means an uncommon exploit, when the
birds are tame, and though very poor *sport*, yet helps to
fill your larder with somewhat better fare than it would
often contain without such assistance. The only thing
that we had to avoid was, aiming at the birds on the
higher branches, as the noise they make in falling
frightens those below. The experienced sportsman
always begins with the lowest bird, and if they sit still
after the first shot, he is almost sure of the rest.

Shooting, however, was not our only amusement:
sometimes, on a fine evening, we used to saddle our horses
and canter over the prairie, till Red River and the fort
were scarcely visible in the horizon; or, following the cart
road along the settlement, called upon our friends and
acquaintances; returning the polite "*bon jour*" of the
French settler, as he trotted past us on his shaggy pony,
or smiling on the pretty half-caste girls, as they passed
along the road. These same girls, by the way, are

generally very pretty; they make excellent wives, and
are uncommonly thrifty. With beads, and brightly coloured porcupines' quills, and silk, they work the most
beautiful devices on the moccasins, leggins, and leather
coats worn by the inhabitants; and during the long
winter months, they spin, and weave an excellent kind
of cloth, from the wool produced by the sheep of the
settlement, mixed with that of the buffalo, brought from
the prairies by the hunters.

About the middle of autumn, the body of Mr Thomas
Simpson, the unfortunate discoverer, who in company
with Mr Dease attempted to discover the Nor'-west
passage, was brought to the settlement for burial. Poor
Mr Simpson had set out with a party of Red River half-
breeds, for the purpose of crossing the plains to St
Lewis, and proceeding thence through the United States
to England. Soon after his departure, however, several
of the party returned to the settlement, stating that Mr
Simpson had, in a fit of insanity, killed two of his men
and then shot himself, and that they had buried him on
the spot where he fell. This story, of course, created a
great sensation in the colony; and as all the party gave
the same account of the affair upon investigation, it was
believed by many that he had committed suicide. A
few, however, thought that he had been murdered, and
had shot the two men in self-defence. In the autumn of
1841, the matter was ordered to be further inquired into;
and, accordingly, Dr Bunn was sent to the place where
Mr Simpson's body had been interred, for the purpose

of raising and examining it. Decomposition, however, had proceeded too far; so the body was conveyed to the colony for burial, and Dr Bunn returned, without having discovered any thing that could throw light on the melancholy subject.

I did not know Mr Simpson personally, but from the report of those who did, it appears that, though a clever and honourable man, he was of rather a haughty disposition, and in consequence was very much disliked by the half-breeds of Red River. I therefore think, with many of Mr Simpson's friends and former companions, that he did *not* kill himself, and that this was only a false report of his murderers. Besides, it is not probable that a man who had just succeeded in making important additions to our geographical knowledge, and who might reasonably expect honour and remuneration upon returning to his native land, would, without any known or apparent cause, first commit murder and then suicide. By his melancholy death the Hudson's Bay Company lost a faithful servant, and the world an intelligent and enterprising man.

Winter, according to its ancient custom, passed away, and spring, not with its genial gales and scented flowers, but with burning sun and melting snow, began to change the face of nature, and break the icy covering of Red River. Duffle coats began to vanish, and a few of the half-breed settlers doffed their fur caps, and donned the "bonnet rouge," while the more hardy and savage contented themselves with the bonnet *noir*, in the shape of

their own thick black hair.   Carioles still continued to
run, but it was merely from the force of habit, and it
was evident they would soon give up in despair.   Sportsmen began to think of ducks and geese, farmers of
ploughs and wheat, and voyageurs to dream of rapid
streams and waterfalls, or distant voyages in light
canoes.

CHAPTER VI.

NORWAY HOUSE.

ORWAY HOUSE, as we have before mentioned, is built upon the shores of Playgreen Lake, close to Jack River, and distant about twenty miles from Lake Winipeg. At its right-hand corner rises a huge abrupt rock, on the top of which stands a flag-staff, and from whence can be obtained a fine view of Playgreen Lake, and the surrounding country. On this rock a number of people were assembled to witness our arrival, and among them Mr R——, who sauntered down to the wharf to meet us as we stepped ashore.

A few days after my arrival, the Council "resolved" that I should winter at Norway House; so next day, in accordance with the resolution of that august assembly, I took up my quarters in the clerks' room, and took possession of the books and papers.

It is an author's prerogative, I believe, to jump from place to place, and to annihilate time at pleasure. Taking advantage, then, of this prerogative, I will pass over the autumn, during which I had hunted, fished, and paddled in canoes to the Indian village at Rossville, a hundred times—and jump at once into the middle of winter.

Norway House no longer boasts of the bustle and excitement of the summer season. No boats arrive, no groups of ladies fair and gentlemen assemble on the rocks to gaze on the sparkling waters. A placid stillness reigns around, except in the immediate vicinity of the fort, where a few axe-men chop the winter firewood, or start with trains of dog-sledges for the lakes, to bring home loads of white fish and venison. Mr R—— is reading the " Penny Cyclopædia" in the hall (as the winter mess-room is called), and I am writing in the dingy little office in the shade, which looks pigstyish in appearance without, but is warm and snug within. Alongside of me, sits Mr C——, a tall, bald-headed, sweet-tempered man of forty-five, who has spent the greater part of his life among the bears and Indians of Hudson's Bay, and is now on a Christmas visit at Norway House. He has just arrived from his post, a few hundred miles off, whence he walked on snow-shoes, and is now engaged in taking off his moccasins and blanket socks, which he spreads out carefully below the stove to dry.

We did not continue long, however, at our different occupations. Mr Evans, the Wesleyan missionary, was to give a feast to the Indians at Rossville, and afterwards to examine the little children who attended the village school. To this feast we were invited; so, in the afternoon, Mr C—— and I put on our moose-skin coats

and snow-shoes, and set off for the village, which was
about two miles distant from the fort.

By the way Mr C—— related an adventure he had
had, while travelling through the country; and as it
may serve to show the dangers that are sometimes encountered by those who wander through the wilds of
North America, I will give it here in his own words.

Mr C——'s Adventure with a Bear.

" It was about the middle of winter," said he, " that I
set off on snow-shoes, accompanied by an Indian, to a
small lake for fish which had been caught in the autumn,
and were then lying frozen in a little house built of logs
to protect them for winter use.   The lake was about ten
miles off; and as the road was pretty level and not much
covered with underwood, we took a train of dogs with us,
and set off before daybreak, intending to return again
before dark; and as the day was clear and cold (the
thermometer was 35° below zero), we went cheerily
along without interruption, except an occasional fall
when a branch caught our snow-shoes, or stopping to
clear the traces when the dogs got entangled among
the trees.   We had proceeded about six miles, and the
first gray streaks of day had lit up the eastern horizon,
when the Indian, who had been walking in advance,
paused, and appeared to be examining some foot-prints
in the snow.   After a few minutes of close observation,
he rose and said, that a bear had passed not long before,
and could not be far off, and asked permission to follow it.

I told him he might do so, and said that I would drive the
dogs in his track, as the bear had gone in the direction
of the fish-house.   The Indian threw his gun over his
shoulder, and was soon lost in the forest.   For a quarter
of an hour I plodded on behind the dogs, now urging
them along, as they flagged and panted in the deep
snow, and occasionally listening for a shot from my
Indian's gun.   At last he fired, and almost immediately
after fired again ; for you must know that some Indians
can load so fast that two shots from their single barrel
sound almost like the discharge in succession of the two
shots from a double-barrelled gun.   Shortly after, I
heard another shot ; and then, as all became silent, I
concluded that he had killed the bear, and that I would
soon find him cutting it up.   Just as I thought this, a
fierce growl alarmed me ; so, seizing a pistol which I
always carried with me, I hastened forward.   As I came
nearer, I heard a man's voice mingled with the growls of
a bear ; and upon arriving at the foot of a small mound,
my Indian's voice, apostrophising death, became distinctly audible.   ' Come, death !' said he, in a contemptuous tone ; ' you have got me at last, but the Indian
does not fear you !'   A loud angry growl from the bear,
as he saw me rushing up the hill, stopped him ; and the
unfortunate man turned his eyes upon me with an im-
ploring look.   He was lying on his back, while the bear
(a black one) stood over him, holding one of his arms in
its mouth.   In rushing up the mound I unfortunately
stumbled, and filled my pistol with snow ; so that when

the bear left the Indian and rushed towards me, it missed fire, and I had only left me the poor, almost hopeless chance, of stunning the savage animal with a blow of the butt end. Just as he was rearing on his hind legs, my eye fell upon the Indian's axe, which fortunately lay at my feet, and seizing it, I brought it down with all my strength on the bear's head, just at the moment that he fell upon me, and we rolled down the hill together. Upon recovering myself, I found that the blow of the axe had killed him instantly, and that I was uninjured. Not so the Indian: the whole calf of his left leg was bitten off, and his body lacerated dreadfully in various places. He was quite sensible, however, though very faint, and spoke to me when I stooped to examine his wounds. In a short time I had tied them up; and placing him on the sledge with part of the bear's carcase, which I intended to dine upon, we returned immediately to the fort. The poor Indian got better slowly, but he never recovered the perfect use of his leg, and now hobbles about the fort, cutting firewood, or paddling about the lake in search of ducks and geese in his bark canoe."

Mr C—— concluded his story just as we arrived at the little bay, at the edge of which the Indian village of Rossville is built. From the spot where we stood, the body of the village did not appear to much advantage; but the parsonage and church, which stood on a small mound, their white walls in strong contrast to the background of dark trees, had a fine picturesque effect. There

were about twenty houses in the village, inhabited entirely
by Indians, most of whom were young and middle-aged
men.   They spent their time in farming during the
summer, and were successful in raising potatoes and a
few other vegetables for their own use.   In winter they
go into the woods to hunt fur-bearing animals, and also
deer ; but they never remain long absent from their
homes.   Mr Evans resided among them, and taught
them and their children writing and arithmetic, besides
instructing them in the principles of Christianity.   They
often assembled in the school-house for prayer and sacred
music, and attended divine service regularly in the church
every Sunday.   Mr Evans, who was a good musician, had
taught them to sing in parts ; and it has a wonderfully
pleasing effect upon a stranger to hear these dingy sons
and daughters of the wilderness raising their melodious
voices in harmony in praise of the Christian's God.

Upon our arrival at the village, we were ushered into
Mr Evans's neat cottage, from the windows of which is a
fine view of Playgreen Lake, studded with small islands,
stretching out to the horizon on the right, and a boundless wilderness of trees on the left.   Here were collected
the ladies and gentlemen of Norway House, and a number of indescribable personages, who seemed to be engaged in mystic preparations for the approaching feast.
It was with something like awe that I entered the school-
room, and beheld two long rows of tables covered with
puddings, pies, tarts, stews, hashes, and vegetables of all
shapes, sizes, and descriptions, smoking thereon.   I feared

for the Indians; for, although they can stand a great deal in the way of repletion, yet I doubted their moderation when such abundance of good things was placed before them. A large shell was sounded after the manner of a bugle, and all the Indians of the village walked into the room and seated themselves, the women on one side of the long tables, and the men on the other. Mr Evans stood at the head, and pronounced an appropriate blessing; and then commenced a work of demolition, the like of which has not been seen since the foundation of the world! The pies had strong crusts, but the knives were stronger; the paste was hard and the interior tough, but Indian teeth were harder and Indian jaws tougher; the dishes were gigantic, but the stomachs were capacious; so that, ere long, numerous skeletons and empty dishes alone graced the board. One old woman, of a dark-brown complexion, with glittering black eyes and awfully long teeth, set up in the wholesale line, and demolished the viands so rapidly, that those who sat beside her, fearing a dearth in the land, began to look angry; fortunately, however, she gave in suddenly, while in the middle of a venison pasty, and reclining languidly backward, with a sweetly contented expression of countenance, while her breath came thickly through her half opened mouth, she gently fell asleep, and thereby, much to her chagrin, lost the tea and cakes which were served out soon afterwards by way of dessert. After they had finished, the juveniles were admitted *en masse*, and they soon cleared away the rem-

nants of their seniors' dinner.   The dress of the Indians
upon this occasion was generally blue cloth capôtes
with hoods, scarlet or blue cloth leggins, quill-worked
moccasins, and no caps.   Some of them, however, were
dressed very funnily, and one or two of the oldest appeared in blue surtouts, which were very ill made, and
much too large for the wearers.   The ladies had short
gowns without plaits, cloth leggins of various colours
highly ornamented with beads, cotton handkerchiefs on
their necks, and sometimes, also, on their heads.   The
boys and girls were just their seniors in miniature.

After the youngsters had finished dinner, the school-
room was cleared by the guests; benches were ranged along the entire room, excepting the upper end,
where a table, with two large candlesticks at either end,
served as a stage for the young actors.   When all was
arranged, the elder Indians seated themselves on the
benches, while the boys and girls ranged themselves
along the wall behind the table.   Mr Evans then began,
by causing a little boy about four years old to recite a
long comical piece of prose in English; having been well
drilled for weeks beforehand, he did it in the most
laughable style.   Then came forward four little girls,
who kept up an animated philosophical discussion as to
the difference of the days in the moon and on the earth.
Then a bigger boy made a long speech in the Seauteaux
language, at which the Indians laughed immensely, and
with which the white people present (who did not understand a word of it) pretended to be greatly delighted,

and laughed loudly too. Then the whole of the little
band, upon a sign being given by Mr Evans, burst at
once into a really beautiful hymn, which was quite unexpected, and consequently all the more gratifying. This
concluded the examination, if I may so call it; and after
a short prayer, the Indians departed to their homes,
highly delighted with their entertainment. Such was
the Christmas feast at Rossville, and many a laugh it
afforded us that night as we returned home across the
frozen lake by the pale moonlight.

Norway House is perhaps one of the best posts in the
Indian country. The climate is dry and salubrious; and
although (like nearly all the other parts of the country)
extremely cold in winter, it is very different from the
damp chilling cold of that season in Great Britain. The
country around is swampy and rocky, and covered with
dense forests. Many of the Company's posts are but
ill provided with the necessaries of life, and entirely destitute of luxuries. Norway House, however, is favoured
in this respect. We always had fresh meat of some kind
or other; sometimes beef, mutton, or venison, and occasionally buffalo meat was sent us from the Swan River
district. Of tea, sugar, butter, and bread, we had abundance; and besides the produce of our garden in the way
of vegetables, the river and lake contributed white-fish,
sturgeon, and pike, or jack-fish, in abundance. The
pike is not a very delicate fish, and the sturgeon is
extremely coarse, but the white-fish is the most delicate and delicious I ever ate. I am not aware of their

existence in any part of the Old World; but the North
American lakes abound with them. It is generally the
size of a good salmon trout, of a bright silvery colour,
and tastes a little like salmon. Many hundreds of fur-
traders live almost entirely on white-fish, particularly at
those far northern posts where flour, sugar, and tea
cannot be had in great quantities, and where deer are
scarce. At these posts the Indians are frequently reduced to cannibalism, and the Company's people have,
on more than one occasion, been obliged to eat their
beaver skins! The beaver skin is thick and oily; so
that, when the fur is burnt off, and the skin well boiled,
it makes a kind of soup that will at least keep one alive.
This was the case one winter in Peel's River, a post
within the Arctic circle, in charge of Mr Bell, a chief
trader in the service; and I remember well reading in
one of his letters, that all the fresh provision they had
been able to procure during the winter, was " two
squirrels and one crow !" During this time they had
existed on a quantity of dried meat which they fortunately had in store, and they were obliged to lock the
gates of the fort, to preserve the remainder from the
wretched Indians, who were eating each other outside
the walls. The cause of all this misery was the entire
failure of the fisheries, together with great scarcity of
wild animals. Starvation is quite common among the
Indians of those distant regions; and the scraped rocks
which they divest of their covering of tripe-de-roche
(which resembles dried-up sea-weed), have a sad mean-

ing and melancholy appearance to the traveller who
journeys through the wilds and solitudes of Rupert's
Land.

Norway House is also an agreeable and interesting
place, from its being in a manner the gate to the only
route to Hudson's Bay ; so that, during the spring and
summer months, all the brigades of boats and canoes
from every part of the northern department must necessarily pass it on their way to York Factory with furs ;
and as they all return in the autumn, and some of the
gentlemen leave their wives and families for a few weeks
till they return to the interior, it is at this sunny season
of the year quite a gay and bustling place ; and the
clerk's house in which I lived was often filled with a
strange and always noisy collection of human beings,
who rested here awhile ere they started for the shores
of Hudson's Bay, the distant regions of M'Kenzie's River,
or the still more distant land of Oregon.

During winter our principal amusement was white
partridge shooting. This bird is a species of ptarmigan,
and is pure white, with the exception of the tips of the
wings and tail. They were very numerous during the
winter, and formed an agreeable dish at our winter mess-
table. I also enjoyed a little skating in the beginning of
winter, but the falling snow soon put an end to this
amusement.

Spring, beautiful spring ! returned again to cheer us
in our solitude, and open into life the waters and the
streams of Hudson's Bay. And yet how different will

be the reader's idea of spring to what it really was! Spring, with its fresh green leaves and opening flowers, its emerald fields and shady groves, filled with the sounds of melody! No, reader, that is not the spring which we depict. Not quite so beautiful, but far more prized is the spring to those who spend a monotonous winter of more than six months in solitude. The sun shines brightly in a cloudless sky, lighting up the pure white fields and plains with dazzling brilliancy. The gushing waters of a thousand rills formed by the melting snow, break sweetly on the ear, like the well-remembered voice of a long absent friend. The whistling wings of wild fowl, as they ever and anon desert the pools of water, now opened in the lake, and hurry o'er the forest trees, accords well with the shrill cry of the yellow-leg and curlew, and the general wildness of the scene; while the now-reviving frogs chirrup gladly in the swamps, to see the breaking up of winter, and welcome back the spring. This is the spring I write of; and, to have a correct idea of the beauties and the sweetness of *this* spring, you must first spend a winter in Hudson's Bay.

As I said, then, spring returned. The ice melted, floated off, and vanished. Jack River flowed gently on its way, as if it had never gone to sleep, and the lake rolled and tumbled on its shores, as if to congratulate them on the happy change. Soon the boats began to arrive : first came the " Portage Brigade," in charge of L'Esperance : there were seven or eight boats ; and, ere long, as many fires burned on the green beside the fort,

with a merry, careless band of wild-looking Canadian
and half-breed voyageurs round each—and a more picturesque set of fellows I never saw. They were all
dressed out in new light blue capôtes, and corduroy
trowsers, which they tied at the knee with beadwork
gaiters. Moose-skin moccasins cased their feet, and
their brawny sunburnt necks were bare ; a scarlet belt
encircled the waist of each ; and while some wore hats
with gaudy feathers, others had their heads adorned with
caps and bonnets, surrounded with gold and silver tinsel
hat-cords. A few, however, despising coats, travelled in
blue and white striped shirts, and trusted in their thickly
matted hair to guard them from the rain and sun. They
were truly a wild yet handsome set of men ; and no one,
while he gazed on their happy faces as they lay or stood
in careless attitudes round the fires, puffing clouds of
smoke from their ever-burning pipes, would have believed that these men had left their wives and families
but the week before, and were yet to start on a five
months' voyage of the most harassing description, fraught
with the dangers of the boiling cataracts and foaming
rapids of the interior.

They stopped at Norway House on their way, to receive the outfit of goods for the Indian trade of Athabasca (one of the interior districts), and were then to
start for " Portage La Roche ; " a place where the whole
cargoes are carried on the men's shoulders overland, for
twelve miles, to the head waters of another river, where
the traders from the northern posts come to meet them ,

and, taking the goods, give in exchange the "returns" in furs of the district.

Next came old Mr M'K—— with his brigade of five boats from Isle à la Crosse, one of the interior districts; and soon another set of camp fires burned on the green, and the clerk's house received another occupant. After them came the Red River brigades in quick succession; careful, funny, uproarious Mr M——t on his way to York for goods expected by the ship (for you must know Mr M——t keeps a store in Red River, and is a man of some importance in the colony); and grasping, comical, close-fisted Mr Mac——t, and quiet Mr S——, all passing onwards to the sea—rendering Norway House quite lively for a while, and then leaving it silent; but not for long, as the Saskatchewan brigade, under the charge of chief trader H——t and young Mr P——, suddenly arrived, and filled the whole country with noise and uproar. The Saskatchewan brigade is the largest and most noisy one that halts at Norway House. It generally numbers from fifteen to twenty boats, which are filled with the wildest men in the service. They come from the prairies and the Rocky Mountains, and are consequently brimful of stories of the buffalo hunt, attacks upon grizzly bears and wild Indians; some of them interesting, and true enough; but the most of them either tremendous exaggerations, or altogether inventions of their own wild fancies.

Soon after, the light canoes arrived from Canada, and in them an assortment of raw material for the service, in the shape of four or five green young men.

The clerks' house now became crammed, and all the quiet elderly folks who had continued to fret at its noisy occupants, now fled in despair to another house, and thereby left room for the new-comers, or green-horns, as they were elegantly styled by their more knowing fellow clerks.

Now, indeed, the corner of the fort in which we lived was avoided by all quiet people, as if it were smitten with the plague ; while the loud laugh, uproarious song, and sounds of the screeching flute or scraping fiddle, issued from the open doors and windows, frightening away the very mosquitoes, and making roof and rafters ring. Suddenly a dead silence would ensue, and then it was conjectured by knowing ones of the place, that Mr P——y was *coming out strong* for the benefit of the new arrivals; for he had a pleasant way of getting the green ones round him, and by detailing some of the wild scenes and incidents of his voyages in the Saskatchewan, lead them on from truth to exaggeration, and from that to fanciful composition, wherein he would detail, with painful minuteness, all the horrors of Indian warfare, and the improbability of any one entering those dreadful regions, ever returning alive !

Norway House was now indeed in full blow; and many a happy hour did I spend upon one of the clerk's beds, every inch of which was generally occupied, listening to the story or the song. The young men there assembled, had arrived from every distant quarter of America, and some of them even from England. Some were in the

prime of manhood, and had spent many years in the
Indian country; some were beginning to scrape the down
from their still soft chins; while others were boys of
fourteen who had just left home, and were listening for
the first time open-mouthed to their seniors' description
of life in the wilderness,

Alas! how soon were those happy, careless young
fellows to separate; and how little probability is there
of their ever meeting again! A sort of friendship had
sprung up among three of us: many a happy hour had
we spent in rambling among the groves and woods of
Norway House; now ranging about in search of wild
pigeons, anon splashing and tumbling in the clear waters
of the lake, or rowing over its surface in a light canoe;
while our inexperienced voices filled the woods with
snatches of the wild yet plaintive songs of the voyageurs, which we had just begun to learn.   Often had
we lain on our little pallet in Bachelor's Hall, recounting to each other our adventures in the wild woods, or
recalling the days of our childhood, and making pro-
mises of keeping up a steady correspondence through all
our separations, difficulties, and dangers.

A year passed away, and at last I got a letter
from one of my friends, dated from the Arctic regions,
near the mouth of the Mackenzie River; the other
wrote to me from among the snow-clad caps of the Rocky
Mountains; while I addressed them from the swampy ice-
begirt shores of Hudson's Bay.

In the Saskatchewan brigade two young bisons were

conveyed to York factory, for the purpose of being shipped for England in the " Prince Rupert."   They were a
couple of the wildest little wretches I ever saw, and were
a source of great annoyance to the men during the voyage.
The way they were taken was odd enough, and as it may
perhaps prove interesting, I shall describe it here.

In the Saskatchewan the chief food both of white men
and Indians is buffalo meat, so that parties are constantly
being sent out to hunt the buffalo. They generally chase
them on horseback, the country being mostly prairie land,
and, when they get close enough, shoot them with guns.
The Indians, however, shoot them oftener with the bow
and arrow, as they prefer keeping their powder and shot
for warfare.   They are very expert with the bow, which
is short and strong, and can easily send an arrow quite
through a buffalo at twenty yards off.   One of these

parties, then, was ordered to procure two calves alive,
if possible, and lead them to the Company's establishment. This they succeeded in doing, in the following

manner :—Upon meeting with a herd, they all set off
full gallop in chase ; away went the startled animals
at a round trot, which soon increased to a full gallop
as the horsemen neared them, and a shot or two told
that they were coming within range. Soon the shots
became more numerous, and here and there a black
spot on the prairie told where a buffalo had fallen.
No slackening of the pace occurred, however, as each
hunter upon killing an animal merely threw down his
cap or mitten to mark it as his own, and continued in
pursuit of the herd, loading his gun as he galloped
along. The buffalo hunters, by the way, are very expert
at loading and firing quickly while going at full gallop,
They carry two or three bullets in their mouths, which
they spit into the muzzles of their guns after dropping
in a little powder, and instead of ramming it down with a
rod, merely hit the butt end of the gun on the pommel
of their saddles ; and in this way fire a great many shots
in quick succession. This, however, is a dangerous mode
of shooting, as the ball sometimes sticks half way down
the barrel and bursts the gun, carrying away a finger, a
joint, and occasionally a hand.

In this way they soon killed as many buffaloes as they
could carry in their carts, and one of the hunters set off
in chase of a calf. In a short time he edged one away
from the rest, and then getting between it and the herd,
ran straight against it with his horse and knocked it
down. The frightened little animal jumped up again
and set off with redoubled speed, but another butt from

the horse again sent it sprawling ; again it rose, and
was again knocked down; and in this way was at last
fairly tired out; when the hunter, jumping suddenly from
his horse, threw a rope round its neck and drove it before
him to the encampment, and soon after brought it to the
fort. It was as wild as ever when I saw it at Norway
House, and seemed to have as much distaste to its thral-
dom as the day it was taken.

As the summer advanced, the heat increased, and the
mosquitoes became perfectly insupportable. Nothing can
save one from the attacks of these little torments. Almost all other insects went to rest with the sun : sand-
flies, which bite viciously during the day, went to sleep at
night; the large *bull-dog*, whose bite is terrible, slum-
bered in the evening ; but the mosquito, the long-legged,
determined, vicious, persevering mosquito, whose ceaseless hum dwells for ever in the ear, *never* went to sleep !
Day and night, the painful, tender, little pimples on our
necks and behind our ears, were being constantly re-
touched by these villanous flies. It was useless killing
thousands of them; millions supplied their place. The
only thing, in fact, that can protect one during the
night (*nothing* can during the day), is a net of gauze
hung over the bed, and as this was looked upon by the
young men as somewhat effeminate, it was seldom resorted to. The best thing for their destruction, we
found, was to fill our rooms full of smoke, either by
burning damp moss, or by letting off large puffs of
gunpowder, and then, throwing the doors and windows

open, allow them to fly out.   This, however, did not
put them all out; so we generally spent an hour or so
before going to bed, in hunting them with candles. Even
this did not entirely destroy them; and often might our
friends, by looking telescopically through the key-hole,
have seen us wandering during the late hours of the
night in our shirts, looking for mosquitoes, like unhappy
ghosts doomed to search perpetually for something they
can never find.   The intense suffocating heat also added
greatly to our discomfort.

In fine weather I used to visit my friend Mr Evans at
Rossville, where I had always a hearty welcome.   I remember on one occasion being obliged to beg the loan of
a canoe from an Indian, and having a romantic paddle
across part of Playgreen Lake.   I had been offered a
passage in a boat which was going to Rossville, but was
not to return. Having nothing particular to do, however,
at the time, I determined to take my chance of finding a
return conveyance of some kind or other.   In due time
I arrived at the parsonage, where I spent a pleasant
afternoon in sauntering about the village, and admiring
the rapidity and ease with which the Indian children
could read and write the Indian language by means
of a syllabic alphabet invented by their clergyman.
The same gentleman afterwards made a set of leaden
types, with no other instrument than a penknife, and
printed a great many hymns in the Indian language.

In the evening I began to think of returning to the
fort, but no boat or canoe could be found small enough

to be paddled by one man, and as no one seemed inclined
to go with me, I began to fear that I should have to remain all night.   At last a young Indian told me he had a
hunting canoe, which I might have, if I chose to venture
across the lake in it, but it was very small.   I instantly
accepted his offer, and bidding adieu to my friends at
the parsonage, followed him down to a small creek over-
shaded by tall trees, where, concealed among the reeds
and bushes, lay the canoe.   It could not, I should think,
have measured more than three yards in length, by eighteen inches in breadth at the middle, whence it tapered at
either end to a thin edge.   It was made of birch bark
scarcely a quarter of an inch thick, and its weight may
be imagined, when I say that the Indian lifted it from the
ground with one hand and placed it in the water, at the
same time handing me a small light paddle.   Into this I
stepped with great care, and the frail bark trembled with
my weight as I seated myself in the bottom, and pushed
out into the lake.   The sun had just set, and his disappearing rays cast a glare upon the overhanging clouds
in the west, while the shades of night were thickly
gathering over the eastern horizon.   Not a breath of
wind disturbed the glassy smoothness of the water, in
which every golden-tinted cloud was mirrored with a
fidelity that rendered it difficult to say which was image
and which was reality. The little bark darted through the
water with the greatest ease, and as I passed now among
the deepening shadows of the lofty pines, and then across
the gilded waters of the bay, a wild enthusiasm seized

me ; I strained with all my strength upon the paddle, and the sparkling drops flew in showers behind me, as the little canoe flew more like a phantom than reality over the water; when suddenly I missed my stroke; my whole weight was thrown on one side, the water gurgled over the gunwale of the canoe, and my heart leapt to my mouth, as I looked for an instant into the dark water. It was only for a moment; in another instant the canoe righted, and I paddled the remainder of the way in a much more gentle manner ; enthusiasm gone, and a most wholesome degree of timidity pervading my entire frame. It was dark when I reached the fort, and upon landing, I took the canoe under my arm and carried it up the bank with nearly as much ease as if it had been a camp-stool.

When the day was warm and the sun bright— when the sky was clear and the water blue—when the air was motionless, and the noise of arrivals and departures had ceased—when work was at a stand, and we enjoyed the felicity of having nothing to do, Mr R—— and I used to saunter down to the water's edge to have an hour or two's fishing.

The fish we fished for were gold-eyes, and the manner of our fishing was this : — pausing occasionally as we walked along, one of us might be observed to bend in a watchful manner over the grass, and gradually assuming the position of a quadruped, fall plump upon his hands and knees. Having achieved this feat, he would rise with a grasshopper between his finger and thumb; a tin box being then held open by the other, the unlucky insect was carefully introduced to the interior, and the lid closed sharply,—some such remark attending each capture, as that "*that* one was safe," or "there went another," and the mystery of the whole proceeding being explained by the fact, that these same incarcerated grasshoppers were intended to form the bait with which we trusted to beguile the unwary gold-eyes to their fate.

Having arrived at the edge of the place where we usually fished, each drew from a cleft in the rock a stout branch of a tree, around the end of which was wound a bit of twine with a large hook attached to it. This we unwound quickly, and after impaling a live grasshopper upon the barbs of our respective hooks, dropped them into the water, and gazed intently at the lines. Mr R——, who was a great lover of angling, now began to get excited, and made several violent pulls at the line under the impression that something had *bitten.* Suddenly his rod, stout as it was, bent with the immense muscular force applied to it, and a small gold-eye, about three or four inches long, flashed like an electric spark from the water, and fell with bursting force on the rocks behind, at the very feet of a small Indian boy, who sat nearly in a state of nature, watching our movements from among the bushes. The little captive was of a bright silvery colour, with a golden eye, and is an excellent fish for breakfast. The truth of the proverb, " It never rains but it pours," was soon verified by the im-

mense number of gold-eyes of every size, from one foot
to four inches, which we began to shower into the bushes
behind us.   Two or three dozen were caught in a few
minutes, and at last we began to get quite exhausted,
and Mr R—— proposed going up to the house for his
new fly-rod, by way of diversifying the sport, and rendering it more scientific.

Down he came again in a few minutes, with a splen-
didly varnished, extremely slim rod, with an invisible
line, and an aërial fly.   This instrument was soon put
up, and Mr R—— letting out six fathoms of line, stood
erect, and making a splendid heave, caught the Indian
boy by the hair!   This was an embarrassing commencement; but being an easy, good-natured man, he
only frowned the Indian boy out of countenance, and
shortened his line.   The next cast was more successful;
the line swept gracefully through the air, and fell in a
series of elegant circles within a few feet of the rock
on which he stood.   Gold-eyes, however, are not particular; and ere he could draw the line strait, a very
large one darted at the fly, and swallowed it.   The rod
bent into a beautiful oval, as Mr R—— made a futile
attempt to whip the fish over his head, according to
custom, and the line straitened with fearful rigidity
as the fish began to pull for its life.   The fisher became
energetic, and the fish impatient, but there was no prospect of its ever being landed; till at last, having got
his rod inextricably entangled among the neighbouring
bushes, he let it fall, and most unscientifically hauled the

fish out by the line, exclaiming, in the bitterness of his heart, "that rods were contemptible childish things, and that a stout branch of a tree was the rod for him." This last essay seemed to have frightened all the rest away, for not another bite did we get after that.

Towards the beginning of June 1843, orders arrived from head-quarters, appointing me to spend the approaching winter at York Factory, the place where I had first pressed American soil. It is impossible to describe the joy with which I received the news. Whether it was my extreme fondness for travelling, or the mere love of change, I cannot tell, but it had certainly the effect of making me very joyful, and I set about making preparation for the journey immediately. The arrival of the canoes from Canada was to be the signal for my departure, and I looked forward to their appearance with great impatience.

In a few days the canoes arrived, and on the fourth of June 1843 I started, in company with several other gentlemen, in two north canoes. These light graceful craft were about thirty-six feet long, by from five to six broad, and were capable of containing eight men and three passengers. They were made entirely of birch bark, and gaudily painted on the bow and stern. In these fairy-like boats, then, we swept swiftly over Playgreen Lake, the bright vermilion paddles glancing in the sunshine, and the woods echoing to the lively tune of *A la claire fontaine*, sung by the two crews in full chorus. We soon left Norway House far behind us, and ere long were rapidly descending the streams that flow through the forests of the interior into Hudson's Bay.

While running one of the numerous rapids with which these rivers abound, our canoe struck upon a rock, which tore a large hole in its side. Fortunately the accident happened close to the shore, and nearly at the usual breakfasting hour; so that while some of the men repaired the damages, which they did in half an hour, we employed ourselves agreeably in demolishing a huge ham, several slices of bread, and a cup or two of strong tea.

This was the only event worth relating that happened to us during the voyage; and as canoe travelling is enlarged upon in another chapter, we will jump at once to the termination of our journey.

CHAPTER VII.

YORK FACTORY.—WINTER AMUSEMENTS, ETC.

ERE you ever, reader, ambitious of dwelling in "a pleasant cot in a tranquil spot, with a distant view of the changing sea?" If so, do not go to York Factory. Not that it is not a pleasant enough place—for I spent two years very happily there—but simply (to give a poetical reason, and explain its character in one sentence) because it is a monstrous blot on a swampy spot, with a partial view of the frozen sea!

First impressions are generally incorrect; and I have little doubt that *your* first impression is, that a "monstrous blot on a swampy spot" cannot by any possibility be an agreeable place. To dispel this impression, and at the same time to enlighten you with regard to a variety of facts with which you are probably unacquainted, I shall describe York Factory as graphically as may be. An outline of its general appearance has been already given in a former chapter, so I will now proceed to particularise the buildings. The principal edifice is the " general store," where the goods, to the amount of two years' outfit for the whole northern department, are stored. On each side of this is a

long, low, whitewashed house, with green edgings, in
one of which visitors and temporary residents during
the summer are quartered. The other is the summer
mess-room. Four roomy fur-stores stand at right angles
to these houses, thus forming three sides of the front
square. Behind these stands a row of smaller buildings
for the labourers and tradesmen; and on the right hand
is the dwelling-house of the gentleman in charge, and
adjoining it the clerk's house, while on the left are the
provision store and Indian trading-shop. A few insignificant buildings, such as the oil-store and ice-house,
intrude themselves here and there; and on the right, a
tall ungainly outlook rises in the air, affording the inhabitants an extensive view of their wild domains.

The climate of York Factory is very bad in the warm
months of the year, but during the winter the intensity
of the cold renders it healthy. Summer is very short;
and the whole three seasons of spring, summer, and
autumn, are included in the months of June, July,
August, and September—the rest being winter.

During part of summer the heat is extreme, and
millions of flies, mosquitoes, &c., render the country
unbearable. Fortunately, however, the cold soon extir-
pates them. Scarcely any thing in the way of vegetables can be raised in the small spot of ground called,
by courtesy, a garden. Potatoes one year, for a wonder,
became the size of walnuts; and sometimes they succeed
in getting a cabbage and a turnip to grow. Yet the
woods are filled with a great variety of wild berries,

among which the cranberry and swampberry are considered the best. Black and red currants, as well as gooseberries, are plentiful, but the first are bitter, and the last small. The swampberry is in shape something like the raspberry, of a light yellow colour, and grows on a low bush, almost close to the ground. They make excellent preserves, and, together with cranberries, are made into tarts for the mess during winter. In the month of September there are generally a couple of weeks or so of extremely fine weather, which is called the Indian summer ; after which, winter, with frost, cold and snow, sets in with rapidity. For a few weeks in October there is sometimes a little warm weather (or rather, I should say, a little *thawy* weather), but after that, until the following April, the thermometer seldom rises to the freezing point. In the depth of winter the thermometer falls from 30 to 40, 45, and even 49 degrees *below zero* of Fahrenheit. This intense cold, however, is not so much felt as one might suppose ; as, during its continuance, the air is perfectly calm. Were the slightest breath of wind to arise when the thermometer stands so low, no man could show his face to it for a moment. Forty degrees below zero, and quite calm, is infinitely preferable to 15° below, or thereabouts, with a strong breeze of wind. Spirit of wine is of course the only thing that can be used in the thermometers, as mercury, were it exposed to such cold, would remain frozen nearly half the winter. Spirit never froze in any cold ever experienced at York Factory, unless when very much

adulterated with water ; and even then, the spirit would
remain liquid in the centre of the mass.*

To resist this intense cold, the inhabitants dress, not
in furs, as is generally supposed, but in coats and trowsers made of smoked deer-skins ; the only piece of fur
in their costume being the cap.   The houses are built of
wood, with double windows and doors.   They are heated
by large iron stoves, fed with wood; yet so intense is the
cold, that I have seen the stove in places *red-hot*, and a
basin of water in the room *frozen* solid.   The average
cold, I should think, is about 15 or 16 degrees below
zero, or 48 degrees of frost.   The country around is a
complete swamp, but the extreme shortness of the warm
weather, and the consequent length of winter, fortunately
prevents the rapid decomposition of vegetable matter.
Another cause of the unhealthiness of the climate during
summer, is the prevalence of dense fogs, which come off
the bay and enshroud the country, and also the liability
of the weather to sudden and extreme changes.†

Summer may be said to commence in July, the preceding month being a fight between summer and winter,
which cannot claim the slightest title to the name of
spring.   As August advances, the heat becomes great ;
but about the commencement of September, nature wears
a more pleasing aspect, which lasts till the middle of

* Quicksilver easily freezes ; and it has frequently been run into a
bullet mould, exposed to the cold air till frozen, and in this state
rammed down a gun barrel, and fired through a thick plank.

† See Table on next page.

AVERAGE RANGE OF FAHRENHEIT'S THERMOMETER DURING FIVE MONTHS

OF THE YEAR 1843.

JANUARY.			FEBRUARY.*			MARCH.			MAY.			JUNE.		
Date	Morning.	Noon.	Date	Morning.	Noon.	Date	Morning.	Noon.	Date	Morning.	Noon.	Date	Morning.	Noon.
1	34 below zero.	22 below zero.	1	32 below zero.	31 below zero.	1	17 below zero.	10 below zero.	1	23 above zero.	26 above zero.	1	24 above zero.	31 above zero.
5	32 —	22 —	4	30 —	25 —	6	11 —	6 —	6	24 —	50 —	4	31 —	36 —
12	29 —	12 —	9	49 below zero.	25 —	8	8 above zero.	5 above zero.	12	40 —	55 —	7	34 —	48 —
20	5 —	1 —	17	32 —	19 —	9	23 below zero.	10 below zero.	20	25 —	45 —	16	40 —	75 —
18	13 above zero.	21 above zero.	23	36 —	15 —	20	36 —	11 —	26	35 —	55 —	22	66 —	79 —
26	9 below zero.	9 below zero.	27	10 above zero.	5 above zero.	27	20 —	5 —	29	28 —	49 —	28	50 —	60 —
31	22 —	23 —	28	13 below zero.	9 below zero.	30	— zero.	16 above zero.	31	23 —	30 —	31	52 —	61 —

* February is invariably the coldest month of the year; and 49 degrees below zero of Fahrenheit is the greatest degree of cold ever experienced. But some years it is even colder, and has been known to fall below 50.

October. It is then clear and beautiful, just cold enough
to kill all the mosquitoes, and render brisk exercise
agreeable. About this time, too, the young ducks begin
to fly south, affording excellent sport among the marshes.
A week or so after this, winter commences, with light
falls of snow occasionally, and hard frost during the
night. Flocks of snow-birds (the harbingers of cold in
autumn, and heat in spring) begin to appear, and soon
the whirring wings of the white partridge may be heard
among the snow-encompassed willows. The first thaw
generally takes place in April, and May is characterised
by melting snow, disruption of ice, and the arrival of the
first flocks of wild-fowl.

The country around the fort is one immense level
swamp, thickly covered with willows, and dotted here and
there with a few clumps of pine-trees. The only large
timber in the vicinity grows on the banks of Hayes and
Nelson Rivers, and consists chiefly of spruce-fir. The
swampy nature of the ground has rendered it necessary
to raise the houses in the fort several feet in the air,
upon blocks of wood, and the squares are intersected by
elevated wooden platforms, which form the only promenade the inhabitants have during the summer, as no one
can venture fifty yards beyond the gates without wetting
his feet. Nothing bearing the most distant resemblance
to a hillock exists in the land. Nelson River is a broad
rapid stream, which discharges itself into Hudson's Bay,
near the mouth of Hayes River, between which lies a
belt of swamp and willows, known by the name of the

point of marsh. Here may be found, during the spring and autumn, millions of ducks, geese, and plover, and during the summer, billions of mosquitoes. There are a great many strange plants and shrubs in this marsh, which forms a wide field of research and pleasure to the botanist and the sportsman; but the lover of beautiful scenery, and the florist, will find little to please the eye or imagination, as nature has here put on her plainest garb; and flowers there are none.

Of the feathered tribes, there are the large and small gray Canada goose, the laughing goose (so called from the resemblance of its cry to laughter), and the wavie or white goose. The latter are not very numerous. There are great numbers of wild-ducks, pintails, widgeons, divers, sawbills, black ducks, and teal; but the prince of ducks (the canvass back) is not there. In spring and autumn the whole country becomes musical with the wild cries and shrill whistle of immense hosts of plover of all kinds; long legs, short legs, black legs, and yellow legs, sand-pipers and snipe, which are assisted in their noisy concerts by myriads of frogs. The latter are really the best songsters in Hudson's Bay.* Bitterns are also found in the marshes; and sometimes, though rarely, a solitary crane finds its way to the coast. In the woods, and among the dry places around, there are

* The thousands of frogs that fill the swamps of America whistle or chirp so exactly like little birds, that many people, upon hearing them for the first time, have mistaken them for the feathered songsters of the groves. Their only fault is, that they scarcely ever cease singing.

a few gray grouse and wood partridges, a great many hawks, and owls of all sizes, from the gigantic white owl, which measures five feet across the back and wings, to the small gray owl, not much bigger than a man's hand.

In winter the woods and frozen swamps are filled with ptarmigan, or, as they are called by the trappers, white partridges. They are not very palatable; but, nevertheless, they form a pretty constant dish at the winter mess-table of York Factory, and afford excellent sport to the inhabitants. There are also great varieties of small birds, among which the most interesting are the snow-birds, or snow-flakes, which pay the country a flying visit at the commencement and termination of winter.

Such is York Fort, the great depôt and gate to the wild regions surrounding Hudson's Bay. Having described its appearance and general characteristics, I shall proceed to introduce the reader to my future companions, and describe our amusements and sports among the marshes.

BACHELOR'S HALL.

On the —— of June 1843, I landed the second time on the wharf of York Fort, and betook myself to Bachelor's Hall, where Mr H——, whom I met by the way, told me to take up my quarters. As I approached the door of the well-remembered house, the most tremendous uproar that ever was heard proceeded from within its dingy walls; so I jumped the paling that stood in front of the windows, and took a peep at the interior before introducing myself.

The scene that met my eye was ludicrous in the extreme. Mounted on a chair, behind a bedroom door, stood my friend C——, with a large pail of water in his arms, which he raised cautiously to the top of the door, for the purpose of tilting it over upon two fellow clerks who stood below, engaged in a wrestling match, little dreaming of the cataract that was soon to fall on their devoted heads. At the door of a room opposite stood the doctor, grinning from ear to ear at the thoughts of sending a thick stream of water in C——'s face from a large syringe which he held in his hands; while near the stove sat the jolly skipper, looking as grave as possible.

The practical joke was just approaching to a climax when I looked in. The combatants neared the door behind which C—— was ensconced. The pail was raised, and the syringe pointed, when the hall door opened, and Mr H—— walked in! The sudden change in the state of things that followed could not have been more rapidly effected had Mr H—— been a magician. The doctor thrust the syringe into his pocket, into which a great deal of the water escaped and dripped from the skirts of his coat as he walked slowly across the room, and began to examine, with a wonderful degree of earnestness, the edge of an amputating knife which lay on his dressing-table. The two wrestlers sprang with one accord into their own room, where they hid their flushed faces behind the door. Certain smothered sounds near the stove, proclaimed that the skipper was revelling in an excruciating fit of suppressed laughter; while poor C——, who slipped his foot in rapidly descending from his chair, lay sprawling in an ocean of water, which he had upset upon himself in his fall.

Mr H—— merely went to Mr W——'s room to ask a few questions, and then departed as if he had seen nothing; but a peculiar twist in the corners of his mouth, and a comical twinkle in his eye, showed that, although he said nothing, yet he had a pretty good guess that his " young men" had been engaged in mischief.

Such were the companions to whom I introduced myself shortly after; and, while they went off to the office, I amused myself in looking round the rooms in which I was to spend the approaching winter.

The house was only one storey high, and the greater part of the interior formed a large hall, from which several doors led into the sleeping apartments of the clerks. The whole was built of wood; and few houses could be found wherein so little attention was paid to ornament or luxury. The walls were originally painted white; but this, from long exposure to the influence of a large smoky stove, had changed to a dirty yellow. No carpet covered the floor, yet, nevertheless, the yellow planks of which it was composed had a cheerful appearance; and gazing at the numerous knots with which it was covered, often afforded me a dreamy kind of amusement when I had nothing better to do. A large

oblong iron box, on four crooked legs, with a funnel
running from it through the roof, stood exactly in the
middle of the room; this was a stove, but the empty
wood-box in the corner showed that its services were not
required at that time. And truly they were not; for it
was the height of summer, and the whole room was filled
with mosquitoes and bull-dog flies, who kept up a per-
petual hum night and day. The only furniture that
graced the room consisted of two small kitchen tables
without table-cloths, five whole wooden chairs, and a
broken one; which latter, being light and handy, was
occasionally used as a missile by the young men when
they happened to quarrel. Several guns and fishing-
rods stood in the corners of the hall; but their dirty
appearance proclaimed that sporting, at that time, was
not the order of the day. The tables were covered with a
miscellaneous collection of articles; and, from the number
of pipes which reposed on little odoriferous heaps of
cut tobacco, I inferred that my future companions were
great smokers. Two or three books, a pair of broken
foils, a battered mask, and several surgical instruments,
over which a huge mortar and pestle presided, completed
the catalogue.

The different sleeping apartments around, were not
only interesting to contemplate, but also extremely characteristic of the pursuits of their different occupants.
The first I entered was very small, just large enough
to contain a bed, a table, and a chest, leaving little
room for the occupant to move about in; and yet, from

the appearance of things, he did move about in it to
some purpose, as the table was strewn with a number
of saws, files, bits of ivory and wood, and in a corner a
small vice held the head of a cane in its iron jaws.
These were mixed with a number of Indian account-
books and an ink-stand; so that I concluded I had
stumbled on the bedroom of my friend Mr W——, the
post-master.

The quadrant case and sea chest in the next room
proved it to be the skipper's, without the additional
testimony of the oiled-cloth coat and sou'-wester which
hung upon the walls.

The doctor's room was filled with dreadful-looking
instruments, suggestive of operations, amputations, bleeding wounds, and human agony; while the accountant's
was equally characterised by methodical neatness, and
the junior clerks' by utter and chaotic confusion.   None
of these bedrooms were carpeted; none of them boasted
of a chair—the trunks and boxes of the persons to whom
they belonged answering instead; and none of the beds
were graced with curtains.   Notwithstanding this emp-
tiness, however, they derived a warmth of appearance
from the number of greatcoats, leather capôtes, fur caps,
worsted sashes, guns, rifles, shot-belts, snow-shoes, and
powder-horns, with which the walls were profusely decorated.   The ceilings of the rooms, moreover, were very
low, so much so, that, by standing on tiptoe, I could
touch them with my hand; and the window in each was
only about three feet high by two and a half broad, so

that upon the whole the house was rather snug than otherwise.

Such was the habitation in which I dwelt, and such the companions with whom I associated at York Factory.

As the season advanced, the days became shorter and the nights more frosty ; and soon a few flakes of snow began to fall, indicating the approach of winter. About the beginning of October the cold damp snowy weather that usually precedes winter set in ; and shortly after Hayes River was full of drifting ice, and the whole country covered with snow. A week or so after this, the river was completely frozen over ; and Hudson's Bay itself, as far as the eye could reach, was covered with a coat of ice. We now settled down into our winter habits. Double windows were fitted in, and double doors also. Extra blankets were put upon the beds ; the iron stove kept constantly alight ; and, in fact, every preparation was made to mitigate the severity of the winter.

The water froze every night in our basins, although the stove was kept at nearly a red heat all day, and pretty warm all night ; and our out-of-door costume was changed from jackets and shooting coats to thick leather capôtes, fur caps, duffle socks, and moccasins.

Soon after this, white partridges began to arrive ; and one fine, clear, frosty morning, after breakfast, I made my first essay to kill some, in company with my fellow-clerk and room-mate, C——, and the worthy skipper.

The manner of dressing ourselves to resist the cold was curious. We will describe C—— as a type of the

rest. After donning a pair of deerskin trousers, he proceeded to put on three pair of blanket socks, and over
these a pair of moose-skin moccasins. Then a pair of
blue cloth leggins were hauled over his trousers, partly
to keep the snow from sticking to them, and partly for
warmth. After this he put on a leather capôte edged
with fur. This coat was very warm, being lined with
flannel, and overlapped very much in front. It was
fastened with a scarlet worsted belt round the waist, and
with a loop at the throat. A pair of thick mittens made
of deerskin hung round his shoulders by a worsted cord,
and his neck was wrapped in a huge shawl, over the
mighty folds of which his good-humoured visage beamed
like the sun on the edge of a fog-bank. A fur cap with
ear-pieces completed his costume. Having finished his
toilet, and tucked a pair of snow-shoes, five feet long,
under one arm, and a double-barrelled fowling-piece
under the other, C—— waxed extremely impatient, and
proceeded systematically to aggravate the unfortunate
skipper (who was always very slow, poor man, except on
board ship), addressing sundry remarks to the stove upon
the slowness of seafaring men in general, and skippers
in particular. In a few minutes the skipper appeared
in a similar costume, with a monstrously long gun over
his shoulder, and under his arm a pair of snow-shoes
gaudily painted by himself; which snow-shoes he used
to admire amazingly, and often gave it as his opinion
that they were "slap-up, tossed-off-to-the-nines" snow-
shoes! Truly they were large enough; the following

sketch will show the proportion the shoe bore to his leg.

In this guise, then, we departed on our ramble. The sun shone brightly in the cold blue sky, giving a warm appearance to the scene, although no sensible warmth proceeded from it to us, so cold was the air. Countless millions of icy particles covered every bush and tree, glittering tremulously in its rays like diamonds—pshaw! that hackneyed simile: diamonds of the purest water never shone like these evanescent little gems of nature. The air was biting cold, obliging us to walk briskly along to keep our blood in circulation; and the breath flew thick and white from our mouths and nostrils, like clouds of steam, and, condensing on our hair and the breasts of our coats, gave us the appearance of being powdered with fine snow. C——'s red countenance assumed a redder hue by contrast, and he cut a very comical figure when his bushy whiskers changed from their natural auburn hue to a pure white, under the influence of this icy covering. The skipper, who all this while had been floundering slowly among the deep snow, through which his short legs were but ill calcu-lated to carry him, suddenly wheeled round, and pre-

sented to our view the phenomenon of a very red warm
face, and an extremely livid cold nose thereunto affixed.
We instantly apprised him of the fact that his nose was
frozen, which he would scarcely believe for some time :
however, he was soon convinced, and after a few minutes'
hard rubbing, it was restored to its usual temperature.

We had hitherto been walking through the thick
woods near the river's bank ; but finding no white partridges there, we stretched out into the frozen swamps,
which now presented large fields and plains of compact
snow, studded here and there with clumps and thickets
of willows.   Among these we soon discovered fresh
tracks of birds in the snow, whereat the skipper became
excited (the sport being quite new to him), and expressed
his belief, in a hoarse whisper, that they were not far off.
He even went the length of endeavouring to walk on
tiptoe, but being unable, from the weight of his snow-
shoes, to accomplish this, he only tripped himself, and,
falling with a stunning crash through a large dried-up
bush, buried his head, shoulders, and gun in the snow.
Whir-r-r ! went the birds—crack ! bang ! went C——'s
gun, and down came two partridges ; while the unfortunate skipper, scarce taking time to clear his eyes from
snow, in his anxiety to get a shot, started up, aimed at
the birds, and blew the top of a willow, which stood a
couple of feet before him, into a thousand atoms.   The
partridges were very tame, and only flew to a neighbouring clump of bushes, where they alighted.   Mean-
while C—— picked up his birds, and while re-loading

his gun, complimented the skipper upon the beautiful manner in which he *pointed*. To this he answered not, but, raising his gun, let drive at a solitary bird, which either from fear or astonishment had remained behind the rest, and escaped detection until now, owing to its resemblance to the surrounding snow. He fortunately succeeded in hitting this time, and bagged it with great exultation. Our next essay was even more successful. The skipper fired at one which he saw sitting near him, killed it, and also two more which he had not seen, but which had happened to be in a line with the shot, and C—— and I killed a brace each when they took wing.

During the whole day we wandered about the woods, sometimes killing a few ptarmigan, and occasionally a kind of grouse, which are called by the people of the country wood partridges. While we were sauntering slowly along in the afternoon, a rabbit darted across our path; the skipper fired at it without even putting the gun to his shoulder, and to his utter astonishment killed it. After this we turned to retrace our steps, thinking that as our game-bags were pretty nearly full, we had done enough for one day. Our sport was not done, however; we came suddenly upon a large flock of ptarmigan, which were so tame that they would not fly, but merely ran from us a little way at the noise of each shot. The firing that now commenced was quite terrific. C—— fired till both barrels of his gun were stopped up; the skipper fired till his powder and shot were done; and I fired till—*I skinned my tongue!* Lest any one should feel surprised at the last statement, I may as well explain *how* this happened. The cold had become so intense, and my hands so benumbed with loading, that the thumb at last obstinately refused to open the spring of my powder-flask. A partridge was sitting impudently before me, so that in the fear of losing the shot, I thought of trying to open it with my teeth. In the execution of this plan, I put the brass handle to my mouth, and my tongue happening to come in contact with it, stuck fast thereto,—or, in other words, was frozen to it. Upon discovering this, I instantly pulled the flask away, and with it a piece of skin about the size of a sixpence. Having achieved this little feat, we once more bent our steps homeward.

During our walk the day had darkened, and the sky insensibly become overcast. Solitary flakes of snow fell here and there around us, and a low moaning sound, as of distant wind, came mournfully down through the sombre trees, and, eddying round their trunks in little gusts, gently moved the branches, and died away in the distance. With an uneasy glance at these undoubted signs of an approaching storm, we hastened towards the fort as fast as our loads permitted us, but had little hope of reaching it before the first burst of the gale. Nature had laid aside her sparkling jewels, and was now dressed in her simple robe of white. Dark leaden clouds rose on the northern horizon, and the distant howling of the cold, cold wind struck mournfully on our ears, as it rushed fresh and bitterly piercing from the Arctic seas, tearing madly over the frozen plains, and driving clouds of hail and snow before it. Whew! how it dashed along—scouring wildly over the ground, as if maddened by the slight resistance offered to it by the swaying bushes, and hurrying impetuously forward to seek a more worthy object on which to spend its bitter fury! Whew! how it curled around our limbs, catching up mountains of snow into the air, and dashing them into impalpable dust against our wretched faces. Oh! it was bitterly, bitterly cold. Notwithstanding our thick wrappings, we felt as if clothed in gauze; while our faces seemed to collapse and wrinkle up as we turned our backs to the wind and hid them in our mittens. One or two flocks of ptarmigan, scared by the storm, flew swiftly past us, and sought shelter in the neighbouring forest. We quickly followed their example, and under the partial shelter of the trees, made the best of our way back to the fort, where we arrived just as it was getting dark, and entered the warm precincts of Bachelor's Hall, like three animated marble statues, so completely were we covered from head to foot with snow.

It was curious to observe the change that took place in the appearance of our gun-barrels, after we entered the warm room. The barrels, and every bit of metal upon them, instantly became white, like ground glass! This phenomenon was caused by the moist atmosphere of the room being condensed and frozen upon the cold iron. Any piece of metal, when brought suddenly out of such intense cold into a warm room, will in this way

become covered with a pure white coating of hoarfrost.
It does not remain long in this state, however, as the
warmth of the room soon heats the metal, and the ice
begins to melt. Thus, in about ten minutes our guns
assumed three different appearances : when we entered
the house, they were clear, polished, and dry ; in five
minutes they were white as snow; and in five minutes
more, they were dripping wet !

On the following morning a small party of Indians
arrived with furs, and Mr W—— went with them to the
trading room, whither I accompanied him.

The trading room, or, as it is frequently called, the
Indian shop, was much like what is called a store in the
United States. It contained every imaginable commodity
likely to be needed by Indians. On various shelves
were piled bales of cloth of all colours, capôtes, blankets,
caps, &c., and in smaller divisions were placed files,
scalping-knives, gun-screws, flints, balls of twine, fire-
steels, canoe-awls, and glass beads of all colours, sizes,
and descriptions. Drawers in the counter contained
needles, pins, scissors, thimbles, fish-hooks, and vermilion for painting their canoes and faces. The floor
was strewn with a variety of copper and tin kettles,
from half-a-pint to a gallon ; and on a stand in the farthest corner of the room, stood about a dozen trading
guns, and beside them a keg of powder and a box of
shot.

Into this room, then, we entered and began to trade.
First of all, an old Indian laid a pack of furs upon the

counter, which Mr W—— proceeded to count and value.
Having done this, he marked the amount opposite to
the old man's name in his "Indian book," and then
handed him a number of small pieces of wood. The
use of these pieces of wood is explained in the third
chapter. The Indian then began to look about him,
opening his eyes gradually, as he endeavoured to find
out which of the many things before him he would like
to have. Sympathising with his eyes, his mouth slowly
opened also; and having remained in this state for some
time, the former looked at Mr W——, and the latter
pronounced *ahcoup* (blanket.) Having received the blanket, he paid the requisite number of bits of wood for it,
and became abstracted again. In this way he bought
a gun, several yards of cloth, a few beads, &c., till all
his sticks were gone, and then made way for another.
They were uncommonly slow about it, however, and Mr
W—— and I returned to the house in a couple of hours,
with very cold toes and fingers, and exceedingly blue
noses.

During winter we breakfasted usually at nine o'clock,
then sat down to the desk till one, when we dined.
After dinner we resumed our pens till six, when we
had tea, and then wrote again till eight, after which
we either amused ourselves with books (of which we
had a few); kicked up a row; or, putting on our snow-
shoes, went off to pay a moonlight visit to our traps.
On Wednesdays and Saturdays, however, we did no
work, and generally spent these days in shooting.

It is only at the few principal establishments of the country where so much writing is necessary, as at these the accounts of the country are collected annually, to be forwarded to the Hudson's Bay House in London.

As the Christmas holidays approached, we began to prepare for the amusements which usually take place during that joyous season.   On the morning before Christmas, a gentleman who had spent the first part of the winter all alone at his outpost, arrived to spend the holidays at York Factory.   We were greatly delighted to have a new face to look at, having seen no one but ourselves since the ship left for England, nearly four months before.

Our visitor, Mr K——, had travelled in a dog cariole. This machine is very narrow, just broad enough to admit one person.   It is a wooden frame covered with deer-skin parchment, painted gaudily, and is generally drawn by four Esquimaux dogs.

Christmas morning dawned, and I opened my eyes to behold the sun flashing brightly on the window, in its endeavours to make a forcible entry into my room, through the thick hoarfrost which covered it.   Presently I became aware of a gentle breathing near me, and turning my eyes slowly round, I beheld my companion C—— standing on tiptoe, with a tremendous grin on his countenance, and a huge pillow in his hands, which was in the very act of descending upon my devoted head.   To collapse into the smallest possible compass, and present the most invulnerable part of my body to

DOG-CARIOLE TRAVELLING.

the blow, was the work of an instant, when down came
the pillow, bang! " Hooroo! hurroo! hurroo! a
merry Christmas to you, you rascal!" shouted C——.
Bang! bang! went the pillow. " Turn out of that, you
lazy lump of plethoric somnolescence," whack!—and,
twirling the ill-used pillow round his head, my facetious
friend rushed from the room to bestow upon the other
occupants of the Hall a similar salutation. Upon recovering from the effects of my pommelling, I sprang
from bed and donned my clothes with all speed, and then
went to pay my friend Mr W—— the compliments of
the season. In passing through the Hall for this purpose,
I discovered C—— struggling in the arms of the skipper, who, having wrested the pillow from him, was now
endeavouring to throttle him partially. I gently shut
and fastened the door of their room, purposing to detain
them there till *very nearly* too late for breakfast, and
then sat down with Mr W——, to discuss our intended
proceedings during the day. These were—firstly, that
we should go and pay a ceremonious visit to the men;
secondly, that we should breakfast; thirdly, that we
should go out to shoot partridges; fourthly, that we
should return to dinner at five; and, fifthly, that we
should give a ball in Bachelor's Hall in the evening, to
which were to be invited all the men at the fort, and *all*
the Indians, men, women, and children, inhabiting the
country for thirty miles round. As the latter, however,
did not amount to above twenty, we did not fear that
more would come than our hall was calculated to accom-

modate. In pursuance, then, of these resolutions, I cleaned my gun, freed my prisoners just as the breakfast bell was ringing, and shortly afterwards went out to shoot. I will not drag the reader after me, however. Suffice it, that we all returned about dusk, with our game-bags full, and with ravenous appetites for dinner.

Our Christmas dinner was a good one, in a substantial point of view, and a very pleasant one, in a social point of view. We ate it in the winter mess-room, and really (for Hudson's Bay) this was quite a snug and highly decorated apartment. True, there was no carpet on the floor, and the chairs were home-made ; but, then, the table was mahogany, and the walls were hung round with several large engravings in bird's-eye maple frames. The stove, too, was brightly polished with black lead, and the painting of the room had been executed with a view to striking dumb those innocent individuals who had spent the greater part of their lives at outposts, and were, consequently, accustomed to domiciles and furniture of the simplest and most unornamental description. On the present grand occasion, the mess-room was illuminated by an argand lamp, and the table covered with a snow-white cloth, whereon reposed a platter, containing a beautiful, fat, plump wild-goose, which had a sort of come-eat-me-up-quick-else-I'll-melt expression about it that was painfully delicious. Opposite to this, smoked a huge roast of beef, to procure which, one of our most useless draught oxen had been sacrificed. This, with a dozen of white partridges, and a large piece of salt pork, composed our dinner. But the greatest rarities on the board were two large decanters of port wine, and two smaller ones of madeira. These were flanked by tumblers and glasses; and truly, upon the whole, our dinner made a goodly show.

" Come away, gentlemen," said Mr H——, as we entered the room and approached the stove where he stood, smiling with that benign expression of countenance peculiar to stout, good-natured gentlemen at this season, and at this particular hour. " Your walk must have sharpened your appetites; sit down, sit down. This way, doctor, sit near me; find a place, Mr B——, beside your friend C—— there; take the foot, Mr W—— ;" and amid a shower of such familiar phrases we seated ourselves and began.

At the top of the table sat Mr H——, indistinctly visible through the steam that rose from the wild-goose before him. On his right and left sat the doctor and the accountant, and down from them sat the skipper, four clerks, and Mr W——, whose honest face beamed with philanthropic smiles at the foot of the table. Loud was the mirth and fun that reigned on this eventful day within the walls of the highly decorated room at York Factory. Bland was the expression of Mr H——'s face, when he asked each of the young clerks to drink wine with him in succession; and great was the confidence which thereby inspired the said clerks, prompting them to the perpetration of several rash and unparalleled pieces of presumption, such as drinking wine with each other (an act of free-will on their part almost unprecedented), and indulging in sundry sly pieces of covert humour, such as handing the vinegar to each other when the salt was requested, and becoming profusely apologetic upon discovering their mistake. But the wildest storm is often succeeded by the greatest calm, and the most hilarious mirth by the most solemn gravity. In the midst of our fun, Mr H—— proposed a toast. Each filled a bumper, and silence reigned around, while he raised his glass, and said, " Let us drink to absent friends." We each whispered " absent friends," and set our glasses down in silence, while our minds flew back to the scenes of former days, and we mingled again in spirit with our dear, dear friends at home. How different the mirth of the loved ones there, circling round the winter hearth, from that of the *men* seated round the Christmas table in the nor'-west wilderness. I question very much if this toast was ever drunk with a more thorough appreciation of its melancholy import, than upon the present memorable occasion. Our sad feelings, however, were speedily put to flight, and our gravity routed, when the skipper, with characteristic modesty, proposed " the ladies ;" which toast we drank with a hearty goodwill, although, indeed, the former included them, inasmuch as they also were *absent* friends—the only one within two hundred and fifty miles of us being Mr H——'s wife.

What a magical effect ladies have upon the male sex, to be sure ! Although hundreds of miles distant from an unmarried specimen of the species, upon the mere mention of their name, there was instantly a perceptible alteration for the better in the looks of the whole party. Mr W—— unconsciously arranged his hair a little more becomingly, as if his ladye-love were actually looking at him; and the skipper afterwards confessed that his heart had bounded suddenly out of his breast, across the snowy billows of the Atlantic, and come smash down on the wharf at Plymouth dock, where he had seen the last wave of Nancy's checked cotton neckerchief, when he left the shores of Old England.

Just as we had reached the above climax, the sound of a fiddle struck upon our ears, and reminded us that our guests, who had been invited to the ball, were ready; so, emptying our glasses, we left the dining-room, and adjourned to the Hall.

Here a scene of the oddest description presented itself. The room was lit up by means of a number of tallow candles, stuck in tin sconces round the walls. On several benches and chairs sat all the Orkneymen and Canadian half-breeds of the establishment, in their Sunday jackets and capotes; while here and there the dark visage of an Indian peered out from among their white faces. But round the stove—which had been removed to one side to leave space for the dancers—the strangest group was collected. Squatting down on the floor, in every ungraceful attitude imaginable, sat about a dozen Indian women, dressed in printed calico gowns, the chief peculiarity of which was the immense size of the balloon-

shaped sleeves, and the extreme scantiness, both in
length and width, of the skirts. They were chatting
and talking to each other with great volubility, occasionally casting a glance behind them, where at least
half a dozen infants stood bolt upright in their tight-
laced cradles. On a chair in a corner near the stove sat
a young good-looking Indian, with a fiddle of his own
making beside him. This was our Paganini; and beside
him sat an Indian boy with a kettle-drum, on which he
tapped occasionally, as if anxious that the ball should
begin. All this flashed upon our eyes; but we had not
much time for contemplating it; as, the moment we entered, the women simultaneously rose, and coming mo-
destly forward to Mr W———, who was the senior of
the party, saluted him, one after another! I had been
told that this was a custom of the *ladies* on Christmas
day, and was consequently not quite unprepared to go
through the ordeal. But when I looked at the superhuman ugliness of some of the old ones, when I gazed at
the immense, and in some cases toothless chasms that
were being pressed on my senior's lips, and gradually
approached, like a hideous nightmare, towards me; and,
when I reflected that these same mouths might have in
former days demolished a few children, my courage for-
sook me, and I entertained for a moment the idea of bolting. The doctor seemed to labour under the same disinclination with myself; for, when they advanced to him,
he refused to bend his head, and, being upwards of six
feet high, they of course were obliged to pass him.

They looked, however, so much disappointed at this, and withal so very modest, that I really felt for them, and prepared to submit to my fate with the best grace possible. A horrible old hag advanced towards me, the perfect embodiment of a nightmare, with a fearful grin on her countenance. I shut my eyes. Suddenly a bright idea flashed across my mind; I stooped down, with apparent good-will, to salute her; just as our mouths were about to meet, I slightly jerked up my head, and she kissed my *chin*. Oh, happy thought! They were all quite satisfied, and attributed the accident, no doubt, to their own clumsiness.

This ceremony over, we each chose partners, the fiddle struck up, and the ball began. Scotch reels were the only dances known by the majority of the guests, so we confined ourselves entirely to them.

The Indian women afforded us a good deal of amusement during the evening. Of all ungraceful beings they are the most ungraceful; and of all accomplishments, dancing is the one in which they shine least. There is no rapid motion of the feet, no lively expression of the countenance; but, with a slow, regular, up-and-down motion, they stalk through the figure with extreme gravity. They seemed to enjoy it amazingly, however, and scarcely allowed the poor fiddler a moment's rest during the whole evening.

Between eleven and twelve o'clock our two tables were put together, and spread with several towels; thus forming a pretty respectable supper table, which would have been perfect, had not the one been three inches higher than the other. On it was placed a huge dish of cold venison, and a monstrous iron kettle of tea. This, with sugar, bread, and a lump of salt butter, completed the entertainment, to which the Indians sat down. They enjoyed it very much, at least so I judged from the rapid manner in which the viands disappeared, and the incessant chattering and giggling kept up at intervals. After all were satisfied, the guests departed in a state of great happiness, particularly the ladies, who tied up the remnants of the supper in their handkerchiefs, and carried them away.

Before concluding the description of our Christmas doings, I may as well mention a circumstance which resulted from the effects of the ball, as it shows in a curious manner the severity of the climate at York Factory. In consequence of the breathing of so many people in so small a room, for such a length of time, the walls had become quite damp, and ere the guests departed, moisture was trickling down in many places. During the night, this moisture was frozen ; and, on rising the following morning, I found, to my astonishment, that Bachelors' Hall was apparently converted into a palace of crystal. The walls and ceiling were thickly coated with beautiful minute crystalline flowers, not sticking flat upon them, but projecting outwards in various directions, thus giving the whole apartment a cheerful light appearance, quite indescribable. The moment our stove was heated, however, the crystals became fluid, and ere long evaporated, leaving the walls exposed in all their original dinginess.

*　　　*　　　*　　　*　　　*　　　*

Winter passed away; but not slowly, or by degrees. A winter of so long duration could not be expected to give up its dominion without a struggle. In October it began, and in November its empire was established. During December, January, February, March, and April, it continued to reign unmolested, in steadfast bitterness; inclosing in its icy bands, and retaining in torpid frigidity, the whole inanimate and vegetable creation. But in May its powerful enemy, caloric, made a decided attack upon its empire, and dealt hoary winter a stunning blow.

About the beginning of April a slight thaw occurred, the first that had taken place since the commencement of winter; but this was speedily succeeded by hard frost, which continued till the second week in May, when thaw set in so steadily, that in a few days the whole country changed in appearance.

On the 12th of May, Hayes River, which had been for nearly eight months covered with a coat of ice upwards of six feet thick, gave way before the floods occasioned by the melting snow; and all the inmates of the fort rushed out to the banks upon hearing the news that the river was " going." On reaching the gate, the sublimity of the spectacle that met our gaze can scarcely be imagined. The noble river, which is here nearly two miles broad, was entirely covered with huge blocks and jagged lumps of ice, rolling and dashing against each other in chaotic confusion, as the swelling floods heaved them up, and swept them with irresistible force towards Hudson's Bay. In one place, where the masses were too closely packed to admit of violent collision, they ground against each other with a slow but powerful motion, that curled their hard edges up like paper, till the smaller lumps, unable to bear the pressure, were ground to powder, and with a loud crash the rest hurried on to renew the struggle elsewhere ; while the ice above, whirling swiftly round in the clear space thus formed, as if delighted at its sudden release, hurried onwards. In another place, where it was not so closely packed, a huge lump suddenly grounded on a shallow; and in a moment the rolling masses, which were hurrying towards the sea with the velocity of a cataract, were precipitated on it with a noise like thunder, and the tremendous pressure from above, forcing block upon block with a loud hissing noise, raised, as if by magic, an icy castle in the air, which, ere its pinnacles had pointed for a second to the sky, fell with stunning violence into the boiling flood from whence it rose. In a short time afterwards the mouth of the river became so full of ice that it stuck there, and in less than an hour the water rose ten or fifteen feet, nearly to a level with the top of the bank. In this state it continued for a week ; and then, about the end of May, the whole floated quietly out to sea, and the cheerful river gurgled along its bed with many a curling eddy and watery dimple rippling its placid face, as if it smiled to think of having overcome its powerful enemy, and at last burst its prison walls.

Although the river was at last free, many a sign of winter yet remained around our forest home. The islands in the middle of the stream were covered with huge masses of ice, many of which were piled up to a height of twenty feet. All along the banks, too, it was strewn thickly; while in the woods snow still lay in many places several feet deep. In time, however, these last evidences of the mighty power of winter gave way before the warm embraces of spring. Bushes and trees began to bud, gushing rills to flow, frogs to whistle in the swamp, and ducks to sport upon the river, while the hoarse cry of the wild-goose, the whistling wings of teal, and all the other sounds and cries of the long absent inhabitants of the marshes, gave life and animation to the scene. Often has nature been described as falling asleep in the arms of winter, and awaking at the touch of spring; but nowhere is this simile so strikingly illustrated as in these hyperborean climes, where, for eight long silent months, nature falls into a sleep so still and unbroken that death seems to be a fitter simile than sleep; and in spring she bursts into a life so bright, so joyous, so teeming with animal and vegetable life, and, especially when contrasted with her previous slumber, so noisy, that awakening from sleep does not give any thing like an adequate idea of the change, and bursting into life, even, falls short of the bright reality.

Now was the time that our guns were cleaned with peculiar care, and regarded with a sort of brotherly affection. Not that we despised the sports of winter, but we infinitely preferred those of spring.

Young C—— and I were inseparable companions; we had slept in the same room, hunted over the same ground, and scribbled at the same desk, during the whole winter, and now we purchased a small hunting canoe from an Indian, for the purpose of roaming about together in spring. Our excursions were always amusing; and as a description of one of them may perhaps prove interesting to the reader, I shall narrate

A Canoe Excursion on the shores of Hudson's Bay.

It is needless to say that the day we chose was fine, that the sun shone brightly, that the curling eddies of the river smiled sweetly, that the jagged pinnacles of the blocks of ice along shore, which had not yet melted, sparkled brilliantly, that the fresh green foliage of the trees contrasted with these white masses oddly, that C—— and I shouldered our canoe between us, after having placed our guns, &c., in it, and walked down to the river bank under our burden lightly. It is needless, I say, to describe all this minutely, as it would be wasting my pens, ink, and paper unnecessarily. It is sufficient to say, that we were soon out in the middle of the stream, floating gently down the current towards the point of marsh which was to be the scene of our exploits.

The day was indeed beautiful, and so very calm and still, that the glassy water reflected every little cloud in the sky; and on the seaward horizon every thing was quivering and magically turned upside down—islands, trees, icebergs, and all! A solitary gull, which stood not far off upon a stone, looked so preposterously huge from the same atmospherical cause, that I would have laughed immoderately had I had energy to do so; but I was too much wrapt in placid enjoyment of the scene to give way to boisterous mirth. The air was so calm that the plaintive cries of thousands of wild fowl which covered the point of marsh struck faintly on our ears. "Ah!" thought I;—but I need not say what I thought. I grasped my powder flask and shook it—it was full, crammed full! I felt my shot-belt—it was fat, very fat, bursting with shot! Our two guns lay side by side, vying in brightness; their flints quite new and sharp, and standing up in a lively, wide-awake sort of way, as much as to say, "If you do not let me go, I'll go bang off by myself!" Happiness is sometimes too strong to be enjoyed quietly; and C—— and I, feeling that we could keep it down no longer, burst simultaneously into a yell that rent the air, and, seizing the paddles, made our light canoe spring over the water, while we vented our feelings in a lively song, which reaching the astonished ears of the aforementioned preposterously large gull, caused it to depart precipitately.

In half an hour we reached the point; and dragging the canoe above high-water mark, shouldered our guns.

and, with long strides, proceeded over the swamp in search of game.

We had little doubt of having good sport, for the whole point away to the horizon was teeming with ducks and plover. We had scarcely gone a hundred yards ere a large widgeon rose from behind a bush, and C——, who was in advance, brought it down. As we plodded on, the faint cry of a wild-goose caused us to squat down suddenly behind a neighbouring bush, from which retreat we gazed round to see where our friends were. Another cry from behind attracted our attention; and far away on the horizon we saw a large flock of geese flying in a mathematically correct triangle. Now, although far out of shot, and almost out of sight, we did not despair of getting one of these birds; for, by imitating their cry, there was a possibility of attracting them towards us. Geese often answer to a call in this way, if well imitated, particularly in spring, as they imagine that their friends have found a good feeding-place, and wish them to alight. Knowing this, C—— and I continued in our squatting position—utterly unmindful, in the excitement of the moment, of the fact that the water of the swamp lay in the same proximity to our persons as a chair does when we sit down on it—and commenced to yell and scream vociferously in imitation of geese; for which, doubtless, many people unacquainted with our purpose would have taken us. At first our call seemed to make no impression on them; but gradually they bent into a curve, and sweeping round in a long circle, came nearer to us, while we continued to shout at the top of our voices. How they ever mistook our bad imitation of the cry for the voices of real geese, I cannot tell—probably they thought we had colds or sore throats; at any rate they came nearer and nearer, screaming to us in return, till at last they ceased to flap their wings, and sailed slowly over the bush behind which we were ensconced, with their long necks stretched straight out, and their heads a little to one side, looking down for their friends. Upon discovering their mistake, and beholding two human beings instead of geese within a few yards of them, the sensation created among them was tremendous, and the racket they kicked up in trying to fly from us was terrific; but it was too late. The moment we saw that they had discovered us, our guns poured forth their contents, and two out of the flock fell with a lumbering smash upon the ground, while a third went off wounded, and after wavering in its flight for a little, sank slowly to the ground. Having bagged our game, we proceeded, and ere long filled our bags with ducks, geese, and plover. Towards the afternoon we arrived at a tent belonging to an old Indian called Morris. With this dingy gentleman we agreed to dine, and accordingly bent our steps towards his habitation. Here we found the old Indian and his wife squatting down on the floor and wreathed in smoke, partly from the wood fire which burned in the middle of the tent, and partly from the tobacco pipes stuck in their respective mouths. Old Morris was engaged in preparing a kettle of pea-soup, in which were boiled several plover, and a large white owl (these same owls, by the way, are, when skinned, comically like very young babies), while his wife was engaged in ornamenting a pair of moccasins with dyed quills. On our entrance, the old man removed his pipe, and cast an inquiring glance into the soup kettle; this apparently gave him immense satisfaction, as he turned to us with a smiling countenance, and remarked (for he could speak capital English, having spent the most of his life near York Factory) that "duck plenty, but he too *h*old to shoot much; obliged to *h*eat *h*owl." This we agreed was uncommonly hard, and after presenting him with several ducks and a goose, proposed an inspection of the contents of the kettle, which being agreed to, we demolished nearly half of the soup, and left him and his wife to "*h*eat" the "*h*owl." After resting an hour with this hospitable fellow, we departed, to prepare our encampment ere it became dark, as we intended passing the night among the swamps, under our canoe. Near the tent we passed a fox-trap set on the top of a pole, and, on inquiring, found that this was the machine in which Old Morris caught his "*h*owls." The white owl is a very large and beautiful bird, sometimes nearly as large as a swan. I shot one which measured five feet three inches across the wings, when expanded. They are in the habit of alighting upon the tops of blighted trees, and poles of any kind, which happen to stand conspicuously apart from the forest trees, for the purpose, probably, of watching for mice and little birds, on which they prey. Taking advantage of this habit, the Indian plants his trap on the top of a bare tree, so that, when the owl alights, it is generally caught by the legs.

Our walk back to the place where we had left the canoe was very exhausting, as we had nearly tired ourselves out before thinking of returning. This is very often the case with eager sportsmen, as they follow the game till quite exhausted, and only then it strikes them that they have got as long a walk back as they had in going out. I recollect this happening once to myself. I had walked so far away into the forest after wild-fowl, that I forgot time and distance in the ardour of the pursuit, and only thought of returning when I was quite knocked up. The walk back was truly wretched. I was obliged to rest every ten minutes, as, besides being tired, I was becoming faint from hunger. On the way I stumbled on the nest of a plover, with one egg in it. This was a great acquisition ; so, seating myself on a stone, I made my dinner of it, raw. Being very small, it did not do me much good, but it inspired me with courage ; and, making a last effort, I reached the encampment in a very unenviable state of exhaustion.

After an hour's walk, C—— and I arrived at the place where we left the canoe.

Our first care was to select a dry spot whereon to sleep, which was not an easy matter in such a swampy place. We found one at last, however, under the shelter of a small willow bush. Thither we dragged the canoe, and turned it bottom up, intending to creep in below it, when we retired to rest. After a long search on the sea shore, we found a sufficiency of drift-wood to make a fire, which we carried up to the encampment, and placed in a heap in front of the canoe. This was soon kindled by means of a flint and steel, and the forked flames began in a few minutes to rise and leap around the branches, throwing the swampy point into deeper shadow, and, by its deep warm light, making the sea look cold and blue, and the ice upon its surface ghost-like. The interior of our inverted canoe looked really quite cheerful and snug, under the influence of the fire's rosy light. And when we had spread our blankets out under it, plucked and cleaned two of the fattest ducks, and stuck them up on sticks before the blaze to roast, we agreed that there were worse things in nature than an encampment in the swamps.

Ere long, the night became pitchy dark; but although we could see nothing, yet ever and anon the whistling wings of ducks became audible, as they passed in flocks overhead. So often did they pass in this way, that at last I was tempted to try to get a shot at them, notwithstanding the apparent hopelessness of such an attempt; so, seizing my gun, and leaving strict injunctions with C—— to attend to the roasting of my widgeon, I sallied forth, and, after getting beyond the light of the fire, endeavoured to peer through the gloom. Nothing was to be seen, however. Flocks of ducks were passing quite near, for I heard their wings whizzing as they flew, but they were quite invisible; so at last, becoming tired of standing up to my knees in water, I pointed my gun at random at the next flock that passed, and fired. After the shot, I listened intently for a few seconds, and the next moment a splash in the water apprised me that the shot had taken effect. After a long search, I found the bird, and returned to my friend C——, whom I threw into a terrible state of consternation, by pitching the dead duck into his lap as he sat winking, and rubbing his hands before the warm blaze.

Supper, in these out-of-the-way regions, is never long of being disposed of, and on the present occasion we finished it very quickly, being both hungry and fatigued. After it was over, we heaped fresh logs upon the fire, wrapped our green blankets round us, and, nestling close together, as much underneath our canoe as possible, began to court the drowsy god. In this courtship I was unsuccessful for some time, and lay gazing on the flickering flames of the watch-fire, which illuminated the grass of the marsh a little distance round; and listening, in a sort of dreamy felicity, to the occasional cry of a wakeful plover, or starting suddenly at the flapping wings of a huge owl, which, attracted by the light of our fire, wheeled slowly round, gazing on us in a kind of solemn astonishment, till, scared by the sounds that proceeded from C——'s nasal organ, it flew with a scream into the dark night air; and again all was silent, save the long, solemn, sweeping boom of the distant waves, as they rolled at long intervals upon the sea shore. During the night we were awakened by a shower of rain falling upon our feet, and as much of our legs as the canoe was incapable of protecting. Pulling them up more under shelter, at the expense of exposing our knees and elbows—for the canoe could not completely cover us—we each gave a mournful grunt, and dropped off again.

Morning broke with unclouded splendour, and we rose from our grassy couch with alacrity to resume our sport; but I will not again drag my patient reader through the point of marsh.

In the afternoon, having spent our ammunition, we launched our light canoe, and after an hour's paddle up the river, arrived, laden with game and splashed with mud, at York Factory.

CHAPTER VIII.

VOYAGE FROM YORK FACTORY TO NORWAY HOUSE IN A SMALL
INDIAN CANOE.

N the afternoon of the 20th of June 1845, I sat in my room at York Fort, musing on the probability of my being sent off to some other part of the Company's wide dominions.

The season was approaching when changes from one part of the country to another might be expected, and boats were beginning to arrive from the interior. Two years of fun and frolic had I spent on the coast, and I was beginning to wish to be sent once more upon my travels, particularly as the busy season was about to commence and the hot weather to set in.

As I sat cogitating, my brother scribblers called me to join them in a short promenade upon the wharf, preparatory to resuming our pens. Just as we reached it, a small Indian canoe from the interior swept round the point above the factory, and came rapidly forward, the sparkling water foaming past her sharp bow as it made towards the landing.

At almost any time an arrival causes a great deal of interest in this out-of-the-way place; but an arrival of this sort, for the canoe was evidently an *express*, threw each of us into a fever of excitement, which was greatly increased when we found that it contained dispatches from head-quarters; and many speculative remarks passed among us as we hurried up to our hall, there to wait in anxious expectation for a letter or an order to appear instanter before Mr H——. Our patience was severely tried, however, and we were beginning to think there was no news at all, when Gibeault, the butler, turned the corner, and came towards our door. We immediately rushed towards it in breathless expectation, and a row of eager faces appeared as he walked slowly up to the door and said, "Mr H—— wishes to see Mr B—— immediately." On hearing this, I assumed an appearance of calm indifference which I was far from feeling, and putting on my cap proceeded to obey the order.

Upon entering Mr H——'s presence, he received me with a benign, patronizing air, and requested me to be seated. He then went on to inform me that letters had just arrived, requesting that I might be sent off immediately to Norway House, where I would be enlightened as to my ultimate destination. This piece of news I received with a mingled expression of surprise and delight, at the same time exclaiming "Indeed!" with peculiar emphasis; and then, becoming suddenly aware of the impropriety of the expression, I endeavoured to follow it up with a look of sorrow at the prospect of leaving my friends, combined with resignation to the will of the Honourable Hudson's Bay Company, in which attempt I failed most signally. After receiving orders to prepare for an immediate start, I rushed out in a state of high glee, to acquaint my fellow scribblers with my good fortune. On re-entering Bachelors' Hall I found my companions as anxious to know where I was destined to vegetate next winter, as they had before been to learn who was going off. Having satisfied them on this point, or rather told them as much as I knew myself regarding it, I proceeded to pack up.

It happened, just at this time, that a brigade of inland boats was on the eve of starting for the distant regions of the interior ; and as the little canoe, destined to carry myself, was much too small to take such an unwieldy article as my "cassette," I gladly availed myself of the opportunity to forward it by the boats, as they would have to pass Norway House *en route*. It would be endless to detail how I spent the next three days; how I never appeared in public without walking very fast, as if pressed with a superhuman amount of business ; how I rummaged about here and there, seeing that every thing was prepared; looking vastly important, and thinking I was immensely busy, when in reality I was doing next to nothing ; I shall, therefore, without further preface, proceed to describe my travelling equipments.

The canoe in which I and two Indians were to travel from York Factory to Norway House, a distance of nearly three hundred miles, measured between five and six yards long, by two feet and a half broad in the middle, tapering

from thence to *nothing* at each end. It was made in the
usual way, and could, with great ease, be carried by one
man. In this we were to embark, with ten days' provisions for three men, three blankets, three small bundles,
and a little travelling case belonging to myself; besides
three paddles wherewith to propel us forward, a tin kettle
for cooking, and an iron one for boiling water. Our craft
being too small to permit my taking the usual allowance
of what are called luxuries, I determined to take pot-luck
with my men, so that our existence, for the next eight or
ten days, was to depend upon the nutritive properties
contained in a few pounds of pemican, a little biscuit, one
pound of butter, and a very small quantity of tea and
sugar. With all this, in addition to ourselves, we calculated upon being pretty deeply laden.

My men were of the tribe called Swampy Crees, and
truly, to judge merely from appearance, they would have
been the very last I should have picked out to travel with;
one being old, apparently upwards of fifty, and the
other, though young, was a cripple. Nevertheless, they
were good hardworking men, as I afterwards experienced.
I did not take a tent with me, as our craft required to be
as light as possible, but I rolled up a mosquito net in my
blanket, as it was a light affair of gauze, and capable of
being compressed into very small compass. Such were
our equipments; and on the 23d of June we started for
the interior.

A melancholy feeling came over me as I turned and
looked, for the last time, upon York Factory, where I

had spent so many happy days with the young men who now stood waving their handkerchiefs from the wharf. Mr H——, too, stood among them, and as I looked on his benevolent manly countenance, I felt that I should ever remember with gratitude his kindness to me while we resided together on the shores of Hudson's Bay. A few minutes more, and the fort was hid from my sight for ever.

My disposition is not a sorrowful one ; I never did and never could remain long in a melancholy mood, which will account for the state of feeling I enjoyed half an hour after losing sight of my late home. The day was fine, and I began to anticipate a pleasant journey, and to speculate as to what part of the country I might be sent to. The whole wide continent of North America was now open to the excursive flights of my imagination, as there was a possibility of my being sent to any one of the myriads of stations in the extensive territories of the Hudson's Bay Company. Sometimes I fancied myself ranging through the wild district of Mackenzie's River, admiring the scenery described by Franklin and Back in their travels of discovery ; and anon, as the tales of my companions occurred to me, I was bounding over the prairies of the Saskatchewan in chase of the buffalo, or descending the rapid waters of the Columbia to the Pacific ocean. Again my fancy wandered, and I imagined myself hunting the grizzly bear in the woods of Athabasca, when a heavy lurch of the canoe awakened me to the fact that I was only ascending the sluggish waters of Hayes River.

The banks of the river were covered with huge blocks of ice, and scarcely a leaf had as yet made its appearance. Not a bird was to be seen, except a few crows and whisky-jacks, which chattered among the branches of the trees ; and nature appeared as if undecided whether or not she should take another nap, ere she bedecked herself in the garments of spring. My Indians paddled slowly against the stream, and I lay back, with a leg cocked over each gunwale, watching the sombre pines as they dropped slowly astern. On our way we passed two landslips, which encroached a good deal on the river, each forming a small rapid round its base. The trees, with which they had formerly been covered, were now scattered about in chaotic confusion, leafless, and covered with mud ; some more than half buried, and others standing with their roots in the air. There is a tradition among the natives that a whole camp of Indians was overwhelmed in the falling of these slips.

A good deal of danger is incurred in passing up these rivers, owing to the number of small landslips which occur annually. The banks, being principally composed of sandy clay, are loosened, and rendered almost fluid in many places, upon the melting of the snow in spring ; and the ice, during the general disruption, tears away large masses of the lower part of the banks, which renders the superincumbent clay liable to slip, upon the first heavy shower of rain, with considerable force into the stream.

About sixteen miles from York Factory we ran bump

against a stone, and tore a small hole in the bottom of our canoe. This obliged us to put ashore immediately, when I had an opportunity of watching the swiftness and dexterity of the Indians in repairing the damage. A small hole, about three inches long, and one inch wide, had been torn in the bottom of the canoe, through which the water squirted with considerable rapidity. Into this hole they fitted a piece of bark, sewed it with wattape (the fibrous roots of the pine-tree,) made a small fire, melted gum, and plastered the place so as to be effectually water-tight, all in about the space of an hour.

During the day we passed a brigade of boats bound for the factory ; but, being too far off, and in a rapid part of the river, we did not hail them. About nine o'clock we put ashore for the night, having travelled nearly twenty miles. The weather was pleasantly cool, so that we were free from mosquitoes. The place we chose for our encampment was on the edge of a high bank, being the only place within three miles where we could carry up our provisions ; and even here it was bad enough to ascend ; but, after we were up, the top proved to be a good spot, covered with soft moss, and well sheltered by trees and bushes. A brook of fresh water rippled at the foot of the bank, and a few decayed trees standing close by afforded us excellent firewood. Here, then, in the bosom of the wilderness, with the silvery light of the moon for our lamp, and serenaded by a solitary owl, we made our first bivouac. Supper was neatly laid out on an oil-cloth, spread before a blazing fire. A huge junk of pemican graced the centre of our rustic table, flanked by a small pile of ship's biscuit on one side, and a lump of salt butter on the other; while a large iron kettle filled with hot water, slightly flavoured with tea-leaves, brought up the rear. Two tin pots and a tumbler performed out-post duty, and were soon smoking full of warm tea. We made an excellent supper, after which the Indians proceeded to solace themselves with a whiff, while I lay on my blanket, enjoying the warmth of the fire, and admiring the apparently extreme felicity of the men, as they sat, with half-closed eyes, watching the smoke curling in snowy wreaths from their pipes, and varying their employment, now and then, with a pull at the tin pots, which seemed to afford them extreme satis-faction. In this manner we lay till the moon waned, and the owl having finished his overture, we rolled ourselves in our blankets, and watched the twinkling stars till sleep closed our eyelids.

Next morning, between two and three o'clock, we began to stretch our limbs, and after a few ill-humoured grunts, prepared for a start. The morning was foggy when we embarked, and once more began to ascend the stream. Every thing was obscure and indistinct till about six o'clock, when the powerful rays of the rising sun began to dispel the mist, and Nature was "herself again." A good deal of ice still lined the shores; but what astonished me most, was the advanced state of vegetation apparent as we pro-ceeded inland. When we left York Factory not a leaf had been visible; but here, though only thirty miles inland, the trees, and more particularly the bushes, were pretty well covered with beautiful light green foliage, which appeared to me quite delightful after the patches of snow, and the leafless willows on the shores of Hudson's Bay.

At eight o'clock we put ashore for breakfast, which was just a repetition of the supper of the preceding night, with this exception, that we discussed it a little more hurriedly, and then proceeded on our way.

Shortly afterwards we met a small canoe, about the size of our own, which contained a postmaster and two Indians, on their way to York Factory with a few packs of otters. After five minutes' conversation we parted, and were soon out of sight of each other. The day, which had hitherto been agreeable, now became oppressively sultry ; not a breath of wind ruffled the water, and as the sun shone down with intense heat from a perfectly cloudless sky, it became almost insufferable. I tried all methods to cool myself, by lying in every position I could think of, sometimes even hanging both legs and arms over the sides of the canoe and trailing them through the water. I had also a racking headach, and, to add to my misery, as the sun began to decline, the mosquitoes began to rise, and bite in a most voracious manner. The Indians, however, did not appear to suffer much, being accustomed, no doubt, to these little annoyances, much in the same way as eels are to being skinned.

In the afternoon we arrived at the forks of Hayes and Steel Rivers, and ascended the latter, till the increasing darkness, and our quickening appetites, reminded us that

it was time to put ashore. We made a hearty supper,
having eaten nothing since breakfast; dinner, while
travelling in a light canoe, being considered quite superfluous.

Our persevering foes, the mosquitoes, now thought it
high time to make their supper also, and attacked us in
myriads, whenever we dared to venture near the woods;
so we were fain to sleep as best we could on the open
beach, without any fire, being much too warm for that;
but even there they found us out, and most effectually
prevented us from sleeping nearly all night.

On the morning of the 25th, we arose, very little refreshed by our short nap, and continued our journey.
The weather was still warm, but a little more bearable,
owing to a light grateful breeze that came down the river.
After breakfast, which we took at the usual hour, and in
the usual way, while proceeding slowly up the current, we
descried on rounding a point, a brigade of boats close to
the bank, on the opposite side of the river; so we embarked our man, who was tracking us up with a line, (the
current being too rapid for the continued use of the paddle,) and crossed over to see who they were.   On landing,
we found that it was the Norway House brigade in charge
of George Kippling, a Red River settler. He shook hands
with us, and then commenced an animated discourse with
my two men, in the Indian language, which being perfectly
unintelligible to me, I amused myself by watching the
operations of the men, who were in the act of cooking
breakfast.

Nothing can be more picturesque than a band of voyageurs breakfasting on the banks of a pretty river. The
spot they had chosen, was a little above the " Burntwood
Creek," on a projecting grassy point, pretty clear of underwood. Each boat's crew, of which there were three, had
a fire to itself, and over these fires were placed gipsy-like
tripods, from which huge tin kettles depended, and above
them hovered three volunteer cooks who were employed
stirring their contents with persevering industry. The
curling wreaths of smoke formed a black cloud among the
numerous fleecy ones in the blue sky; while all around,
in every imaginable attitude, sat, stood, and reclined, the
sun-burnt savage-looking half-breeds, chatting, laughing, and smoking, in perfect happiness. They were all
dressed alike, in light cloth capotes with hoods, corduroy
trousers, striped shirts, open in front; with cotton
kerchiefs tied sailor-fashion loosely round their swarthy
necks. A scarlet worsted vest strapped each man's coat
tightly to his body, and Indian moccasins defended their
feet. Their head-dresses, however, were as various as
they were fanciful; while some wore caps of coarse cloth,
others wore coloured handkerchiefs, turban-fashion, round
their heads, and one or two, who might be looked upon as
voyageur fops, sported black beaver hats, covered so
plenteously with bullion tassels, and feathers, as to be
scarcely recognisable.

The breakfast consisted solely of pemican and flour,
boiled into a sort of thick soup, dignified by the name of
robbiboo. It is not, as might be expected, a very delicate

dish, but is, nevertheless, exceedingly nutritious; and those
who have lived long in the country, particularly the
Canadians, are very fond of it. I think, however, that
another of their dishes, composed of the same materials,
but fried instead of boiled, is much superior to it. They
call it *richeau ;* it is uncommonly rich, and very little will
suffice for an ordinary man.

After staying about a quarter of an hour, chatting with
Kippling about the good folks of Red River and Norway
House, we took our departure just as they commenced
the first vigorous attack upon the capacious kettles of
robbiboo.

Shortly after, we arrived at the mouth of Hill River,
which we began to ascend. The face of the country was
now greatly changed, and it was evident that here spring
had long ago dethroned winter. The banks of the river
were covered from top to bottom with the most luxuriant
foliage, while dark clumps of spruce-fir varied and improved the landscape. In many places the banks, which
appeared to be upwards of a hundred feet high, ran
almost perpendicularly down to the water's edge, perfectly
devoid of vegetation except at the top, where large trees
overhung the precipice, some hanging by their roots
ready to fall. In other places the banks sloped from
nearly the same height, gradually, and with slight undulations, down to the stream, thickly covered with vegetation, and teeming with little birds—whose merry voices,
warbling a cheerful welcome to the opening buds, greatly
enhanced the pleasures of the scene.

We soon began to experience great difficulty in tracking the canoe against the rapidity of the stream which now opposed us. From the steepness of the banks in some places, and their being clothed with thick willows in others, it became a slow and fatiguing process for our men to drag us against the strong current, and sometimes the poor Indians were clinging like flies against nearly perpendicular cliffs of slippery clay, and at others tearing through the almost impervious bushes. They relieved each other by turns every hour at this work, the one steering the canoe while the other tracked, and they took no rest during the whole day, except when at breakfast. Indeed, any proposal to do so would have been received by them with great contempt, as being a very improper and useless waste of time.

When the track happened to be at all passable, 1 used to get out and walk, to relieve them a little, as well as to stretch my cramped limbs, it being almost impossible, when there is any luggage in a small Indian canoe, to attain a comfortable position.

At sunset we put ashore for the night, on a point covered with a great number of *lopsticks*. These are tall pine-trees, denuded of their lower branches, a small tuft being left at the top. They are generally made to serve as landmarks, and sometimes the voyageurs make them in honour of gentlemen who happen to be travelling for the first time along the route, and those trees are chosen which, from their being on elevated ground, are conspicuous objects. The traveller for whom they are made is always expected to acknowledge his sense of the honour conferred upon him, by presenting the boat's crew with a pint of grog, either on the spot or at the first establishment they meet with. He is then considered as having paid for his footing, and may ever afterwards pass scot-free.

We soon had our encampment prepared, and the fire blazing; but hundreds of mosquitoes were, as usual, awaiting our arrival, and we found it utterly impossible to sup, so fiercely did they attack us; so we at last went to leeward of the fire and devoured it hastily in the smoke, preferring to risk being suffocated, or smoke-dried, to being eaten up alive! It was certainly amusing to see us rush into the thick smoke, bolt a few mouthfuls of pemican, and then rush out again for fresh air; our hands swinging like the sails of a windmill round our heads, while every now and then, as a mosquito fastened on a tender part, we gave ourselves a resounding slap on the side of the head, which, had it come from the hand of another, would certainly have raised in us a most pugnacious spirit of resentment. In this manner we continued rushing out of and into the smoke, till supper was finished, and then prepared for sleep. This time, however, I was determined not to be tormented; so I cut four stakes, drove them into the ground, and over them threw my gauze mosquito-net, previously making a small fire, with wet grass on it, to raise a smoke and prevent intruders from entering while I was in the act of putting it on; then, cautiously raising one end, I bolted in after

the most approved harlequinian style, leaving my dis-
comfited tormentors wondering at the audacity of a man
who could snore in a state of unconcerned felicity in the
very midst of the enemy's camp!

On the following morning we started at an early hour.
The day was delightfully cool, and mosquitoes scarce,
so that we felt considerably comfortable as we glided
quietly up the current.   In this way we proceeded
till after breakfast, when we came in sight of the first
portage, on which we landed.   In a surprisingly short
time our luggage, &c., was pitched ashore, and the
canoe carried over by the Indians, while I followed with
some of the baggage; and in half an hour we were ready
to start from the upper end of the portage.   While carrying across the last few articles, one of the Indians
killed two fish called suckers, which they boiled on the
spot and devoured immediately.

Towards sunset we paddled quietly up to the " White
Mud Portage," where there is a fall, of about seven or
eight feet, of extreme rapidity, shooting over the edge in
an arch of solid water, which falls hissing and curling
into the stream below.   Here we intended to encamp.   As
we approached the cataract, a boat suddenly appeared on
the top of it, and shot with the speed of lightning into
the boiling water beneath, its reckless crew shouting,
pulling, laughing, and hallooing, as it swept round a
small point at the foot of the fall, and ran aground in a
bay or hollow, where the eddying water, still covered
with patches of foam after its mighty leap, floated quietly

round the shore. They had scarcely landed, when another boat appeared on the brink, and, hovering for an instant, as if to prepare itself for the leap, flashed through the water, and the next moment was aground beside the first. In this manner seven boats successively ran the fall, and grounded in the bay.

Upon our arriving, we found them to be a part of the Saskatchewan brigade, on its way to the common point of rendezvous, York Factory. It was in charge of two friends of mine; so I accosted them, without introducing myself, and chatted for some time about the occurrences of the voyage. They appeared a little disconcerted, however, and looked very earnestly at me two or three times. At last, they confessed that they had forgotten me altogether! And, indeed, it was no wonder; for the sun had burned me nearly as black as my Indian friends, while my dress consisted of a blue capote, sadly singed with the fire—a straw hat, whose shape, from exposure and bad usage, was utterly indescribable—a pair of corduroys, and Indian moccasins, which so metamorphosed me, that my friends, who perfectly recollected me the moment I mentioned my name, might have remained in ignorance to this day, had I not enlightened them on the subject.

After supper, Mr M——, one of these gentlemen, offered me a share of his tent, and we turned in together, but not to sleep; for we continued gossiping till long after the noisy voices of the voyageurs had ceased to disturb the tranquillity of night.

At the first peep of day our ears were saluted with the usual unpleasant sound of "*Lève! lève! lève!*" issuing from the leathern throat of the guide. Now this same "*Lève!*" is in my ears a peculiarly harsh and disagreeable word, being associated with frosty mornings, uncomfortable beds, and getting up in the dark before half enough of sleep has been obtained. The way in which it is uttered, too, is particularly exasperating; and often, when partially awakened by a stump boring a hole in my side, have I listened with dread to hear the detested sound, and then, fancying it must surely be too early to rise, have fallen gently over on the other side, when a low, muffled sound as if some one were throwing off his blanket would strike upon my ear, then a cough or grunt, and finally, as if from the bowels of the earth, a low and scarcely audible "*Lève! lève!*" would break the universal stillness, growing rapidly louder, "*Lève! lève! lève!*" and louder, "*Lève! lève!*" till at last a final stentorian "*Lève! lève! lève!*" brought the hateful sound to a close, and was succeeded by a confused collection of grunts, groans, coughs, grumbles, and sneezes, from the unfortunate sleepers thus rudely roused from their slumbers. The disinclination to rise, however, was soon overcome; and up we got, merry as larks, the men loading their boats, while I and my Indians carried our luggage, &c., over the portage.

Our troubles now commenced: the longest and most difficult part of the route lay before us, and we prepared for a day of toil. Far as the eye could reach, the river

was white with boiling rapids and foaming cascades,
which, though small, were much too large to ascend,
and consequently we were obliged to make portages at
almost every two or three hundred yards. Rapid after
rapid was surmounted; yet still, as we rounded every
point and curve, rapids and falls rose, in apparently
endless succession, before our wearied eyes. My Indians,
however, knew exactly the number they had to ascend,
so they set themselves manfully to the task. I could not
help admiring the dexterous way in which they guided
the canoe among the rapids. Upon arriving at one, the
old Indian, who always sat in the bow, (this being
the principal seat in canoe travelling,) rose up on his
knees and stretched out his neck to take a look before
commencing the attempt; and then, sinking down again,
seized his paddle, and pointing significantly to the chaos
of boiling waters that rushed swiftly past us, (thus indicating the route he intended to pursue to his part-
ner in the stern,) dashed into the stream. At first
we were borne down with the speed of lightning, while
the water hissed and boiled to within an inch of the
gunwale, and a person unaccustomed to such navigation
would have thought it folly our attempting to ascend;
but a second glance would prove that our Indians had
not acted rashly. In the centre of the impetuous current
a large rock rose above the surface, and from its lower
end a long eddy ran like the tail of a comet for about
twenty yards down the river. It was just opposite this
rock that we entered the rapid and paddled for it with all

our might.   The current, however, as I said before, swept
us down, and when we got to the middle of the stream we
just reached the extreme point of the eddy, and after a
few vigorous strokes of the paddles were floating quietly
in the lee of the rock. We did not stay long, however—
just long enough to look for another stone, and the old
Indian soon pitched upon one a few yards higher up, but a
good deal to one side ; so, dipping our paddles once more,
we pushed out into the stream again, and soon reached the
second rock.   In this way, yard by yard, did we ascend
for miles, sometimes scarcely gaining a foot in a minute,
and at others, as a favouring bay or curve presented a
long piece of smooth water, advancing more rapidly.   In
fact our progress could not be likened to any thing more
aptly than to the ascent of a salmon as he darts rapidly
from eddy to eddy, taking advantage of every stone and
hollow that he finds : and the simile may be still further
carried out ; for, as the salmon is sometimes driven back
tail foremost in attempting to leap a fall, so were we, in
a similar attempt, driven back by the overpowering force
of the water.   It happened thus : we had surmounted a
good many rapids, and made a few portages, when we
arrived at a perpendicular fall of about two feet in
height, but from the rapidity of the current it formed
only a very steep shoot.   Here the Indians paused to
breathe, and seemed to doubt whether it was possible to
ascend ; however, after a little conversation on the subject, they determined to try it, and got out their poles
for the purpose, (poles being always used when the

current is too strong for the paddles). We now made a dash, and turning the bow to the current the Indians fixed their poles firmly in the ground, while the water rushed like a mill-race past us. They then pushed forward, one keeping his pole fixed while the other refixed his a little more ahead. In this way we advanced inch by inch, and had almost got up—the water rushed past us in a thick black body, hissing sharply in passing the side of our canoe, which trembled like a reed before the powerful current, when suddenly the pole of the Indian in the stern slipped, and almost before I knew what had happened, we were floating down the stream about a hundred yards below the fall. Fortunately the canoe went stern foremost, so that we got down in safety. Had it turned round even a little in its descent, it would have been rolled over and over like a cask. Our second attempt proved more successful; and after a good deal of straining and puffing we arrived at the top, where the sight of a longer stretch than usual of calm and placid water rewarded us for our exertions during the day. In passing over a portage we met the English River brigade; and, after a little conversation, we parted. The evening was deliciously cool and serene as we glided quietly up the now tranquil river. Numbers of little islets, covered to the very edge of the rippling water with luxuriant vegetation, rose like emeralds from the bosom of the broad river, shining brightly in the rays of the setting sun; sometimes so closely scattered as to veil the real size of the river, which, upon again emerging from among them, burst upon our delighted vision a broad sheet of clear pellucid water, with beautiful fresh banks covered with foliage of every shade, from the dark and sombre pine to the light drooping willow; while near the shore a matronly-looking duck swam solemnly along, casting now and then a look of warning to a numerous family of little yellow ducklings that frisked and gamboled in very wantonness, as if they too enjoyed and appreciated the beauties of the scene. Through this terrestrial paradise we wended our way, till rapids again began to disturb the water, and a portage at last brought us to a stand. Here we found M'Nab, who had left York Factory three days before us with his brigade, just going to encamp; so we also brought up for the night. When supper was ready I sent an invitation to M'Nab to come and sup with me, which he accepted, at the same time bringing his brother with him. The elder was a bluff, good-natured Red River settler, with whom I had become acquainted while in the colony; and we chatted of bygone times and mutual acquaintances over a cup of excellent hyson, till long after the sun had gone down, leaving the blazing camp-fires to illuminate the scene.

Next morning we started at the same time with the boats; but our little canoe soon passed them in the rapids, and we saw no more of them. Our way was not now so much impeded by rapids as it had hitherto been; and by breakfast-time we had surmounted them all and arrived at the Dram-stone, where we put ashore for our morning meal. In the morning I shot a duck, being the first that had come within range since I left York Factory. They were very scarce, and the few that we did see were generally accompanied by a numerous offspring not much bigger than the eggs which originally contained them. While taking breakfast we were surprised by hearing a quick rushing sound a little above us, and the next moment a light canoe came sweeping round a point and made towards us. It was one of those called " north canoes," which are calculated to carry eight men as a crew, besides three passengers. The one now before us was built much the same as an Indian canoe, but somewhat neater, and ornamented with sundry ingenious devices painted in gaudy colours on the bows and stern. It was manned by eight men and apparently one passenger, to whom I hallooed once or twice; but they took me, no doubt, for an Indian, and so passed on without taking any notice of us. As the noble bark bounded quickly forward and was hid by intervening trees, I bent a look savouring slightly of contempt upon our little Indian canoe, and proceeded to finish breakfast. A solitary north canoe, however, passing thus in silence, can give but a faint idea of the sensation felt on seeing a brigade of them arriving at a post after a long journey. It is then that they appear in wild perfection. The voyageurs upon such occasions are dressed in their best clothes; and gaudy feathers, ribbons, and tassels stream in abundance from their caps and gaiters. And the bright canoes painted gaily and ranged side by side, like contending chargers, skim swiftly over the water, bounding under the vigorous and rapid strokes of the small but numerous paddles, while the powerful voyageurs strain every muscle to urge them quickly on. And while yet in the distance, the beautifully simple and lively yet plaintive paddling song, so well suited to the surrounding scenery, and so different from any other air, breaks sweetly on the ear; and one reflects, with a kind of subdued and pleasing melancholy, how far the singers are from their native land, and how many long and weary days of danger and of toil will pass before they can rest once more in their Canadian homes. How strangely, too, upon their nearer approach, is this feeling changed for one of exultation, as the deep and manly voices swell in chorus over the placid waters, while a competition arises among them who shall first arrive; and the canoes dash over the water with arrow-speed to the very edge of the wharf, where they come suddenly, and as if by magic, to a pause. This is effected by each man backing water with his utmost force; after which they roll their paddles on the gunwale simultaneously, enveloping themselves in a shower of spray as they thus shake the dripping water from their bright vermilion blades. Truly it is an animating, inspiriting scene, the arrival of a brigade of light canoes.

Our route now lay through a number of small lakes and rivers, with scarcely any current in them; so we proceeded happily on our way with the cheering prospect of uninterrupted travelling. We had crossed Swampy Lake, and after making one or two insignificant portages,

entered Knee Lake. This body of water obtained its
name from turning at a sharp angle near its centre and
stretching out in an opposite direction from its preceding
course; thus forming something like a knee. Late in
the evening we encamped on one of the small islands
with which it is here and there dotted. Nothing could
exceed the beauty of the view we had of the lake from
our encampment. Not a breath of wind stirred its glassy
surface, which shone in the ruddy rays of the sun setting
on its bosom in the distant horizon; and I sat long upon
the rocks admiring the lovely scene, while one of my
Indians filled the tea-kettle, and the other was busily
engaged in skinning a minx for supper. Our evening
meal was further enriched by the addition of a great
many small gulls' eggs, which we had found on an
island during the day, which, saving one or two that
showed evident symptoms of being far advanced towards
birdhood, were excellent. On the following morning the
scene was entirely changed. Dark and lowering clouds
flew across the sky, and the wind blew furiously, with a
melancholy moaning sound through the trees. The lake,
which the night before had been so calm and tranquil,
was now of a dark leaden hue and covered with foaming
waves. However, we determined to try to proceed, and
launched our canoe accordingly; but, soon finding that
the wind was too strong for us, we put ashore on a small
island and breakfasted. As the weather moderated
after breakfast, we made another attempt to advance.
Numerous islets studded the lake, and on one of them we

landed to collect gulls' eggs. Of these we found enough; but among them were a number of little yellow gulls, chattering vociferously, and in terrible consternation at our approach, while the old ones kept uttering the most plaintive cries overhead. The eggs were very small, being those of a small species of gull which frequents those inland lakes in great numbers. The wind again began to rise; and after a little consultation on the subject we landed, intending to spend the remainder of the day on shore. We now, for the first time since leaving York Factory, prepared dinner, which we expected would be quite a sumptuous one, having collected a good many eggs in the morning; so we set about it with alacrity. A fire was quickly made, the tea-kettle on, and a huge pot containing upwards of a hundred eggs placed upon the fire. These we intended to boil hard and carry with us. Being very hungry, I watched the progress of dinner with much interest, while the Indians smoked in silence. While sitting thus, my attention was attracted by a loud whistling sound that greatly perplexed me, as I could not discover whence it proceeded. I got up once or twice to see what it could be, but found nothing, although it sounded as if close beside me. At last one of the Indians rose, and, standing close to the fire, bent in a very attentive attitude over the kettle of eggs, and after listening a little while took up one and broke it, when out came a young gull with a monstrous head and no feathers, squeaking and chirping in a most indefatigable manner! "So much for our dinner!" thought I, as he threw the bird into the lake, and took out a handful of eggs which all proved to be much in the same condition. The warmth of the water put life into the little birds, which, however, was speedily destroyed when it began to boil. We did not despair, nevertheless, of finding a few good ones amongst them; so, after they were well cooked, we all sat round the kettle and commenced operations. Some were good and others slightly spoiled, while many were intersected with red veins, but the greater part contained boiled birds. The Indians were not nice, however, and we managed to make a good dinner off them after all.

In the afternoon the weather cleared up and the wind moderated, but we had scarcely got underweigh again when a thunder-storm arose and obliged us to put ashore; and there we remained for four hours sitting under a tree, while the rain poured down in torrents. In the evening Nature began to tire of teasing us; and the sun shone brightly out as we once more resumed our paddles. To make up for lost time we travelled until about two o'clock next morning, when we put ashore to rest a little; and, as the night was fine, we just threw our blankets over our shoulders and tumbled down on the first convenient spot we could find, without making a fire or taking any supper. We had not lain long, however, when I felt a curious chilly sensation all along my side, which effectually awakened me; and then I saw, or rather heard, that a perfect deluge of rain was descending upon our luckless heads, and that I had been reposing in the centre of a large puddle. This state of things was desperate; and as the poor Indians seemed to be as thoroughly uncomfortable as they possibly could be, I proposed to start again, which we did, and before daylight were many a mile from our wretched encampment. As the sun rose the weather cleared up, and soon after we came to the end of Knee Lake and commenced the ascent of Trout River. Here I made a sketch of the Trout Falls while the men were making a portage to avoid them. A few Indians were encamped on this portage with whom we exchanged a little pemican for some excellent white-fish, which proved a great treat to us after living so long on pemican and tea; for our biscuit had run short a few days before, and the pound of butter which we brought from York Factory had melted into oil from the excessive heat, and vanished through the bottom of the canvass bag in which it had been put. Trout River, though short, has a pretty fair share of falls and rapids, which we continued ascending all day. The scenery was pleasing and romantic; but there was nothing of grandeur in it, the country being low, flat, and, excepting on the banks of the river, uninteresting. In the afternoon we came to the end of this short river, and arrived at Oxford House. We landed in silence, and I walked slowly up the hill, but not a soul appeared; at last, as I neared the house, I caught a glimpse of a little boy's face at the window, who no sooner saw me than his eyes opened to their widest extent, while his mouth followed their example, and he disappeared with

a precipitancy that convinced me he was off to tell his
mother the astounding news that somebody had arrived.
The next moment I was shaking hands with my old
friend Mrs G—— and her two daughters, whom I found
employed in the interesting occupation of preparing tea.
From them I learned that they were entirely alone, with
only one man to take care of the post, Mr G——, whom
they expected back every day, having gone to Norway
House. I spent a delightful evening with this kind and
hospitable family, talking of our mutual friends, and
discussing the affairs of the country, till a tall box in a
corner of the room attracted my attention. This I discovered to my delight was no less than a barrel organ,
on which one of the young ladies at my request played a
few tunes. Now barrel organs, be it known, were things
that I had detested from my infancy upwards; but this
dislike arose principally from my having been brought
up in the dear town o' Auld Reekie, where barrel organ
music is, as it were, crammed down one's throat without
permission being asked or received, and even, indeed,
where it is decidedly objected to. Every body said, too,
that barrel organs were a nuisance, and of course I
believed them; so that I left my home with a decided
dislike to barrel organs in general. Four years' residence, however, in the bush had rendered me much less
fastidious in music as well as in many other things; and
during the two last years spent at York Factory, not a
solitary note of melody had soothed my longing ear, so
that it was with a species of rapture that I now ground

away at the handle of this organ, which happened to be a very good one, and played in perfect tune. "God save the Queen," "Rule Britannia," "Lord M'Donald's Reel," and the "Blue Bells of Scotland" were played over and over again; and, old and threadbare though they be, to me they were replete with endearing associations, and sounded like the well-known voices of long, long absent friends. I spent indeed a delightful evening, and its pleasures were the more enhanced from the circumstance of its being the first, after a banishment of two years, which I had spent in the society of the fair sex.

Next morning was fine, though the wind blew pretty freshly, and we started before breakfast, having taken leave of the family the night before. This was the 1st of July. We had now been eight days on the route, which is rather a long time for a canoe to take to reach Oxford House; but, as the most of the portages were now over, we calculated upon arriving at Norway House in two or three days.

In the afternoon the wind began to blow again, and obliged us to encamp on a small island, where we remained all day. While there, a couple of Indians visited us, and gave us an immense trout in exchange for some pemican. This trout I neglected to measure, but I am convinced it was more than three feet long and half a foot broad: it was very good, and we made a capital dinner off it. During the day, as it was very warm, I had a delightful swim in the lake, on the lee of the island.

The wind moderated a little in the evening, and we

again embarked, making up for lost time by travelling till midnight, when we put ashore and went to sleep without making a fire or taking any supper. About four o'clock we started again, and in a couple of hours came to the end of Oxford Lake, after which we travelled through a number of small swamps or reedy lakes, and stagnant rivers, among which I got so bewildered that I gave up the attempt to chronicle their names as hopeless; and indeed it was scarcely worth while, as they were so small and overgrown with bulrushes that they were no more worthy of a name in such a place as America than a *dub* would be in Scotland. The weather was delightfully cool, and mosquitoes not troublesome, so that we proceeded with pleasure and rapidity.

While thus threading our way through narrow channels and passages, upon turning a point we met three light canoes just on the point of putting ashore for breakfast, so I told my Indians to run ashore near them. As we approached, I saw that there were five gentlemen assembled with whom I was acquainted, so that I was rather anxious to get ashore; but alas! fortune had determined to play me a scurvy trick, for no sooner had my foot touched the slippery stone on which I intended to land, than down I came squash on my breast in a most humiliating manner, while my legs kept playfully waving about in the cooling element This unfortunate accident I saw occasioned a strange elongation in the lateral dimensions of the mouths of the party on shore, who stood in silence admiring the scene. I knew, however, that to appear annoyed would only make matters worse ; so, with a desperate effort to appear at ease, I rose, and while shaking hands with them expressed my belief that there was nothing so conducive to health as a cold bath before breakfast. This set all right, and after a laugh at my expense we sat down to breakfast. One of the gentlemen gave me a letter from the Governor, and I now learned for the first time, that I was to take a passage in one of the light canoes for Montreal. Here, then, was a termination to my imaginary rambles on the Rocky Mountains, or the undulating prairies of the Saskatchewan ; and instead of massacreing buffalo and deer in the bush, I was in a short time to endeavour to render myself a respectable member of civilised society. I was delighted with the idea of the change, and it was with a firmer step and lighter heart that I took my leave and once more stepped into the canoe.

After passing through a succession of swamps and narrow channels, we arrived at Robinson's Portage, where we found voyageurs running about in all directions, some with goods on their backs, and others returning light to the other end of the portage. We found that they belonged to the Oxford House boats, which had just arrived at the other end of the portage, where they intended to encamp, as it was now late. Robinson's Portage is the longest on the route, being nearly a mile long ; and as all the brigades going to York Factory must pass over it twice in going and returning, the track is well beaten into a good broad road, and pretty firm,

although it is rather uneven, and during heavy rains
somewhat muddy. Over this, all the boats are dragged,
and launched at the upper or lower end of the portage, as
the brigades may happen to be ascending or descending
the stream. Then all the cargoes are in like manner
carried over. Packs of furs and bales of goods are
generally from 80 to 100 lbs. weight each, and every
man who does not wish to be considered a lazy fellow,
or to be ridiculed by his companions, carries two of
those *pieces*, as they are called, across all portages. The
boats are capable of containing from seventy to ninety
of these pieces, so that it will be easily conceived that a
voyageur's life is any thing but an easy one; indeed, it
is one of constant and harassing toil, even were the
trouble of ascending rapid rivers, where he is often
obliged to jump into the water at a moment's notice, to
lighten the boat in shallows, left entirely out of the
question. This portage is made to avoid what are
called the White Falls, a succession of cataracts up
which nothing but a fish could possibly ascend. After
carrying over our canoe and luggage, we encamped at
the upper end. The river which we commenced ascending next morning was pretty broad, and after a short
paddle in it we entered the Echimamis. This is a
sluggish serpentine stream, about five or six yards
broad, though in some places so narrow that boats
scrape the banks on either side. What little current
there is, runs in a contrary direction to the rivers we
had been ascending, so that this is looked upon as a

height of land. Musquitoes again attacked us as we
glided down its gloomy current, and nothing but swamps
filled with immense bulrushes was visible around. Here,
in days of yore, the beaver had a flourishing colony, and
numbers of their dams and cuttings were yet visible ; but
they have long since deserted this much-frequented
waste, and one of their principal dams now serves to
heighten the water, which is not deep, for the passage
of brigades in dry seasons. At night, when we encamped
on its low, damp banks, we were attacked by myriads of
musquitoes, so that we could only sleep by making two
or three fires round us, the smoke from which partially
protected us. About three o'clock in the morning, which
was very warm, we re-embarked, and at noon arrived
at the Sea Portage, (why so called I know not, as it is
hundreds of miles inland), which is the last on the route.
This portage is very short, and is made to surmount a
pretty large waterfall. Almost immediately afterwards
we entered Playgreen Lake, and put ashore on a small
island to alter our attire before arriving at Norway
House. Here, with the woods for our closet, and the
clear lake for our basin as well as looking-glass, we
proceeded to scrub our sunburnt faces, and in half an
hour, having made ourselves as respectable as circumstances would permit, we paddled swiftly over the lake.
It is pretty long, and it was not until evening that I
caught the first glimpse of the bright spire of the Wesleyan church at Rossville.

We were now approaching the termination of our

journey, for the time being at least; and it was with pleasing recollections that I recognised the well-known rocks where I had so often wandered three years before. When we came in sight of the Fort it was in a state of bustle and excitement as usual, and I could perceive from the vigorous shaking of hands going forward, the number of voyageurs collected on the landing place, and boats at the wharf, that there had just been an arrival. Our poor little canoe was not taken any notice of as it neared the wharf, until some of the people on shore began to observe that there was some one in the middle of it sitting in a very lazy, indolent position, which is quite uncommon among Indians.   In another minute we gained the bank, and I was grasping the hand of my kind friend and former master, chief factor R——.   We had now been travelling twelve days, which is rather slow work for a canoe, and had passed over upwards of thirty portages during our voyage.

CHAPTER IX.

VOYAGE TO CANADA BY THE GREAT LAKES OF THE INTERIOR.

T Norway House I remained for nearly a month, with my old friend, Mr R——, who, in a former part of this veracious book, is described as being a very ardent and scientific fisher, extremely partial to strong rods and lines, and entertaining a powerful antipathy to slender rods and flies.

Little change had taken place in the appearance of the Fort. The clerks' house was still as full, and as noisy, as when P—— told frightful stories to the greenhorns on the point of setting out for the wild countries of Mackenzie's River and New Caledonia. The Indians of the village at Rossville plodded on in their usual peaceful way, under the guidance of their former pastor; and the ladies of the establishment were as blooming as ever.

One fine morning, just as Mr R—— and I were sauntering down to the river with our rods, a north canoe, full of men, swept round the point above the fort, and grounded near the wharf. Our rods were soon cast aside, and we were speedily congratulating Mr and Mrs B—— on their safe arrival. These were to be my companions on the impending voyage to Canada, and the canoe in which they had arrived was to be our conveyance.

Mr B—— was a good-natured, light-hearted Highlander, and his lady a pretty lass of twenty-three; so that we were likely to turn out a merry triumvirate.

On the following morning all was ready; and soon after breakfast we were escorted down to the wharf by all the people in the fort, who crowded on the rocks to witness our departure.

Our men, eight in number, stood leaning on their paddles near the wharf; and, truly, a fine athletic set of fellows they were. The beautifully-shaped canoe floated lightly on the river, notwithstanding the heavy cargo which she carried, and the water rippled gently on her sides as it swept slowly past. This frail bark, on which our safety and progression depended, was made of rolls of birch-bark sewed together, lined in the inside with thin laths of wood, and pitched on the seams with gum. It was about thirty-six feet long, and five broad in the middle, from whence it tapered either way to a sharp edge. It was calculated to carry from twenty to twenty-five cwt., with eight or nine men, besides three passengers, and provisions for nearly a month. And yet, so light was it, that two men were capable of carrying it a quarter of a mile without resting. Such was the machine in which, on the 20th August 1845, we embarked; and, after bidding our friends at Norway House adieu, departed for Canada, a distance of nearly two thousand three hundred miles through the uninhabited forests of America.

Our first day was propitious, being warm and clear: and we travelled a good distance ere the rapidly thickening shades of evening obliged us to put ashore for the night. The place on which we encamped was a flat rock which lay close to the river's bank, and behind it the thick forest formed a screen from the north wind. It looked gloomy enough on landing; but, ere long, a huge fire was kindled on the rock, our two snow-white tents pitched, and supper in course of preparation, so that things soon began to wear a gayer aspect. Supper was spread in Mr B——'s tent by one of the men, whom we appointed to the office of cook and waiter. And, when we were seated on our blankets and cloaks upon the ground, and Mr B—— had squinted at the fire for five minutes, and then at his wife (who presided at the *board*) for ten, we began to feel quite jolly, and gazed with infinite satisfaction at the men who ate their supper, out of the same kettle, in the warm light of the camp-fire. Our first bed was typical of the voyage, being hard and rough, but, withal, much more comfortable than many others we slept upon afterwards, and we were all soon as sound asleep upon the rock in the forest, as if we had been in feather-beds at home.

Early on the following morning, long before daylight, we were roused from our slumbers to re-embark, and now our journey may be said to have commenced in earnest. Slowly and silently we stepped into the canoe, and sat down in our allotted places, while the men advanced in silence, and paddled up the quiet river in a very melancholy sort of mood. The rising sun, however, dissipated these gloomy feelings, and after breakfast, which we took on a small island near the head of Jack River, we revived at once, and started with a cheering song, in which all joined. Soon after, we rounded a point of the river, and Lake Winnipeg, calm, and clear as crystal, glittering in the beams of the morning sun, lay stretched out before us to the distant, and scarcely perceptible horizon. Every pleasure has its alloy, and the glorious calm, on which we felicitated ourselves not a little, soon became ruffled by a breeze, which speedily increased so much as to oblige us to encamp near Montreal Point, being too strong for us to venture across the traverse of five or six miles which now lay before us. Here, then, we remained the rest of the day and night, rather disappointed that interruptions should have occurred so soon.

Next day we left our encampment early, and travelled prosperously till about noon, when the wind again increased to such a degree that we were forced to put ashore on a point, where we remained for the next two days in grumbling inactivity.

There is nothing more distressing and annoying than being wind-bound in these wild and uninhabited regions. One has no amusement except reading, or promenading about the shores of the lake. Now, although this may be very delightful to a person of a romantic disposition, it was any thing but agreeable to us, as the season was pretty far advanced, and the voyage long; besides, I had no gun, having parted with mine before leaving Norway House, and no books had been brought, as we did not calculate upon being wind-bound. I was particularly disappointed at not having brought my gun, for, while we were lying on the rocks one fine day, gazing gloomily on the foaming lake, a black bear was perceived walking slowly round the bottom of the bay, formed by the point on which we were encamped. It was hopeless to attempt killing him, as Mr Bruin was not fool enough to permit us to attack him with axes. After this, a regular course of high winds commenced, which retarded us very much, and gave us a good deal of uneasiness as well as annoyance. A good idea of the harassing nature of our voyage across Lake Winnipeg may be obtained from the following page or two of my journal, as I wrote it on the spot:—

Monday, 25th August.—The wind having moderated this morning, we left the encampment at an early hour, and travelled uninterruptedly till nearly eight o'clock, when it began to blow so furiously, that we were obliged to run ashore and encamp. All day the gale continued, but in the evening it moderated, and we were enabled to proceed a good way ere night closed in.

Tuesday 26th.—Rain fell in torrents during the night. The wind, too, was high, and we did not leave our encampment till after breakfast. We made a good day's journey, however, travelling about forty miles, and at night pitched our tents on a point of rock, the only camping place, as our guide told us, within ten miles. No dry ground was to be found in the vicinity, so we were fain to sleep upon the flattest rock we could find, with only one blanket under us. This bed, however, was not so disagreeable as one might imagine, its principal disadvantage being, that should it rain, the water, instead of sinking into the ground, forms a little pond below you, which is deep or shallow, according to the hollowness or flatness of the rock on which you repose.

Wednesday 27th.—Set out early this morning, and travelled till noon, when the wind *again* drove us ashore, where we remained, in no very happy humour, all day. Mr B—— and I played the flute for pastime.

Thursday 28th.—The persevering wind blew so hard that we remained in the encampment all day. This was indeed a dismal day; for, independent of being delayed, which is bad enough, the rain fell so heavily that it began to penetrate through our tents, and, as if not content with this, a gust of wind more violent than usual tore the fastenings of my tent out of the ground, and dashed it over my head, leaving me exposed to the pitiless pelting of the storm. Mr B——'s tent being in a more sheltered spot, fortunately escaped.

Friday 29th.—The weather was much improved today, but still continued to blow sufficiently to prevent our starting. As the wind moderated, however, in the evening, the men carried the baggage down to the beach to have it in readiness for an early start on the morrow.

Saturday 30*th*.—In the morning we found that the wind had *again* risen so as to prevent our leaving the encampment. This detention is really very tiresome. We have no amusement except reading a few uninteresting books, eating without appetite, and sleeping inordinately. Oh, that I were possessed of the Arabian Nights' *mat*, which transported its owner whithersoever he listed! There is nothing for it, however, but patience, and assuredly I have a good example in poor Mrs B——, who, though little accustomed to such work, has not given utterance to a word of complaint since we left Norway House. It is now four days since we pitched our tents on this vile point. How long we may still remain is yet to be seen.

Sunday 31*st*.—The wind was more moderate this morning, and about ten o'clock we were enabled to resume our journey. The Sabbath day in such a voyage as this cannot be a day of rest, as, from the lateness of the season, every hour is of the utmost importance. Delay may cause our being arrested by ice when we reach the heights of land; and even now we fear that, unless the season is a late one, we shall experience great difficulty in reaching Canada. The proper observance of the Sabbath is, I am happy to say, becoming more general throughout the Hudson's Bay Company's territories than it used to be. Many of the gentlemen who travel with brigades of boats and canoes, remain in the encampment on the Lord's day, particularly those who have not long journeys to perform. But those who,

from circumstances, cannot begin their journeys till late
in the autumn, and have long distances to travel, dare
not spend the Sabbath in inactivity, as, by so doing,
they would risk being frozen in by the ice, and probably
cause the loss of the whole crews.

Monday, Sept. 1.—This morning we started very early,
and travelled rapidly along till about noon, when the wind
again spitefully put us ashore, where we remained during
the remainder of the day.   Towards evening it increased
to a gale, accompanied with heavy rain ; and during the
night, while I was sleeping calmly under my blanket,
unmindful of the raging storm, a sudden gust *again*
upset my tent, and I was awakened by the clammy folds
of the wet canvass flapping about my head and ears.   The
strength of the wind precluded the possibility of my
pitching it ; so throwing a large block of drift wood on
it to keep it from blowing away altogether, I ran to the
canoe, which was turned bottom up at no great distance,
and lay down under its shelter beside the men.

Tuesday, 2*d*.—Still blowing too hard to proceed ; but
about noon the wind fell sufficiently to allow us to travel
till four o'clock, when it commenced to blow again so
furiously that we were, after being nearly swamped in
our endeavours to continue our journey, obliged to put
ashore.   There was something peculiarly aggravating in
this day's detention ; as, had we been able to continue
paddling for only two hours longer, we would then have
come to the end of Lake Winnipeg, and arrived at Fort
Alexander, which was not more than eight miles distant.

As it was, here we were; and, if the wind chose, here we *might* be for a week to come. In the afternoon two Indians stumbled on our encampment. They had just come overland from the fort, where they had got some potatoes; and they good-naturedly gave us a few, together with some unripe plums, in exchange for a few inches of twist tobacco. They were of the Cree tribe, dressed in the ordinary coarse cloth capotes and leggings of the low countries.

Wednesday, 3d.—Spent the "lee lang day" on the same rascally point, enjoying the tantalising knowledge that a couple of hours would put us beyond the reach of Winnipeg's obstinate waves. More Indians visited us us during the day. Mr B—— and I amused ourselves by alternately playing the flute and grumbling at our hard fate, much to the enjoyment of Mrs B——, who is really blessed with a most equable and enviable temper.

Thursday, 4th.—The wind was still very strong this morning; but so impatient had we become at our repeated detentions, that with one accord we consented to do or die! So, after launching and loading the canoe with great difficulty, owing to the immense waves which thundered on the shore, we all embarked and pushed off. After great difficulty, and much shipping of water, we at last came to the mouth of the Winnipeg River, after proceeding up which a short distance we arrived at Fort Alexander.

Thus had we taken fifteen days to coast along Lake

Winnipeg, a journey that is usually performed in a third
of that time.

This fort belongs to the Lac la Pluie district; but
being a small post, neither famous for trade nor for
appearance, I will not take the trouble of describing it.
We only remained a couple of hours to take in provisions
in the shape of a ham, a little pork, and some flour, and
then re-embarking commenced the ascent of Winnipeg
River.

The travelling now before us was widely different from
that of the last fifteen days. Our men could now no
longer rest upon their paddles when tired, as they used
to do on the level waters of the lake. The river was a
rapid one; and towards evening we had an earnest of
the rough work in store for us by meeting in rapid succession with three waterfalls, to surmount which we were
obliged to carry the canoe and cargo over the rocks and
launch them above the falls. While the men were engaged in this laborious duty, Mr B—— and I discovered
a great many plum-trees laden with excellent fruit, of
which we ate as many as we conveniently could, and
then filling our caps and handkerchiefs embarked with
our prize. They were a great treat to us after our long
abstinence from every thing but salt food, and I believe
we demolished enough to have killed a whole parish
school—boys, master, usher, and all! But in voyages
like these one may take great liberties with one's health
with perfect impunity.

About sunset we encamped in a picturesque spot, near

the top of a huge waterfall, whose thundering roar, as
it mingled with the sighing of the night wind through
the bushes and among the precipitous rocks around us,
formed an appropriate and somewhat romantic lullaby.

On the following morning we were aroused from our
slumbers at daybreak; and in ten minutes our tents were
down and ourselves in the canoe, bounding merrily up
the river, while the echoing woods and dells responded
to the lively air of " Rose blanche," sung by the men as
we swept round point after point and curve after curve
of the noble river, which displayed to our admiring gaze
every variety of wild and woodland scenery. Now
opening up a long vista of sloping groves of graceful
trees, beautifully variegated with the tints of autumnal
foliage, and sprinkled with a profusion of wild flowers,
and anon surrounding us with immense cliffs and precipitous banks of the grandest and most majestic appearance;
at the foot of which the black waters rushed impetuously
past, and gurgling into white foam, as they sped through
a broken and more interrupted channel, finally sprang
over a mist-encompassed cliff, and after boiling madly onwards for a short space, resumed their silent, quiet course
again through peaceful scenery. As if to enhance the romantic wildness of the scene, upon rounding a point we
came suddenly upon a large black bear, which was walking leisurely along the banks of the river. He gazed at
us in surprise for a moment; and then, as if it had suddenly occurred to him that guns *might* be in the canoe,
away he went helter-skelter up the bank, tearing up the

ground in his precipitate retreat, and vanished among the bushes. Fortunately for him there was *not* a gun in the canoe, else his chance of escape would have been very small indeed, as he was only fifty yards or so from us when we first discovered him.

We made ten portages of various lengths during the course of the day; none of them exceeded a quarter of a mile, while the most were merely a few yards. They were very harassing, however, being close to each other; and often we loaded, unloaded, and carried the canoe and cargo over land several times in the distance of half a mile.

On the 7th we left the encampment at an early hour, and made one short portage a few minutes after starting. After breakfast, as we were paddling quietly along, we descried three canoes coming towards us, filled with Indians of the Seauteaux tribe. They gave us a few fresh ducks in exchange for some pork and tobacco, with which they were much delighted. After a short conversation with one of our men who understood the language, we left them and proceeded on our way. A little rain fell during the day, but in the afternoon the sun shone out and lighted up the scenery. The forests about this part of the river wore a much more cheerful aspect than those of the lower countries, being composed chiefly of poplar, birch, oak, and willows, whose beautiful light green foliage had a very pleasing effect upon eyes long accustomed to the dark pines along the shores of Hudson's Bay.

In the afternoon we met another canoe, in which we

saw a gentleman sitting. This strange sight set us all speculating as to who it could be; for we knew that all the canoes accustomed annually to go through these wilds had long since passed. We were soon enlightened, however, on the subject. Both canoes made towards a flat rock that offered a convenient spot for landing on; and the stranger introduced himself as Dr Rae. He was on his way to York Factory for the purpose of fitting out at that post an expedition for the survey of the small part of the North American coast left unexplored by Messrs Dease and Simpson, which will then prove beyond a doubt whether or not there is a communication by water between the Atlantic and Pacific oceans round the north of America. Dr Rae appeared to be just the man for such an expedition. He was very muscular and active, full of animal spirits, and had a fine intellectual countenance. He was considered, by those who knew him well, to be one of the best snow-shoe walkers in the service, was also an excellent rifle-shot, and could stand an immense amount of fatigue. Poor fellow! greatly will he require to exert all his abilities and powers of endurance. He does not proceed as other expeditions have done—namely, with large supplies of provisions and men, but merely takes a very small supply of provisions and ten or twelve men. These, however, are all to be of his own choosing, and will, doubtless, be men of great experience in travelling among the wild regions of North America. The whole expedition is fitted out at the expense of the Hudson's Bay Company. The party

are to depend almost entirely on their guns for provisions; and after proceeding in two open boats round
the north-western shores of Hudson's Bay as far as they
may find it expedient or practicable, are to land, place
their boats in security for the winter, and then penetrate
into these unexplored regions on foot. After having
done as much as possible towards the forwarding of the
object of his journey, Dr Rae and his party are to spend
the long dreary winter with the Esquimaux, and commence operations again early in the spring. He is of
such a pushing, energetic character, however, that there
is every probability he will endeavour to prosecute his
discoveries during winter, if at all practicable. How
long he will remain exploring among these wild regions
is uncertain, but he may be two, perhaps three years.
There is every reason to believe that this expedition will
be successful, as it is fitted out by a company intimately
acquainted with the difficulties and dangers of the country
through which it will have to pass, and the best methods
of overcoming and avoiding them. Besides, the Doctor
himself is well accustomed to the life he will have to lead,
and enters upon it, not with the vague and uncertain
notions of Back and Franklin, but with a pretty correct
apprehension of the probable routine of procedure, and
the experience of a great many years spent in the service
of the Hudson's Bay Company.* After a few minutes'

* Since this sheet was prepared for press, I have heard of the return of Dr Rae from his *successful* discoveries. As a full account of
them has appeared in the newspapers, any notice of them would be
superfluous here.

conversation we parted, and pursued our respective journeys.

Towards sunset, we encamped on the margin of a small lake, or expanse of the river ; and soon the silence of the forest was broken by the merry voices of our men, and the crashing of the stately trees, as they fell under the axes of the voyageurs. The sun's last rays streamed across the water in a broad, red glare, as if jealous of the huge camp-fire, which now rose crackling among the trees, casting a ruddy glow upon our huts, and lighting up the swarthy faces of our men as they assembled round it to rest their weary limbs, and watch the operations of the cook while he prepared their evening meal.

In less than an hour after we landed, the floor of our tent was covered with a smoking dish of fried pork, a huge ham, a monstrous tea-pot, and various massive slices of bread, with butter to match. To partake of these delicacies, we seated ourselves in Oriental fashion, and sipped our tea in contemplative silence, as we listened to the gentle murmur of a neighbouring brook, and gazed through the opening of our tent at the voyageurs, while they ate their supper round the fire, or, reclining at length upon the grass, smoked their pipes in silence.

Supper was soon over, and I went out to warm myself, preparatory to turning in for the night. The men had supped, and their huge forms were now stretched around the fire, enveloped in clouds of tobacco smoke, which curled in volumes from their unshaven lips. They were chatting and laughing over tales of bygone days; and just as I came up, they appeared to be begging Pierre, the guide, to relate a tale of some sort or other. "Come, Pierre," said a tall, dark-looking fellow, whose pipe, eyes, and hair were of the same jetty hue, " tell us how that Ingin was killed on the Labrador coast by a black bear. Baptiste, here, never heard how it happened, and you know he's fond of wild stories." " Well," returned the guide, "since you must have it, I'll do what I can; but don't be disappointed if it isn't so interesting as you would wish. It's a simple tale, and not over long." So saying, the guide disposed himself in a more comfortable attitude, refilled his pipe, and after blowing two or three thick clouds to make sure of its keeping alight, gave, in nearly the following words, an account of

The Death of Wapwian.

" It is now twenty years since I saw Wapwian, and during that time I have travelled far and wide in the plains and forests of America, I have hunted the buffalo with the Scauteaux, in the prairies of the Saskatchewan, —I have crossed the Rocky Mountains with the Blackfeet,—and killed the black bear with the Abinikies, on the coasts of Labrador,—but never, among all the tribes that I have visited, have I met an Indian like Wapwian. It was not his form or his strength that I admired— though the first was graceful, and the latter immense ; but his disposition was so kind, and affectionate, and noble, that all who came in contact with him loved and respected him; yet, strange to say, he was never converted by the few Roman Catholic missionaries who, from time to time, visited his village. He listened to them with respectful attention, but always answered that he could worship the Great Manitou better as a hunter in the forest than as a farmer in the settlements of the white men.

" Well do I remember the first time I stumbled upon the Indian village in which he lived. I had set out from Montreal, with two trappers, to pay a visit to the Labrador coast; we had travelled most of the way in a small Indian canoe, coasting along the northern shore of the Gulf of St Lawrence, and reconnoitring in the woods for portages to avoid rounding long capes and points of land, and sometimes in search of game—for we depended almost entirely upon our guns for food.

" It was upon one of the latter occasions that I went off, accompanied by one of the trappers, while the other remained to watch the canoe and prepare our encampment for the night. We were unsuccessful, and after a long walk began to think of returning to our camp empty-handed, when a loud whirring sound in the bushes attracted our attention, and two partridges perched upon a tree quite near us. We shot them, and fixing them in our belts, retraced our way towards the coast with lighter hearts. Just as we emerged from the dense forest, however, on one side of an open space, a tall muscular Indian strode from among the bushes

and stood before us. He was dressed in the blanket
capote, cloth leggins, and scarlet cap, usually worn by
the Abinikies, and other tribes of the Labrador coast.
A red-deer skin shot-pouch, and a powder-horn, hung
round his neck ; and at his side hung a beautifully ornamented fire-bag and scalping knife. A common gun lay
in the hollow of his left arm, and a pair of ornamented
moccasins covered his feet. He was, indeed, a handsome
looking fellow, as he stood scanning us rapidly with his
jet-black eyes, while we approached him. We accosted
him, and informed him (for he understood a little French)
from whence we came, and our object in visiting his
part of the country. He received our advances kindly,
accepted a piece of tobacco that we offered him, and
told us that his name was Wapwian, and that we were
welcome to remain at his village—to which he offered
to conduct us—as long as we pleased. After a little
hesitation we accepted his invitation to remain a few
days ; the more so, as by so doing we would have an
opportunity of getting some provisions to enable us to
continue our journey. In half-an-hour we reached the
brow of a small eminence, from whence the curling
smoke of the wigwams became visible. The tents were
pitched on the shores of a small bay or inlet, guarded
from the east wind by a high precipice of rugged rocks,
around which hundreds of sea-fowl sailed in graceful
flights. Beyond this headland stretched the majestic
Gulf of St Lawrence,—while to the left, the village was
shaded by the spruce fir, of which most of this part

of the forest is composed. There were, in all, about a dozen tents, made of dressed deer-skin, at the openings of which might be seen groups of little children, playing about on the grass, or running after their mothers as they went to the neighbouring rivulet for water, or launched their canoes and proceeded to examine the trout nets in the bay.

"Wapwian paused to gaze an instant on the scene, and then, descending the hill with rapid strides, entered the village, and dispatched a little boy for our companion in the encampment.

"We were ushered into a tent which stood a little elevated above the others, and were soon reclining on a soft pile of pine branches, smoking in company with our friend Wapwian, while his pretty little squaw prepared a kettle of trout for supper.

"Two days we spent happily in the village—hunting deer with our Indian friend, and assisting the squaws in their fishing operations. On the third morning we remained in the camp to dry the venison, and prepare for our departure; while Wapwian shouldered his gun, and calling to his nephew, a slim active youth of eighteen, bade him follow with his gun, as he intended to bring back a few ducks for his white brothers.

"The two Indians proceeded for a time along the shore, and then, striking off into the forest, threaded their way among the thick bushes in the direction of a chain of small lakes where wild-fowl were numerous.

"For some time they moved rapidly along under the

sombre shade of the trees, casting, from time to time, sharp glances into the surrounding underwood. Suddenly the elder Indian paused and threw forward his gun, as a slight rustling in the bushes struck his ear. The boughs bent and crackled a few yards in advance; and a large black bear crossed the path and entered the underwood on the other side. Wapwian fired at him instantly—and a savage growl told that the shot had taken effect. The gun, however, had been loaded with small shot; and although when he fired the bear was only a few yards off, yet the improbability of its having wounded him badly, and the distance they had to go ere they reached the lakes, inclined him to give up the chase. While Wapwian was loading his gun, Miniquan (his nephew) had been examining the bear's track, and returned, saying that he was sure the animal must be badly wounded as there was much blood on the track. At first the elder Indian refused to follow it; but seeing that his nephew wished very much to kill it, he at last consented. As the trail of the bear was much covered with blood, they found no difficulty in tracking it; and after a short walk they found him extended on his side at the foot of a large tree, apparently lifeless. Wapwian, however, was too experienced a hunter to trust himself incautiously within its reach; so he examined the priming of his gun, and then, advancing slowly to the animal, pushed it with the muzzle. In an instant the bear sprang upon him, regardless of the shot lodged in its breast; and in another moment Wapwian lay stunned and bleeding at the mon-

ster's feet.   Miniquan was at first so thunderstruck, as
he gazed in horror at the savage animal tearing with
bloody jaws the senseless form of his uncle, that he stood
rooted to the ground.   It was only for a moment—the
next, his gun was at his shoulder; and after firing at, but
unfortunately, in the excitement of the moment, missing
the bear, he attacked it with the but of his gun, which
he soon shivered to pieces on its skull.   This drew the
animal for a few moments from Wapwian; and Miniquan,
in hopes of leading it from the place, ran off in the direction of the village.   The bear, however, soon gave up
the chase, and returned again to its victim.   Miniquan
now saw that the only chance of saving his relative was
to alarm the village; so, tightening his belt, he set off
with the speed of the hunted deer in the direction of the
camp.   In an incredibly short time he arrived, and soon
returned with the trappers and myself.   Alas! alas!"
said the guide, with a deep sigh, "it was too late.   Upon
arriving at the spot, we found the bear quite dead, and
the noble, generous Wapwian extended by its side, torn
and lacerated in such a manner that we could scarcely
recognise him.   He still breathed a little, however, and
appeared to know me, as I bent over him and tried to
close his gaping wounds.   We constructed a rude couch
of branches, and conveyed him slowly to the village.
No word of complaint or cry of sorrow escaped from his
wife as we laid his bleeding form in her tent.   She
seemed to have lost the power of speech, as she sat, hour
after hour, gazing in unutterable despair on the mangled

form of her husband. Poor Wapwian lingered for a
week in a state of unconsciousness. His skull had been
fractured, and he lay almost in a state of insensibility,
and never spoke, save when, in a fit of delirium, his
fancy wandered back to bygone days, when he ranged
through the forest with a tiny bow in chase of little birds
and squirrels; or fancied that he strode again, in the
vigour of early manhood, over frozen plains of snow, or
dashed down foaming currents and mighty rivers in his
light canoe. Then a shade would cross his brow as he
thought, perhaps, of his recent struggle with the bear,
and he would relapse again into silence.

" He recovered slightly before his death; and once he
smiled, as if he recognised his wife, but he never spoke
to any one. We scarcely knew when his spirit fled, so
calm and peaceful was his end.

" His body now reposes beneath the spreading branches
of a lordly pine, near the scenes of his childhood; where
he had spent the vigour of his youth, and where he met
with his untimely end."

      *   *   *   *   *   *

The guide paused, and looked round upon his auditors.
Alas! for the sympathy of man—the half of them had
gone to sleep; and Baptiste, for whose benefit the story
had been related, lay or rather sprawled upon the turf
behind the fire, snoring loudly, his shaggy head resting on
the rotten stump of an old tree, and his empty pipe hanging
gracefully from his half-open mouth. A slight "humph"
escaped the worthy guide, as he shook the ashes from

his pipe, and, rolling his blanket round him, laid his head upon the ground.

Early on the following morning we raised the camp and continued our journey. The scenery had now become more wild and picturesque. Large pines became numerous; and the rocky fissures, through which the river rushed in a black unbroken mass, cast a gloomy shadow upon us as we struggled to ascend. Sometimes we managed to get up these rapids with the paddles, and, when the current was too powerful, with long poles, which the men fixed in the ground, and thus pushed slowly up ; but, when both of these failed, we resorted to the tracking line, upon which occasions four of the men went on shore and dragged us up, leaving four in the canoe to paddle and steer it. When the current was too strong for this, they used to carry parts of the cargo to the smooth water further up, and drag the canoe up light, or, taking it on their shoulders, carry it over-land. We made nine or ten of these portages in two days. In the afternoon we came in view of a Roman Catholic mission station, which was snugly situated at the bottom of a small bay or creek ; but, as it was a little out of our way, and from its quiet appearance seemed to be deserted, we did not stop.

In the afternoon of the following day, the 9th of September, we arrived at the Company's post called Rat Portage House, where we were hospitably entertained for a few hours by Mr M'Kenzie, the gentleman in charge. On the portage, over which we had to carry

our canoe and baggage, a large party of Indians of both
sexes and all ages were collected to witness our departure;
and Mr M'Kenzie advised us to keep a sharp look-out,
as they were much addicted to appropriating the pro-
perty of others to their own private use, provided they
could find an opportunity of doing so unobserved; so,
while our men were running backwards and forwards,
carrying the things over the rocks, Mr B—— and his
lady remained at one end to guard them and I at the
other. Every thing, however, was got safely across; the
Indians merely stood looking on, apparently much amused
with our proceedings, and nothing seemed further from
their thoughts than stealing. Just as we paddled from
the bank one of our men threw them a handful of tobacco,
for which there was a great scramble, and their noisy
voices died away in the distance as we rounded an
abrupt point of rocks, and floated out upon the glorious
expanse of Lac du Bois, or, as it is more frequently
called, the Lake of the Woods.

There is nothing, I think, more calculated to awaken
the more solemn feelings of our nature, (unless, indeed,
it be the thrilling tones of sacred music), than one of
these noble lakes, studded with innumerable islets, suddenly bursting on the traveller's view, as he emerges
from one of the sombre, wood-encompassed rivers of the
American wilderness. The clear unruffled water, stretching out to the horizon—here, embracing the heavy and
luxuriant foliage of a hundred wooded isles, or reflecting
the wood-clad mountains on its margin, clothed in all

the variegated hues of autumn; and there, glittering with dazzling brilliancy, in the bright rays of the evening sun, or rippling among the reeds and rushes of some shallow bay, where hundreds of wild-fowl chatter, as they feed, with varied cry, rendering more apparent, rather than disturbing, the solemn stillness of the scene: all tends to "raise the soul from nature up to nature's God," and remind one of the beautiful passage of Scripture,—"O Lord, how manifold are thy works! in wisdom hast thou made them all: the earth is full of thy riches."

At night we encamped at the farthest extremity of the lake, on a very exposed spot, from whence we looked out upon the starlit scene, while our supper was spread before us in the warm light of the fire, which blazed and crackled as the men heaped log after log upon it, sending up clouds of bright sparks into the sky.

Next morning we commenced the ascent of Lac la Pluie River. This is decidedly the most beautiful river we had yet traversed, not only on account of the luxuriant foliage, of every hue, with which its noble banks are covered, but chiefly from the resemblance it bears in many places to the scenery of England, recalling to mind the grassy lawns and verdant banks of Britain's streams, and transporting the beholder from the wild scenes of the western world to his native home. The trees along its banks were larger and more varied than any we had hitherto seen,—ash, poplar, cedar, red and white pines, oak, and birch, being abundant, while many flowers of gaudy hues enhanced the beauty of the scene.

Towards noon our guide kept a sharp look-out for a convenient spot whereon to dine ; and ere long, a flat shelving rock, partly shaded by trees and partly exposed to the blaze of the sun, presented itself to view. The canoe was soon alongside of it, and kept floating about half-a-foot from the edge by means of two branches, the two ends of which were fastened to the bow and stern of the canoe, and the other two held to the ground by means of huge stones. It is necessary to be thus careful with canoes, as the gum or pitch with which the seams are plastered breaks off in lumps, particularly in cold weather, and makes the craft leaky. A snow-white napkin was spread on the flattest part of the rock, and so arranged that, as we reclined around it on cloaks and blankets, our bodies, down to the knees, were shaded by the luxuriant foliage behind us, while our feet were basking in the solar rays ! Upon the napkin was presently placed, by our active waiter, Gibault, three pewter plates, a decanter of port wine, and a large ham, together with a turret of salt butter, and a loaf of bread, to the demolition of which viands we devoted ourselves with great earnestness. At a short distance, the men circled round a huge lump of boiled pork, each with a large slice of bread in one hand and a knife in the other, with which he *porked* his bread in the same way that civilised people *butter* theirs ! Half-an-hour concluded our midday meal, and then, casting off the branches from the canoe, we were out of sight of our temporary diningroom in five minutes.

In the evening of the following day we arrived at the
Company's post, Fort Frances, so called in honour of the
lady of Sir George Simpson. The fort is rather an old
building, situated at the bottom of a small bay or curve
in the river, near the foot of a waterfall, whose thundering roar forms a ceaseless music to the inhabitants. We
found the post in charge of a chief trader, who had no
other society than that of three or four labouring men ;
so, as may be supposed, he was delighted to see us. Our
men carried the canoe, &c., over the portage to avoid
the waterfall, and, as it was then too late to proceed
further that night, we accepted Mr F——'s pressing
invitation to pass the night at the fort. There was only
one spare bed in the house, but this was a matter of
little moment to us after the variety of beds we had had
since starting ; so, spreading a buffalo robe upon the
floor for a mattras, I rolled myself in my blankets and
tried to sleep. At first I could not manage it, owing to
the unearthly stillness of a room, after being so long
accustomed to the open air and the noise of rivers and
cataracts, but at last succeeded, and slept soundly till
morning. Dame Fortune does not always persecute her
friends ; and although she had retarded us hitherto a
good deal, with contrary winds and rain, she kindly
assisted us when we commenced crossing Lac la Pluie
next morning, by raising a stiff, fair breeze. Now, be it
known, that a canoe, from having no keel, and a round
bottom, cannot venture to hoist a sail unless the wind
is directly astern—the least bit to one side would be

sure to capsize it ; so that our getting the wind precisely
in the proper direction at the commencement, was a
great piece of good fortune, inasmuch as it enabled us
to cross the lake in six hours, instead of (as is generally
the case) taking one, two, or three days. In the evening
we arrived, in high spirits, at a portage, on which we
encamped. Our progress, after this, became a little
more interrupted by portages and small lakes, or rather
ponds, through which we sometimes passed with difficulty,
owing to the shallowness of the water in many places.
Soon after this we came to the Mecan River, up which
we prepared to ascend. In making a portage, we suddenly discovered a little Indian boy, dressed in the
extreme of the Indian summer fashions—in other words,
he was in a perfect state of nakedness, with the exception of a breech-cloth ; and upon casting our eyes across
the river we beheld his father, in a similar costume,
busily employed in catching fish with a hand-net. He
was really a wild, picturesque-looking fellow, notwithstanding the scantiness of his costume, and I was much
interested in his proceedings. When I first saw him, he
was standing upon a rock close to the edge of a foaming
rapid, into the eddies of which he gazed intently, with
the net raised in the air, and his muscular frame motionless, as if petrified while in the act of striking. Suddenly
the net swung through the air, and his body quivered as
he strained every sinew to force it quickly through the
water : in a moment it came out with a beautiful white-
fish, upwards of a foot long, glittering like silver as it

struggled in the meshes. In the space of half an hour
he had caught half-a-dozen in this manner, and we
bought three or four of the finest for a few plugs of
tobacco. His wigwam and family were close at hand,
so, while our men crossed the portage, I ran up to see
them.

The tent, which was made of sheets of birch-bark
sewed together, was pitched beneath the branches of a
gigantic pine, upon the lower limbs of which hung a pair
of worn-out snowshoes, a very dirty blanket, and a short
bow, with a quiver of arrows near it. At the foot of it,
upon the ground, were scattered a few tin pots, several
pairs of old moccasins, and a gun ; while against it leaned
an Indian cradle, in which a small very brown baby,
with jet-black eyes and hair, stood bolt upright, basking
in the sun's rays, and bearing a comical resemblance to
an Egyptian mummy. At the door of the tent a child
of riper years amused itself, by rolling about among the
chips of wood, useless bits of deer-skin and filth, that is
always strewn around a wigwam. On the right hand
lay a pile of firewood, with an axe beside it, near which
crouched a half-starved, wretched-looking, nondescript
dog, who kicked up a tremendous row the moment he
cast eyes upon me. Such was the outside. The interior,
which was filled with smoke from the fire and Indians'
pipes, was, if possible, even dirtier. Amid a large pile
of rabbit-skins reclined an old woman, who was busily
employed plucking the feathers from a fine duck, which
she preserved carefully (the feathers, not the duck) in a

bag, for the purpose of trading them with the Company
at a future period.   Her dress was a coat of rabbit-skins,
so strangely shaped that no one could possibly tell how
she ever got it off or on.   This, however, was doubtless
a matter of little consequence to her, as Indians seldom
take the trouble of changing their clothes, or even of
undressing at all.   The coat was fearfully dirty, and
hung upon her in a way that led me to suppose she had
worn it for six months, and that it would fall off her in a
few days.   A pair of faded blue cloth leggins completed
her costume — her dirty shoulders, arms, and feet being
quite destitute of covering; while her long black hair fell
in tangled masses upon her neck, and it was evidently a
long time since a comb had passed through it.   On the
other side sat a younger woman similarly attired, employed in mending a hand-net; and on a very much
worn buffalo robe sat a young man (probably the brother
of the one we had seen fishing), wrapped in a blanket,
smoking his pipe in silence.   A few dirty little half-naked
boys lay sprawling among several packages of furs, tied
up in birch bark, and disputed with two or three ill-
looking dogs for the most commodious place whereon to
lie.   The fire in the middle of the tent sent up a cloud
of smoke which escaped through an aperture at the top,
and from a cross-bar depended a few slices of deers-meat,
which was undergoing the process of being smoked.

I had merely time to note all this, and say "what
cheer" to the Indians, who returned the compliment
with a grunt, when the loud voice of our guide ringing

through the glades of the forest, informed me that the canoe was ready to proceed.

The country through which we now passed was very interesting, on account of the variety of the scenes and places through which we wound our way. At times we were paddling with difficulty against the strong current of a narrow river, which, on our turning a point of land, suddenly became a large lake ; and then, after crossing this, we arrived at a portage : after passing over it, there came a series of small ponds and little creeks, through which we pushed our way with difficulty ; and then arrived at another lake, and more little rivers, with numerous portages. Sometimes ludicrous accidents happened to us, which, though bad enough at the time, were subjects of mirth afterwards.

One cold, frosty morning, (for the weather had now become cold, from the elevation of the country through which we passed), while the canoe was going quietly over a small reedy lake, or ford, I was awakened out of a nap into which I had fallen, and told that the canoe was aground, and I must get out and walk a little way to lighten her. Hastily pulling up my trousers, (for I always travelled barefoot), I sprang over the side into the water, and the canoe left me. Now all this happened so quickly, that I was scarcely awake ; but the bitterly cold water, which nearly reached my knees, cleared up my faculties most effectually, and I then found that I was fifty yards from the shore, with an unknown depth of water around me, the canoe out of sight ahead of me, and Mr B—— (who had been turned out while half asleep also) standing with a rueful expression of countenance beside me. After feeling our way cautiously—for the bottom was soft and muddy—we reached the shore; and then, thinking that all was right, proceeded to walk round to join the canoe. Alas! we found the bushes so thick, that they were very nearly impenetrable; and worse than all, that they, as well as the ground, were covered with thorns, which scratched and lacerated our feet most fearfully at every step. There was nothing for it, however, but to persevere; and after a painful walk of a quarter of a mile, we overtook the canoe, vowing never to leap before we looked, upon any other occasion whatsoever.

In this way we proceeded, literally over hill and dale, in our canoe, and in the course of a few days ascended Mecan River, and traversed Cross Lake, Malign River, Sturgeon Lake, Lac du Mort, Mille Lac, besides a great number of smaller sheets of water without names, and many portages of various lengths and descriptions, till the evening of the 19th, when we ascended the beautiful little river called the Savan, and arrived at the Savan Portage.

Thirty years' ago, in the time of the North-West Company, the echoes among these wild solitudes were far oftener and more loudly awakened than they are now. The reason of it was this. The North-West Company, having their headquarters in Montreal, and being composed chiefly of Canadian adventurers, imported their whole supplies into the country, and exported all their furs out of it, in north canoes, by the same route over which we were now travelling. As they carried on business on a large scale, it may be supposed that the traffic was correspondingly great. No less than ten brigades (each numbering twenty canoes) used to pass through these scenes during the summer months. No one who has not experienced it can form an adequate idea of the thrilling effect the passing of these brigades must have had upon a stranger. I have seen four canoes sweep round a promontory suddenly, and burst upon my view; while at the same moment, the wild, romantic song of the voyageurs, as they plied their brisk paddles, struck upon my ear, and I have felt the thrilling enthusiasm caused by such a scene : what, then, must have been the feelings of those who had spent a long, dreary winter in the wild North-West, far removed from the bustle and excitement of the civilised world, when thirty or forty of these picturesque canoes burst unexpectedly upon them, half inshrouded in the spray that flew from the bright, vermilion paddles, while the men, who had overcome difficulties and dangers innumerable during a long voyage through the wilderness, urged their light craft over the troubled water with the speed of the reindeer, and with joyful hearts at the happy termination of their trials and privations, sang with all the force of three hundred manly voices, one of their lively airs, which, rising and falling faintly in the distance as it was borne, first lightly on the breeze, and then more steadily as they

approached, swelled out in the rich tones of many a
mellow voice, and burst into a long enthusiastic shout of
joy!

Alas! the forests no longer echo to such sounds. The
passage, once or twice a-year, of three or four canoes,
is all that breaks the stillness of the scene; and nought,
save narrow pathways over the portages, and rough
wooden crosses over the graves of the travellers who
perished by the way, remains to mark that such things
were.

Of these marks, the Savan Portage, at which we had
arrived, was one of the most striking. A long succession
of boiling rapids and waterfalls, having, in days of yore,
obstructed the passage of the fur-traders, they had
landed at the top of them, and cut a pathway through
the woods, which happened at this place to be exceedingly swampy—hence, the name Savan, or swampy,
Portage. To render the road more passable, they had
cut down trees, which they placed side by side along its
whole extent, which was about three miles, and over
this wooden platform carried their canoes and cargoes
with perfect ease. After the coalition of the two companies, and the consequent carriage of the furs to England
by Hudson's Bay, instead of to Canada by the lakes and
rivers of the interior, these roads were neglected and
got out of repair; and, consequently, we found the logs
over the portage decayed, and trees fallen across them,
so that our men, instead of running quickly over, were
constantly breaking through the rotten wood, sinking

PORTAGE DU CHIEN.

up to the knees in mud, and scrambling over trees and branches. We got over at last, however, in about two hours, and after proceeding a little farther arrived at and encamped upon the Prairie Portage, by the side of a voyageur's grave, which was marked as usual with a wooden cross, on which some friendly hand had cut a rude inscription; time had now rendered it quite illegible. This is the height of land, dividing the waters which flow northward into Hudson's Bay from those which flow in a southerly direction though the great lakes into the Atlantic ocean.

A few pages from my journal, here, may serve to give a better idea of the characteristics of our voyage than could be conveyed in narrative.

Saturday, 20th September.— We crossed the Prairie Portage this morning, a distance of between three and four miles, and breakfasted at the upper end of it. Amused myself by sketching the view from a neighbouring hill. After crossing over two more portages, and a variety of small lakes, we launched our canoe on the bosom of the river Du Chien, and began for the first time since the commencement of our journey to *descend*, having passed over the height of land. We saw several gray grouse here, and in the evening one of our men caught one in a curious manner. They were extremely tame, and allowed us to approach them very closely, so Baptiste determined to catch one for supper. Cutting a long branch from a neighbouring tree, he tied a running noose on one end of it, and, going quietly up to the bird, put the noose gently over its head and pulled it off the tree! This is a common practice among the Indians, particularly when they have run short of gunpowder.

Sunday, 21st.—Crossed Lac du Chien, and made the portage of the same name, from the top of which we had a most beautiful view of the whole country for miles round. Having crossed this portage, we proceeded down the Kamenistaquoia River, on the banks of which, after making another portage, we pitched our tents.

Monday, 22d.—Rain obliged us to put ashore this morning. Nothing can be more wretched than travelling in rainy weather. The men, poor fellows, do not make the least attempt to keep themselves dry; but the passengers endeavour, by means of oiled cloths, to keep out the wet,—and under this they broil and suffocate, till at last they are obliged to throw off the covering. Even were this not the case, we would still be wretched, as the rain always finds its way in somewhere or other; and I have been often awakened from a nap by the cold trickling of moisture down my back, and have discovered, upon moving, that I was lying in a pool of water. Ashore, we are generally a little more comfortable, but not much. After dinner we again started, and advanced on our journey till sunset.

Tuesday, 23d.—To-day we advanced very slowly, owing to the shallowness of the water, and crossed a number of portages. During the day, we ran several rapids. This is an exceedingly exciting thing: upon nearing the heads of a large rapid, the men strain every muscle to urge the canoe more quickly forward than the water, so that it may steer better. The bowsman and steersman stand erect, guiding the frail bark through the more unbroken places in the fierce current, which hisses and foams around, as if eager to swallow us up. Now we rush, with lightning force, towards a rock, against which the water dashes in fury, and, to an uninitiated traveller, we appear to be on the point of destruction;—but one vigorous stroke from the bowsman and steersman, (for they always act in concert), sends the light craft at a sharp angle from the impending danger, and away we plunge again over the surging waters,—sometimes floating for an instant in a small eddy, and hovering, as it were, to choose our path, and then plunging swiftly forward again through the windings of the stream,—till, having passed the whole in safety, we float in the smooth water below. Accidents, as may be supposed, often happen; and to-day we found that there is danger as well as pleasure in running the rapids. We had got over a great part of the day in safety, and were in the act of running the first part of the Rose rapid, when our canoe struck upon a rock, and wheeling round with its broadside to the stream, began to fill quickly. I could hear the timbers cracking beneath me under the immense pressure—another minute, and we should have been gone; but our men, who were active fellows, and well accustomed to such dangers, sprang simultaneously over the side of the canoe, which, being thus lightened, passed over the rock, and rushed down the remainder of the rapid stern-foremost, ere the men could scramble in and resume their paddles. When rapids were very dangerous, most of the cargo was generally disembarked, and while one-half of the crew carried it round to the still water below, the other half ran down light. Crossed two small portages, and the Mountain Portage in the afternoon, on the latter of which I went to see a waterfall, which I was told was in its vicinity. I had great difficulty in finding it at first, but its thundering roar soon guided me to a spot from whence I could see it. Truly, a grander waterfall I never saw! The whole river, which was pretty broad, plunged in one broad, white sheet over a precipice, higher, by a few feet, than the famous Falls of Niagara; and the spray from the foot sprang high into the air, bedewing the wild, precipitous rocks, with which the fall is encompassed, and the gloomy pines that hang about the clefts and fissures of the rocks. Travellers have given it the name of the Mountain Fall, from a peculiar mountain in its vicinity,—but the natives call it the *Kackabecka* Falls. After making a sketch of it, and getting myself thoroughly wet in so doing, I returned to the canoe. In the evening we encamped within nine miles of Fort William, having lost one of our men, who went ashore to lighten the canoe while we ran a rapid. After a good deal of trouble we found him again, but too late to admit of our proceeding to the fort that night.

Wednesday, 24th.—Early this morning we left the encampment, and after two hours' paddling, Fort William burst upon our enraptured gaze, mirrored in the limpid waters of that immense fresh-water sea, Lake Superior, whose rocky shores and rolling billows vie with the ocean in grandeur and magnificence.

Fort William was once one of the chief posts in the Indian country; and, when it belonged to the North-West Company, contained a great number of men. Now, however, much of its glory has departed. Many of the buildings have been pulled down, and those that remain are very rickety-looking affairs. It is still, however, a very important fishing station, and many hundreds of beautiful whitefish, with which Lake Superior swarms, are salted there annually for the Canada markets. These whitefish are indeed excellent, and it is difficult to say whether they, or the immense trout, which are also caught in abundance, have the most delicate flavour. These trout, as well as whitefish, are caught in nets, and the former sometimes measure three feet long, and are proportionately broad. The one we had to breakfast on the morning of our arrival, must have been very nearly this size.

The fur trade of the post is not very good, but the furs traded are similar to those obtained in other parts of the country.

A number of *canôtes de maître*, or very large canoes, are always kept in store here, for the use of the Company's travellers. These canoes are of the largest size, exceeding the north canoe in length by several feet, besides being much broader and deeper.

They are used solely for the purpose of travelling on Lake Superior, being much too large and cumbersome for travelling with through the interior. They are carried by four men instead of two, like the north canoe, and, besides being capable of carrying twice as much cargo, are paddled by fourteen or sixteen men. Travellers from Canada to the interior generally change their *canôtes de maitre* for north canoes at Fort William, before entering upon the intricate navigation though which we had already passed ; while those going from the interior to Canada, change the small for the large canoe. As we had few men, however, and the weather appeared settled, we determined to risk coasting round the northern shore of the lake in our north canoe.

The scenery around the fort is very pretty. In its immediate vicinity the land is flat, covered with small trees and willows, which are agreeably suggestive of partridges and other game ; but in the distance rise stupendous mountains ; and on the left hand, the noble expanse of the Lake Superior, with rocky islands on its mighty bosom, and abrupt hills on its shores, stretches out to the horizon. The fort is built at the mouth of the Kamenistaquoia River, and from its walls a beautiful view of the surrounding country can be obtained.

As the men wanted a little rest, and our canoe a little repair, we determined to remain all day at Fort William ; so some of the men employed themselves re-gumming the canoe, while others spread out our blankets and tents to dry. This last was very necessary, as on the journey we have little time to spare from eating and sleeping while on shore, and many a time have I in consequence slept in a wet blanket.

The fair lady of the gentleman in charge of the fort, was the *only lady* at the place, and indeed the only one within a circuit of six hundred miles, which space, being the primeval forest, was inhabited only by wild beasts and a few Indians. She was consequently very much delighted to meet with Mrs B——, who, having for so many days seen no one but rough voyageurs, was equally delighted to meet her. While they went off to make the most of each other, Mr B—— and I sauntered about in the vicinity of the fort, admiring the beauty of the scenery, and paid numerous visits to a superb dairy in the fort, which overflowed with milk and cream. There was a number of cows at the post, a few of which we encountered during our walk, and also a good many pigs and sheep.

In the evening we returned, and at tea-time were introduced to a post-master, who had been absent when we arrived. This post-master turned out to be a first-rate player of Scottish reels on the violin. He was self-taught, and truly the sweetness and precision with which he played every note and trill of the rapid reel and strathspey, whould have made Neil Gow himself envious. So beautiful and inspiriting were they, that Mr B—— and our host, who were both genuine Highlanders, jumped simultaneously from their seats, in an ecstasy

of enthusiasm, and danced to the lively music till the
very walls shook, much to the amusement of the two
ladies, who having been both born in Canada, could
not so well appreciate the music.　Indeed, the musician
himself looked a little astonished, being quite ignorant
of the endearing recollections and associations recalled
to the memory of the two Highlanders by the rapid
notes of his violin.　They were not, however, to be
contented with one reel ; so, after fruitlessly attempting
to make the ladies join us, we sent over to the men's
houses for the old Canadian wife of Pierre Lattinville,
and her two blooming daughters.　They soon came, and
after much coyness, blushing, and hesitation, at last stood
up, and under the inspiring influence of the violin, we

> " Danced till we were like to fa'
> The reel o' Tullochgorum ! "

and did not cease till the lateness of the hour, and the
exhaustion of our musician, compelled us to give in.

On the following morning we bade adieu to the good
people at Fort William, and began our journey along
the northern shore of Lake Superior, which is upwards
of three hundred miles in diameter.　Fortune, however,
is proverbially fickle, and she did not belie her character
on this particular day.　The weather, when we started,
was calm and clear, which pleased us much, as we had
to make what is called a traverse—that is, to cross from
one point of land to another—instead of coasting round a
very deep bay.　The traverse which we set out to make
on leaving Fort William, was fourteen miles broad, which

made it of some consequence our having a calm day to cross it, in our little egg-shell of a canoe. Away we went, then, over the clear lake, singing Rose Blanche vociferously. We had already gone a few miles of the distance, when a dark cloud rose on the seaward horizon. Presently the water darkened under the influence of a stiff breeze; and in less than half an hour the waves were rolling and boiling around us like those of the Atlantic. Ahead of us lay a small island, about a mile distant, and towards this the canoe was steered; while the men urged it forward as quickly as the roughness of the sea would allow. Still the wind increased, and the island was not yet gained. Some of the waves had broken over the edge of the canoe, and she was getting filled with water; but a kind providence permitted us to reach the island in safety, though not in comfort, as most of the men were much wet, and many of them a good deal frightened.

On landing, we pitched our tents, made a fire, and proceeded to dry ourselves; and in less than an hour we were as comfortable as possible. The island on which we had encamped, was a small rocky one, covered with short heathery-looking shrubs, among which we found thousands of blae-berries. On walking round to the other side of it, I discovered an Indian encamped with his family. He supplied us with a fine whitefish, for which our men gave him a little tobacco and a bit of the fresh mutton with which we had supplied ourselves on leaving Fort William.

Three days we remained on this vile island, while the wind and waves continued unceasingly to howl and lash around it, as if they wished in their disappointment to beat it down and swallow us up, island and all ; but, towards the close of the third day, the gale moderated, and we ventured again to attempt the traverse. This time we succeeded, and in two hours passed Thunder Point, on the other side of which we encamped.

The next day we could only travel till breakfast time, as the wind again increased so much as to oblige us to put ashore. We comforted ourselves, however, with the prospect of a good mutton-chop. The fire was soon made, the kettle on, and every thing in preparation, when the dreadful discovery was made that the whole of the fresh mutton had been forgotten ! Words cannot paint our consternation at this discovery. Poor Mrs B—— sat in mute despair, thinking of the misery of being reduced again to salt pork ; while her husband, who had hitherto stood aghast, jumped suddenly forward, and seizing a bag of fine potatoes that had been given to the men, threw it, in a transport of rage, into the lake, vowing that as we were by their negligence to be deprived of our mutton, they certainly should also be sufferers with us.

It was very laughable to behold the rueful countenances of the men, as their beautiful, large, white potatoes sank to the bottom of the clear water, and shone brightly there, as if to tantalise them, while the rippling water caused them to quiver so much, that the lake seemed to rest on a pavement of huge potatoes! None of them dared, however, attempt to recover one; but, after a while, when Mr B——'s back was turned, one of the men crept cautiously down to the water's-edge, and gathered as many as were within reach,—always, however, keeping an eye on his master, and stooping in an attitude that would permit of his bolting up on the slightest indication of a wrathful movement.

It would be tedious, as well as unnecessary, to recount here all the minutiæ of our voyage across Lake Superior; I shall merely touch on a few of the more particular incidents. On the 1st of October we arrived at the Pic House,* where we spent the night; and, after a rough voyage, reached Michipicoton on the 4th. Our voyage along Lake Superior was very stormy and harassing, reminding us often of Lake Winnipeg. Sometimes we were paddling along over the smooth water, and at other times *lying-by*, while the lake was lashed into a mass of foam and billows by a strong gale. So much detention, and the lateness of the season, rendered it necessary to take advantage of every lull and calm hour that occurred, so that we travelled a good deal during the night. This sort of travelling was very romantic. I will describe a night of it. On one occasion, after having been ashore for two days, the wind moderated in the afternoon, and we determined to proceed if possible. The sun set gloriously, giving promise

* It must be borne in mind that all the establishments we passed on the way belonged to the Hudson's Bay Company.

of fine weather. The sky was clear and cloudless, and the lake calm. For an hour or so, the men sang as they paddled, but, as the shades of evening fell, they ceased ; and, as it was getting rather chilly, I wrapped myself in my green blanket, (which served me for a boat-cloak as well as a bed,) and soon fell fast asleep. How long I slept I know not, but when I awoke, the regular, rapid hiss of the paddles struck upon my ear, and upon throwing off the blanket, the first thing that met my eye was the dark sky spangled with the most gorgeous and brilliant stars I ever beheld. The whole scene, indeed, was one of the most magnificent and awful than can be imagined. On our left hand rose tremendous precipices and cliffs, around the bottom and among the caverns of which, the black waters of the lake curled quietly, (for a most deathlike, unearthly calm prevailed,) sending forth a faint hollow murmur, as of distant waters, which ended at long intervals in a slow melancholy cadence. Before and behind us, abrupt, craggy islands rose from the water, assuming every imaginable and unimaginable shape in the uncertain light; while on the right, the eye ranged over the inky lake, till it was lost in thick darkness. A thin, transparent night-fog added to the mystical appearance of the scene, upon which I looked with mingled feelings of wonder and awe. The only distinct sound that could be heard, was the measured sound of the paddles, which the men plied in silence, as if unwilling to break the stillness of the night. Suddenly the guide uttered in a hoarse whisper, " A terre!" startling the sleepy men, and rendering the succeeding silence still more impressive. The canoe glided noiselessly through a maze of narrow passages among the tall cliffs, and grounded on a stony beach. Every thing was then carried up, and the tents pitched in the dark, as no wood could be conveniently found for the purpose of making a fire ; and, without taking any supper, or even breaking the solemn silence of the night, we spread our beds as we best could upon the round stones, (some of which were larger than a man's foot,) and sank into repose. In a couple of hours we were roused by the anxious guide, and told to embark again. In this way we travelled at night or by day, as the weather permitted, and even, upon one or two occasions, both night and day, till the 12th of October, when we arrived at the *Sault de Ste Marie,* which is situated at the termination of Lake Superior, just as our provisions were exhausted. We had thus taken eighteen days to coast the lake. This was very slow going indeed, the usual time for coasting the lake in a north canoe being from eight to ten days. The Sault de Ste Marie is a large rapid, which carries the waters of Lake Superior into Lake Huron. It separates the British from the American possessions, and is forti-fied on the American side by a large wooden fort, in which a body of soldiers are constantly resident. There is also a pretty large village of Americans, which is rapidly increasing. The British side is not fortified, and, indeed, there are no houses of any kind except the few belonging to the Hudson's Bay Company. This may be considered the extreme outskirts of civilisation, being the first place where I had seen any number of people collected together, who were unconnected with the Hudson's Bay Company.

I was not destined, however, to enjoy the sight of new faces long; for next morning we started to coast round the northern and uninhabited shores of Lake Huron, and so down the Ottawa to Montreal. Mr and Mrs B—— left me here, and proceeded by the route of the Lakes.

During the next few days we travelled through a number of rivers and lakes of various sizes; among the latter were Lakes Huron and Nipisingue. In crossing the latter, I observed a point on which were erected fourteen rough wooden crosses : such an unusual sight excited my curiosity, and upon inquiring, I found that they were planted there to mark the place where a canoe, containing fourteen men, had been upset in a gale, and every soul been lost. The lake was clear and smooth when we passed the melancholy spot, and many a rolling year has defaced and cast down the crosses since the unfortunate men, whose sad fate they commemorate, perished in the storm.

While searching about the shore one night for wood to make a fire, one of our men found a large basket made of bark filled with fine bear's-grease, which had been hid by some Indians. This was considered a great wind-fall, and ere two days were past, the whole of it was eaten by the men, who buttered their flour cakes with it profusely.

Not long after this we passed a large waterfall, where a friend of mine was very nearly lost. A projecting point obliges the traveller to run his canoe rather near the head of the fall, for the purpose of landing, to make the portage. From long habit the guides had been accustomed to this, and always effected the doubling of the point in safety. Upon this occasion, however, either from carelessness or accident, the canoe got into the strong current, and almost in an instant was swept down towards the fall. To turn the head of the canoe up the stream, and paddle for their lives, was the work of a moment; but before they got it fairly round they were on the very brink of the cataract, which, had they gone over it, would have dashed them to a thousand atoms. They paddled with the strength of desperation, but so strong was the current, that they remained almost stationary. At last they began slowly to ascend, an inch at a time, and finally reached the bank in safety.

On Sunday the 19th of October, we commenced descending the magnificent river Ottawa, and began to feel that we were at last approaching the civilised nations of the earth. During the day we passed several small log-huts, or shantys, which are the temporary dwelling-places of men who penetrate thus far into the forest for the purpose of cutting timber. A canoe full of these adventurous pioneers also passed us; and in the evening we reached Fort Mattawan, one of the Company's stations. At night we encamped along with a party of men who were taking provisions to the wood-cutters.

The scenery on the Ottawa is beautiful, and as we descended the stream it was rendered more picturesque and interesting by the appearance, occasionally, of that, to us unusual sight, a farm-house. They were too few and far between, however, to permit of our taking advantage of the inhabitants' hospitality; and for the next four days we continued to make our encampments in the woods as heretofore. At one of these frontier farms, our worthy guide discovered, to his unutterable astonishment and delight, an old friend and fellow voyageur, to greet whom, he put ashore. The meeting was strange : instead of shaking hands warmly, as I had expected, they stood for a moment gazing in astonishment, and then, with perfect solemnity, kissed each other — not gently on the cheek, but with a good, hearty smack on their sunburnt lips. After conversing for a little, they parted with another kiss.

On the fourth day after this event, we came in sight of the village of Aylmer, which lay calmly on the sloping banks of the river, its church spires glittering in the sun, and its white houses reflected in the stream.

It is difficult to express the feelings of delight with which I gazed upon this little village, after my long banishment from the civilised world. It was like recovering from a trance of four long dreamy years ; and

I wandered about the streets, gazing in joy and admiration upon every thing and every body ; but, especially upon the ladies, who appeared quite a strange race of beings to me, and all of them looked quite beautiful in my eyes, (so long accustomed to Indian dames,) insomuch that I fell in love with every one individually that passed me in the village. In this happy mood I sauntered about, utterly oblivious of the fact, that my men had been left in a public-house, and would infallibly, if not prevented, get dead drunk. I was soon awakened to this startling probability by the guide, who walked up the road in a very solemn, I'm-not-at-all-drunk sort of manner, peering about on every side, evidently in search of me. Having found me, he burst into an expression of unbounded joy, and then, recollecting that this was inconsistent with his assumed character of sobriety, became awfully grave, and told me that we must start soon, as the men were all getting tipsy.

The following day we arrived at Bytowne. This town is picturesquely situated on the brow of a stupendous cliff, which descends precipitously into the Ottawa. Just above the town a handsome bridge stretches across the river, near which the Kettle Fall thunders over a a high cliff. We only staid a few minutes here, and then proceded on our way. During the day, we passed the locks of the Rideau Canal, which rise, to the number of eight or ten, one over another like steps ; and immediately below them appeared the Curtain Falls. These Falls are not very picturesque, but their great height, and curtain-like smoothness, render them an interesting object. After this, villages and detached houses became numerous all the way down the river ; and late in the evening of the 24th, we arrived at a station belonging to the Hudson's Bay Company, on the Lake of the Two Mountains, where we passed the remainder of the night.

Here, for the first time since leaving home, I was ushered into a civilised drawing-room; and when I found myself seated on a *cushioned* chair, with my moccasined feet pressing a soft carpet, and several real, *bonâ-fide ladies* (the wife and daughters of my entertainer) sitting before me, and asking hundreds of questions about my long voyage, — the strange species of unbelief in the possibility of again seeing the civilised world, which had beset me for the last three years, began to give way, and at last entirely vanished, when my host showed me into a handsomely furnished bedroom, and left me for the night. The first thing that struck me on entering the bed-room, was the appearance of one of our voyageurs, dressed in a soiled blue capote, dilapidated corduroy trousers, and moccasins; while his deeply sunburnt face, under a mass of long, straggling hair, stared at me in astonishment ! It will, doubtless, be supposed that I was much horrified at this apparition. I was, indeed, much surprised ; but, seeing that it was my own image reflected in a full-length looking-glass, I cannot say that I felt extremely horrified. This was the first time that I had seen myself—if I may so speak—

since leaving Norway House ; and, truly, I had no reason
to feel proud of my appearance.

The following morning, at four o'clock, we left the
Lake of the Two Mountains ; and in the afternoon of
the 25th October 1845, arrived at Lachine, where, for
the time, my travels came to a close—having been jour-
neying in the wilderness for sixty-six days.

    *   *   *   *   *   *

The village of Lachine is prettily situated on the
banks of the St Lawrence, about nine miles above Montreal. The country around it is populous and pretty,
and the view across the river is beautiful. Just in front
of the Hudson's Bay House—where I was soon installed
—is the Lachine Canal, up and down which, steamers
and barges are constantly passing. Beyond this flows
the majestic river St Lawrence, which is here nearly two
miles broad ; and on the opposite shore lies the village
of Ookanawagan, inhabited by a tribe of Iroquois Indians. Lachine itself is very small ; the only street in it,
however, is well peopled, and the houses of which it is
composed scattered over a large space of ground. The
Hudson's Bay House is the most imposing building about
the place, but it does not reflect much credit on its
architect. There are three churches in the village :—a
Presbyterian, Episcopalian, and Roman Catholic church,
the latter being most generally attended by the inhabitants, who are mostly all French Canadians.

Soon after my arrival, winter set in, and I began to
become acquainted with a few of the inhabitants of

Lachine. The moment the snow fell, wheeled carriages were superseded by carioles and sleighs of all descriptions. These beautiful vehicles are mounted on runners, or large skates, and slide very smoothly and easily over the snow, except when the road is bad, and then, owing to the want of springs, sleighs become very rough carriages indeed. They are usually drawn by one horse, the harness and trappings of which are profusely covered with small round bells. These bells are very necessary appendages, as little noise is made by the approach of a sleigh over the soft snow, and they serve to warn travellers in the dark. The cheerful tinkling music thus occasioned on the Canadian roads, is very pleasing. Sleighs vary a good deal in structure, and costliness of decoration; and one often meets a rough, cheerful Canadian *habitant* sitting in his small box of a sledge, (which is painted sometimes red and sometimes green,) lashing away at his shaggy pony, in a fruitless attempt to keep up with the large graceful sleigh of a wealthy inhabitant of Montreal, who, wrapped up in furs, drives tandem, with two strong horses and loudly tinkling bells.

Reader,—I had very nearly come to the resolution of giving you a long account of Canada and the Canadians, but I dare not venture on it. I feel that it would be encroaching upon the ground of civilised authors ; and, as I do not belong to this class, but profess to write of savage life—and nothing but savage life—I hope that you will extend to me your kind forgiveness, if I conclude this chapter rather abruptly.

It is a true saying, that the cup of happiness is often dashed from the lips that are about to taste it. I have sometimes proved this to be the case. The cup of happiness, on the present occasion, was the enjoyment of civilised and social life ; and the dashing of it away was my being sent, with very short warning, to an out-of-the-way station, whose name, to me, was strange— distance uncertain, but long—appearance unknown, and geographical position a most profound mystery.

CHAPTER X.

T was on a bright winter's day, in the month of January 1846, that I was sent for by the Governor, and told to hold myself in readiness to start early the following morning with Mr B—— for Tadousac, adding, that probably I should spend the approaching summer at Seven Islands.

Tadousac, be it known, is a station about three hundred miles below Montreal, on the mouth of the river Saguenay,—and Seven Islands is two hundred miles below Tadousac; so that the journey is not a short one. The greater part of the road runs through an uninhabited country, and the travelling is bad.

In preparation for this journey, then, I employed myself during the remainder of the day; and before night all was ready.

Next morning I found that our journey was postponed to the following day, so I went into Montreal to make a few purchases: and passed the rest of the day in a state of intense thought, endeavouring to find out if any thing had been forgotten. Nothing, however, recurred to my memory, and going to bed only half undressed, in order to be ready at a moment's notice, I soon fell into a short disturbed slumber, from which the servant awakened me long before daylight, by announcing that the sleigh was at the door. In ten minutes I was down stairs, where shortly after, Mr B—— joined me ; and after seeing our traps safely deposited in the bottom of the sleigh, we jumped in, and slid noiselessly over the quiet street of Lachine.

The stars shone brightly out as we glided over the crunching snow, and the sleigh-bells tinkled merrily as our horse sped over the deserted road. Groups of white cottages, and solitary gigantic trees, flew past us, looking, in the uncertain light, like larger snow-drifts ; save where the twinkling of a candle, or the first blue flames of the morning fire, indicated that the industrious *habitant* had risen to his daily toil. In silence we glided on our way, till the distant lights of Montreal awakened us from our reveries, and we began to pass at intervals a solitary pedestrian, or a sleigh-load of laughing, fur-encompassed faces, returning probably from an evening party.

About seven o'clock we arrived at the hotel from which the stage was to start for Quebec,—but when did stage-coach, or sleigh either, keep to its time ? No sign of it was to be seen, and it required no small appli-cation of our knuckles and toes at the door to make the lazy waiter turn out to let us in. No misery, save being too late, can equal that of being too soon ; at least so I thought, while walking up and down the coffee-room of the hotel, upon the table of which were scattered the remains of last night's supper, amid a confusion of newspapers, and fag-ends of cigars ; while the sleepy waiter made unavailing efforts to coax a small spark of fire to contribute some warmth to one or two damp billets of wood.

About an hour after its appointed time, the sleigh drove up to the door, and we hastened to take our places. The stage, however, was full, but the driver informed us that an " extra," (or separate sleigh of smaller dimensions than the stage,) had been provided for us ; so that we enjoyed the enviable advantage of having it all to ourselves. Crack went the whip, and off went the leader with a bound, the wheeler following at a pace between a trot and a gallop, and our " extra" keeping close in the rear. The lamps were still burning as we left the city, although the first streaks of dawn illumined the eastern sky. In fifteen minutes more we had left Montreal far behind.

There is something very agreeable in the motion of a sleigh along a good road. The soft muffled sound of the runners gliding over the snow, harmonises well with the tinkling bells ; and the rapid motion through the frosty air, together with the occasional jolt of going into a hollow, or over a hillock, is very exhilarating, and we enjoyed our drive very much for the first hour or so. But, alas ! human happiness is seldom of long duration, as we soon discovered ; for just as I was falling into a comfortable doze, bang ! went the sleigh into a deep " cahoe," which most effectually wakened me. Now

these same "cahoes" are among the disadvantages attending sleigh travelling in Canada. They are nothing
more or less than deep hollows, or undulations, in the
road, into which the sleighs unexpectedly plunge, thereby
pitching the traveller roughly forward ; and upon the
horses jerking the vehicles out of them, throwing him
backward in a way that is pretty sure to bring his head
into closer acquaintance with the back of the sleigh
than is quite agreeable ; particularly if he be a novice
in sleigh travelling.   Those which we now encountered
were certainly the worst I ever travelled over, rising in
succession, like the waves of the sea, and making our
conveyance plunge, sometimes so roughly, that I expected it to go to pieces.   Indeed, I cannot understand how
wood and iron could stand the crashes to which we were
exposed.   In this way we jolted along, sometimes over
good, sometimes over bad roads, till about nine o'clock,
when we stopped at a neat, comfortable-looking inn,
where the driver changed his horses, and the passengers
sat down to a hurried breakfast.

The morning turned out beautifully clear and warm,
at least in comparison with what it had been ; and upon
re-entering the sleigh we all looked extremely happy,
and disposed to be pleased with every thing and every
body.   The country through which we now passed, was
picturesque and varied.   Hills and valleys, covered with
glittering snow and dark pines, followed each other in
endless succession ; while in every valley, and from
every mountain-top, we saw hundreds of hamlets and

Canadian villages, whose little streets and thoroughfares
were crowded with busy habitants, engaged in their
various occupations and winter traffic. The laughing
voices of merry little Canadian children, romping along
the roads, accorded harmoniously with the lively tinkling of their parents' sleigh bells as they set out for the
market with the produce of their farms ; or dressed in
their whitest blanket capote and smartest *bonnet rouge,*
accompanied their wives and daughters to a marriage
or a festival. The scene was rendered still more pleasing by the extreme clearness of the frosty air, and the
deep blue of the sky ; while the weather was just cold
enough to make the rapid motion of our sleighs agreeable and necessary. The roads were in some places
extremely precipitous ; and when we arrived at the foot
of a large hill, we used generally to get out and walk,
preferring this, to being dragged slowly up by the jaded
horses. During the day our sleighs were upset several
times ; but Mr B—— and I, in the "extra," suffered
more in this way than those of the regular stage, as
it was much narrower, and, consequently, more liable
to tip over. Upon upsetting, it unaccountably happened,
that poor Mr B—— was always undermost. But he
submitted to his fate most stoically ; although, from the
nature of things, my elbow invariably thrust him deep
into the snow, on which, after being extricated, a splendid profile impression was left, to serve as a warning
to other travellers, and show them that a gentleman had
been *cast* there.

SLEIGH TRAVELLING IN CANADA.

As very little danger, however, attended these accidents, they only afforded subject for mirth at the time, and conversation at the end of the stage,—except once, when the sleigh turned over so rapidly that I was thrown with considerable force against the roof, which, being of a kind of slight framework, covered with painted canvass, offered but small opposition to my flight; my head, consequently, went quite through it, and my unfortunate nose was divested to rather an alarming extent of its cutaneous covering. With this exception, we proceeded safely and merrily along, and about seven o'clock in the evening, arrived at the small town of Three Rivers.

Early next morning we resumed our journey, and about four in the afternoon arrived at the famous city of Quebec, without having encountered any very interesting adventures by the way.

The first sight we had of Quebec was certainly any thing but prepossessing. A recent fire in the lower town had completely destroyed a large portion of it; and the first street I passed through was nothing but a gaunt row of blackened chimneys and skeleton houses, which had a very melancholy ghostlike appearance, when contrasted with the white snow. As we advanced, however, to where the fire had been checked, the streets assumed a more agreeable aspect,—shops were open here and there, and workmen busily employed in repairing damaged houses, and pulling down dangerous ones. Upon arriving at the steep street which leads from the lower town to within the walls, the immense strength of the ramparts and fortifications struck me forcibly.   The road up which we passed to the gate, was very narrow : on one side a steep hill descended to the lower town ; and on the other, towered the city walls, pierced all over with loop-holes, and bristling with cannon.   At the head of the road, in an angle of the wall, two silent but grim-looking guns pointed their muzzles directly down the road, so as to command it from one end to the other.   All the other parts of the walls that I happened to see, were even more strongly fortified than this.

The streets of Quebec are very steep, much more so than those of Edinburgh ; and it is no small exertion to mount one or two without stopping to breathe at the top.   Upon the whole, it is any thing but a pretty town, (at least in winter,)—the houses being high, and the streets very narrow.   The buildings, too, are common-place, and the monument to Wolfe and Montcalm is a very insignificant affair.   In fact, Quebec can boast of little else than the magnificent views it commands from the ramparts, and the impregnable strength of its for-tifications.   Some of the suburban villas, however, are very beautiful ; and although I saw them in winter, yet I could form some idea of the enchanting places they must be in summer,   After spending three pleasant days here, we got into our sleigh again, and resumed our journey.

No stages ran below Quebec, so that we now travelled

in the sleigh of a farmer, who happened to be going down part of the way.

Soon after leaving the city, we passed quite close to the famous falls of Montmorenci : they are as high, if not higher, than those of Niagara, but I thought them rather tame, being nothing but a broad curtain of water, falling over an even cliff, and quite devoid of picturesque scenery. A curious cone of ice, formed by the spray, rose nearly half-way up the falls.

The scenery below Quebec is much more rugged and mountainous than that above,—and as we advanced, the marks of civilisation began gradually to disappear ; villages became scarcer, and roads worse, till at last we came to the shanties of the wood-cutters, with here and there a solitary farm-house. Still, however, we occasionally met a few sleighs, with the conductors of which our driver seemed to be intimately acquainted. These little interruptions broke, in a great degree, the monotony of the journey ; and we always felt happier for an hour after having passed and exchanged with a Canadian a cheerful *bon jour.*

Our driver happened to be a very agreeable man, and more intelligent than most Canadians of his class ; moreover, he had a good voice, and when we came to a level part of the road, I requested him to sing me a song, which he did at once, — singing with a clear, strong, manly voice, the most beautiful French air I ever heard,—both the name and air, however, I have now forgotten. He then asked me to sing, which I did without further ceremony, treating him to one of the ancient melodies of Scotland ; and thus, with solos and duets, we beguiled the tedium of the road, and filled the woods with melody ! much to the annoyance of the unmusical American feathered tribes, and to the edification of our horse, who pricked up his ears, and often glanced backwards apparently in extreme surprise.

Towards evening, the driver told us that we would soon arrive at Baie de St Paul, and in half an hour more our weary horse dragged us slowly to the top of a hill, from which we had a splendid view of the village.   Over all the miles of country I had passed, I never saw any thing to equal the exquisite beauty of the Vale of Baie de St Paul.   From the hill on which we stood the whole valley, of many miles in extent, was visible.   It was perfectly level, and covered from end to end with thousands of little hamlets, and several churches, with here and there a few small patches of forest.   The course of a little rivulet, which meanders through it in summer, was apparent, even though covered with snow.   At the mouth of this, several schooners and small vessels lay embedded in ice ; beyond which, rolled the dark, ice-laden waves of the Gulf of St Lawrence.   The whole valley was teeming with human life.   Hundreds of Canadians, in their graceful sleighs and carioles, flew over the numerous roads which intersected the country ; and the faint sound of tinkling bells floated gently up the mountain side, till it reached the elevated position on which we stood.   The whole scene was exquisitely calm and peaceful, forming a strange and striking contrast to the country round it. Like the Happy Valley of Rasselas, it was surrounded by the most wild and rugged mountains, which rose in endless succession, one behind another, stretching away in the distance, till they resembled a faint blue wave on the horizon. In this beautiful place we spent the night; and the following at Mal Baie. This village was also pretty, but after Baie de St Paul I could but little admire it.

Next night we slept in a shanty belonging to the timber-cutters on the coast of the Gulf, which was truly the most wretched abode, except an Indian tent, I ever had the chance (or mischance) to sleep in. It was a small log-hut, with only one room; a low door—to enter which we had to stoop—and a solitary square window, filled with parchment in lieu of glass. The furniture was of the coarsest description, and certainly not too abundant. Every thing was extremely dirty, and the close air was farther adulterated with thick clouds of tobacco smoke, which curled from the pipes of half-a-dozen wood-choppers. Such was the place in which we passed the night, and glad was I when the first blush of day summoned us to resume our travels. We now entered our sleigh for the last time, and after a short drive arrived at the termination of the horse road. Here we got out, and rested a short time in a shanty, preparatory to taking to our snow-shoes.

The road now lay through the primeval forest, and fortunately it proved to be pretty well beaten. so we

walked lightly along, with our snow-shoes under our
arms.   In the afternoon we arrived at another shanty,
having walked about eighteen miles.   Here we found a
a gentlemen who superintended the operations of the
lumberers, or wood-cutters.   He kindly offered to drive
us to Canard River, a place not far distant from the
termination of our journey.   I need scarcely say we
gladly accepted his offer, and in a short time arrived at
the river Saguenay.   This river, owing to its immense
depth, never freezes over at its mouth ; so, we crossed it
in a boat, and about tea-time, on the evening of the 7th
of February, we arrived at the post of Tadousac.

This establishment belongs to the Hudson's Bay Company, and is situated at the bottom of a large and deep
bay, adjoining the mouth of the river Saguenay.   Unlike
the posts of the north, it is merely a group of houses,
scattered about in a hollow of the mountains, without any
attempt at arrangement, and without a stockade.   The
post, when viewed from one of the hills in the neighbourhood, is rather picturesque ; it is seen embedded in the
mountains, and its white-topped houses contrast prettily
with the few pines around it. [See Frontispiece.] A little
to the right, rolls the deep, unfathonable Saguenay, at
the base of precipitous rocks and abrupt mountains,
which are in some places covered with stunted pines,
but for the most part their fronts are bald.   Up the
river the view is interrupted by a large rock, nearly
round, which juts out into the stream, and is named the
" Bull."   To the right lies the bay of St Catherine,

with a new settlement at its head ; and above this, flows the majestic St Lawrence, compared to which, the broad Saguenay is but a thread.

Tadousac Bay is one of the finest natural harbours in the St Lawrence ; being very deep quite close to the shore, it is consequently much frequented by vessels and craft of every description and dimension. Ships, schooners, barques, brigs, and batteaux, are seen lying calmly at anchor within a stone's throw of the bushes on shore ; others are seen beating about at the mouth of the harbour, attempting to enter ; while numerous pilot boats sail up and down, almost under the windows of the house; and in the offing may be seen hundreds of vessels, whose white sails glimmer on the horizon like the wings of sea-gulls, as they beat up for anchorage, or proceed on their course for England or Quebec. The magnificent panorama is closed by the distant hills of the opposite shore, blending with the azure sky. This, however, is the only view, the land being a monotonous repetition of bare granite hills and stunted pines.*

Here, then, for a time, my travels came to a close, and I set about making myself as comfortable in my new quarters as circumstances would permit.

Tadousac I found to be similar, in many respects, to the forts in the north. The country around was wild,

* It may be well to mention, that the above description applies to the country only in the summer and autumn months of the year. During winter, the navigation of the St Lawrence is completely stopped by ice ; and Tadousac then appears as represented in the frontispiece.

mountainous, and uninhabited, save by a few Indians and wild animals.   There was no society, excepting that of Mr B——'s family ; the only other civilised being, above the rank of a labourer, being a gentleman who superintended a timber-cutting and log-sawing establishment, a quarter of a mile from the Company's post.

My *bourgeois* Mr B——, was a very kind man, and an entertaining companion.   He had left Scotland, his native land, when very young ; and had, ever since, been travelling about and dwelling in the wild woods of America.   A deep scar on the bridge of his nose showed that he had not passed through these savage countries scatheless.   The way in which he came by this scar, was curious ; so I may relate it here.

At one of the solitary forts, in the wild regions on the west side of the Rocky Mountains, where my friend Mr B—— dwelt, the Indians were in the habit of selling horses—of which they had a great many—to the servants of the Hudson's Bay Company.   They had also, however, an uncommonly disagreeable propensity to steal these horses again, the moment a convenient opportunity presented itself; and to guard against the gratification of this propensity was one of the many difficulties that the fur-traders had to encounter.   Upon one occasion, a fine horse was sold by an Indian to Mr B—— ; the price (probably several yards of cloth and a few pounds of tobacco) paid, and the Indian went away. Not long after, the horse was stolen ; but, as this was an event that often happened, it was soon forgotten. Winter passed away, and spring began to thaw the lakes and rivers around ; and soon a party of Indians arrived, with furs and horses to trade. They were of the Blackfoot tribe, and a wilder set of fellows one would hardly wish to see. Being much in the habit of fighting with the neighbouring tribes, they were quite prepared for battle, and decorated with many of the trophies of war. Scalp-locks hung from the skirts of their leather shirts and leggins. Eagles' feathers and beads ornamented their heads ; and their faces were painted with stripes of black and red paint.

After conversing with them a short time, they were admitted through the wicket one by one, and their arms taken from them, and locked up. This precaution was rendered necessary at these posts, as the Indians used to buy spirits, and often quarrelled with each other ; but, having no arms, of course they could do themselves little damage. When about a dozen of them had entered, the gate was shut, and Mr B—— proceeded to trade their furs, and examine their horses. Upon going forward, he beheld, to his surprise, the horse which had been stolen from him the summer before ; and, upon asking to whom it belonged, the same Indian who had formerly sold it to him, stood forward and said it was his. Mr B—— (who was an exceedingly quiet, good-natured man, but, like many men of this stamp, very passionate when roused) no sooner witnessed the Indian's audacity, than he seized a gun from one of his men, and shot the horse. The Indian instantly sprang upon him ; but, being a less powerful man than Mr B——, and withal unaccustomed to use his fists, he was soon overcome, and pommelled out of the fort. Not content with this, Mr B—— followed him down to the Indian camp, pommelling him all the way. The instant, however, that the Indian found himself surrounded by his own friends, he faced about, and, with a dozen warriors, attacked Mr B——, and threw him to the ground, where they continued to kick and bruise him severely ; while several boys of the tribe hovered round with bows and arrows, waiting for a favourable opportunity to shoot him. Suddenly a savage came forward with a large stone in his hand, and, standing over his fallen enemy, raised it high in the air, and dashed it down in his face. Mr B——, when telling me the story, said that he had just time, upon seeing the stone in the act of falling, to commend his spirit to God, ere he was rendered insensible. The merciful God, to whom he had looked for help in what may be called the eleventh hour, did not desert him in the time of need. Several men belonging to the fort, upon seeing the turn that things were taking, hastily armed themselves, and, hurrying out to the rescue, arrived just at the critical moment when the stone was dashed in his face. Though too late to prevent this, they were in time to prevent a repetition of the blow ; and, after a short scuffle with the Indians, without any bloodshed, they succeeded in carrying their master up to the fort, where he soon recovered.

The deep cut made by the stone, however, on the bridge of his nose, left an indelible scar upon his countenance.

Besides Mr B——, I had another companion, namely, Mr J——, a clerk, who inhabited the same office with me, and slept in the same bedroom, during the whole winter. He was a fine-looking athletic half-breed, who had been partially educated, but had spent much more of his life among Indians than among civilised men. He used to be sent about the country to trade with the natives, and, consequently, led a much more active life than I did. One part of his business, during the early months of spring, was hunting seals. This was an amusing, though, withal, rather a murderous kind of sport. The manner of it was this.

My friend J—— chose a fine day for his excursion; and, embarking in a boat with six or seven men, sailed a few miles down the St Lawrence, till he came to a low flat point. In a small bay near this, he drew up the boat, and then went into the woods with his party, where each man cut a large pole or club. Arming themselves with these, they waited until the tide receded and left the point dry. In a short time, one or two seals crawled out of the sea, and began to bask upon the shore; soon several more appeared; and, ere long, a band of more than a hundred lay sunning themselves upon the beach. The ambuscade now prepared to attack the enemy. Creeping stealthily down, as near as possible without being discovered, they simultaneously rushed upon the astonished animals; and the tragic scene of

slaughter, mingled with melodramatic and comic incidents that ensued, baffles all description. In one place
might be seen my friend J—— swinging a huge club
round with his powerful arms, and dealing death and
destruction at every blow; while, in another place, a
poor weazened-looking Scotchman (who had formerly
been a tailor! and to whom the work was new) advanced, with cautious trepidation, towards a huge seal,
which spluttered and splashed fearfully in its endeavours
to reach the sea, and dealt it a blow on the back. He
might as well have hit a rock. The slight rap had only
the effect of making the animal show its teeth, at which
sight the tailor retreated precipitately, and, striking his
heel against a rock, fell backwards into a pool of water,
where he rolled over and over, impressed, apparently,
with the idea that he was attacked by all the seals in the
sea. His next essay, however, was more successful, and
in a few minutes he killed several, having learned to hit
on the head instead of on the back. In less than a
quarter of an hour, they killed between twenty and
thirty seals, which were stowed in the boat and conveyed to the post.

Nothing worth mentioning took place at Tadousac
during my residence there. The winter became severe
and stormy ; confining us much to the house, and obliging
us to lead very humdrum sort of lives. Indeed, the
only thing that I can recollect as being at all interesting
or amusing, was my becoming, on one occasion, a dis-
ciple of Æsculapius. The Indians who were living near

the post at the time had been very unhealthy; and, one afternoon, an old sickly-looking fellow came to me and said that he was not at all well, and wanted medicine. Upon hearing this, I questioned him very closely regarding the nature of his complaint; and, after much consideration, came to the conclusion that he had consumption, or something of that sort. Being ignorant of the precise treatment necessary for this disease, I struck out a new line of treatment of my own; so, going to the medicine chest, I took out a strengthening plaster and clapped it on his back; and then, by way of counteracting its effects, placed a blister on his chest, and, thus doctored, sent him away, with a recommendation not to go about much for a few days! In a short time he became much better; but whether from the effects of my treatment, or other causes, I will not take upon myself to say.

This last essay of mine must have frightened the good people with whom I lived, and induced them to petition for my being sent away — or, perhaps, Dame Fortune took a special pleasure in knocking me about the world; but certain it is, that very shortly after the medical transaction mentioned in the foregoing paragraph, I received orders again to prepare for a journey; and, as on many a former occasion, the time given me for preparation was not long.

CHAPTER XI.

T was on a cold bleak morning, about the beginning of March 1846, that I awoke from a comfortable snooze in my bedroom at Tadousac, and recollected that in a few hours I must take leave of my present quarters, and travel, on snow-shoes, sixty miles down the Gulf of St Lawrence to the post of Isle Jeremie.

The wind howled mournfully through the leafless trees, and a few flakes of snow fell upon the window, as I looked out upon the cheerless prospect. Winter—cold, biting, frosty winter—still reigned around. The shores of Tadousac Bay were still covered with the same coat of ice that had bound them up four months before,—and the broad St Lawrence still flowed on, black as ink, and laden with immense fields and hummocks of dirty ice, brought down from the banks of the river above. The land presented one uniform chilling prospect of bare trees and deep snow, over which I was soon to traverse many a weary mile.

There is nothing, however, like taking things philosophically; so, after venting my spite at the weather in one or two short grumbles, I sat down, in a passable state of equanimity, to breakfast. During the meal I discussed with Mr B—— the prospects of the impending journey, and indulged in a few excursive remarks upon snow-shoe travelling, during which he related a few incidents of his own eventful career in the country. On one occasion, he was sent off upon a long journey over the snow, where the country was so mountainous, that snow-shoe walking was rendered exceedingly painful by the feet slipping forward against the front bar of the shoe when descending the hills. After he had accomplished a good part of his journey, two large blisters rose under the nails of his great toes; and, soon after, the nails came off. Still he must go on, or die in the woods; so he was obliged to *tie* the nails on his toes each morning before starting, for the purpose of protecting the tender parts beneath; and every evening he wrapped them up carefully in a piece of rag, and put them into his waistcoat pocket,—*being afraid of losing them if he kept them on all night.*

After breakfast, I took leave of my friends at Tadousac; and, with a pair of snow-shoes under my arm, followed my companion J—— to the boat which was to convey me the first twenty miles of the journey, and then land me, with one man, who was to be my only companion. In the boat was seated a Roman Catholic priest, on his way to visit a party of Indians a short distance down the Gulf. The shivering men shipped their oars in silence; and we glided through the black water, while the ice grated harshly against the boat's sides, as we rounded Point Rouge :—another pull, and Tadousac was hidden from our view.

Few things can be more comfortless or depressing, than a sail down the Gulf of St Lawrence on a gloomy winter's day, with the thermometer at zero ! The water looks so black and cold, and the sky so gray, that it makes one shudder as he turns to look upon the land. But there no cheering prospect meets the view. Rocks— cold, hard, misanthropic rocks, grin from beneath volumes of snow; and the few stunted black-looking pines that dot the banks here and there, only tend to render the scene more desolate. No birds fly about to enliven the traveller ; and the only sound that meets the ear, besides the low sighing of the cold, cold wind, is the crashing of immense fields of ice, as they meet and war in the eddies of opposing currents. Fortunately, however, there was no ice near the shore, and we met with little interruption on the way. The priest bore the cold like a stoic ; and my friend J——, being made, metaphorically speaking, of iron, treated it with the contemptuous indifference that might be expected from such metal.

In the evening we arrived at Esquimain river, where we took up our quarters in a small log-hut belonging to a poor seal-fisher, whose family, and a few men who attended a saw-mill, a short distance off, were the only inhabitants of this little hamlet. Here we remained all night, and prepared our snow-shoes for the morrow, as the boat was there to leave us and return to

Tadousac. The night was calm and frosty, and every thing gave promise of fine weather for our journey. But who can tell what an hour will bring forth? Before morning, the weather became milder, and soon it began to *thaw*. A fine warm day, with a bright sun, be it known, is one of the most dreadful calamities that can befall a snow-shoe traveller, as the snow then becomes soft and sticky, thereby drenching the feet and snow-shoes, which become painfully heavy from the quantity of snow which sticks to, and falls upon them. In cold frosty weather, the snow is dry, crisp and fine, so that it falls through the net-work of the snow-shoe without leaving a feather's weight behind, while the feet are dry and warm; but a thaw!—Oh! it is useless attempting to recapitulate the miseries attending a thaw; my next day's experience will show what it is.

Early on the following morning, I jumped from my bed on the floor of the hut, and proceeded to equip myself for the march. The apartment in which I had passed the night presented a curious appearance. It measured about sixteen feet by twelve, and the greater part of this space was occupied by two beds, on which lay, in every imaginable position, the different members of the half-breed family to whom the mansion belonged. In the centre of the room stood a coarsely constructed deal table, on which lay in confusion the remains of the preceding night's supper. On the right of this, a large gaudily painted Yankee clock graced the wall, and stared down upon the sleeping figures of the men. This, with a few rough wooden chairs, and a small cupboard, comprised all the furniture of the house.

I soon singled out *my* man from among the sleeping figures on the floor, and bade him equip himself for the road, or rather for the march, for road we had none. In half an hour we were ready; and having fortified ourselves with a cup of weak tea, and a slice of bread, left the house, and commenced our journey. As our costumes were rather odd, I may as well describe them.

My man Bezeau (a French Canadian) was dressed in a blue striped cotton shirt, of very coarse quality, and a pair of corduroys, which were strapped round his waist with a scarlet belt. Over these he wore a pair of blue cloth leggins, neatly bound with orange-coloured ribbon. A Glengary bonnet covered his head, and two pairs of flannel socks, under a pair of raw sealskin shoes, protected his feet from the cold. His burden consisted of my carpet-bag, two days' provisions, and a blue cloth capote, which latter he carried over his shoulder as the weather was warm. My dress consisted of a scarlet flannel shirt, and a pair of *étoffe du pays* trousers, which were fastened round my waist by a leathern belt, from which depended a small hunting-knife; a foraging cap, and deerskin moccasins, completed my costume. My burden was a large green blanket, a greatcoat, and a tin tea-kettle. Our only arms of offence, or defence, were, the little hunting-knife before mentioned, and a small axe for felling trees, should we wish to make a fire. We brought no guns, as there was little prospect of meeting any game on the road, and it behoves one, when travelling on foot, to carry as little as possible.

Thus we started from Esquimain River. The best joke, however, of all was, that neither I nor my man had ever travelled that way before! All we knew was, that we had to walk fifty miles through an uninhabited country; and that then we would, or at least ought to, reach Isle Jeremie. There were two solitary houses, however, that we had to pass on the way; the one an outpost of the Hudson's Bay Company, the other, a sawmill belonging to one of the lumber companies (or timber traders) in Quebec. In fact, the best idea of our situation may be had from the following lines, which may be supposed to have been uttered by the establishment to which we were bound :—

" Through the woods, through the woods, follow and find me,
    Search every hollow and dingle and dell;"
To the right, left, or front, you may pass, or behind me,
    Unless you are careful and look for me well.

The first part of our road lay along the shores of the St Lawrence. The sun shone brightly, and the drifting ice in the Gulf glittered in its rays as it flowed slowly out to sea; but ere long the warm rays began to act upon the snow, and rendered walking toilsome and fatiguing. After about an hour's walk along the shore, we arrived at the last hut we were likely to see that day. It was inhabited by an Indian and his family. Here we rested a few minutes, and I renewed my snow-shoe lines, the old ones having broken by the way.

Shortly after this we passed the wreck of what had once been a fine ship. She lay crushed and dismasted among the rocks and lumps of ice which lined the desolate shore; her decks and the stumps of her masts drifted over with snow. Six short months before, she had bounded over the Atlantic wave in all the panoply of sail and rigging pertaining to a large three-master, inclosing in her sturdy hull full many a daring heart beating high with sanguine hopes, and dreaming of fame and glory, or perchance of home. But now, how great the change! her sails and masts uprooted, and her helm—the seaman's confidence and safeguard—gone; her bed upon the rocks and pebbles of a dreary shore; and her shattered hull hung round with icicles, and wrapped in the cold embraces of the wintry ocean. Few things I think can have a more inexpressibly melancholy appearance than a wreck upon a rocky and deserted shore in winter.

The road now began to get extremely bad. The ice, over which we had to walk for miles, had been covered with about six inches of water and snow. A sharp frost during the night had covered this with a cake of ice sufficiently strong to bear us up until we got fairly upon it, and were preparing to take another step, when down it went; so that we had a sort of natural treadmill to exercise ourselves upon all day, while every time we sank, as a matter of course, our snow-shoes were covered with a mixture of water, snow, and broken ice; to extricate our

our feet from which, almost pulled our legs out of the
sockets. In this way we plodded slowly and painfully
along, till we came to a part of the shore where the ice
had been entirely carried off, leaving the sandy beach
uncovered for about two miles. We gladly took advantage of this, and pulling off our snow-shoes, walked
along among the shells and tangle of the sea-shore. At
this agreeable part of our journey, while we walked
lightly along, with our snow-shoes under our arms, I fell
into a reverie upon the superior advantages of travelling
in cold weather, and the delights of walking on sandy
beaches in contrast with wet snow. These cogitations,
however, were suddenly interrupted by our arrival at
the place where the ice had parted from the general
mass, so, with a deep sigh, we resumed our snow-shoes.
My feet, from the friction of the lines, now began to feel
very painful; so, having walked about ten miles, I proposed taking a rest. To this my man, who seemed
rather tired, gladly acceded, and we proceeded to light a
fire under the stem of a fallen tree which opportunely
presented itself.

Here we sat down comfortably together; and, while
our wet shoes and socks dried before the blazing fire,
and our chafed toes wriggled joyously at being relieved
from the painful harness of the snow-shoes, we swallowed
a cup of congou with a degree of luxurious enjoyment
impossible to be appreciated except by those who have
walked themselves into a state of great exhaustion after
a hurried breakfast.

This greatly refreshed us, and we resumed our journey
in better spirits, and even affected to believe we were
taking an agreeable afternoon walk for the first mile or
so. We soon, however, fell to zero again, as we gazed
wistfully upon the long line of coast, stretching away to
the horizon. But there was no help for it ; so, on we
splashed, sometimes through ice, water, and snow, and
sometimes across the shingly beach, till the day was far
spent, when I became so exhausted, that I could scarcely
drag one foot after the other, and moved along almost
mechanically. My man, too, strong as he was, began to
exhibit symptoms of fatigue ; though, to do him justice,
he was at least seven times more heavily laden than I.
While we jogged slowly along in this enviable condition,
a lump of ice offered so tempting a seat, that we simultaneously proposed to sit down. This was very foolish.
Resting without a fire is bad at all times ; and the exhausted condition we were then in, made it far worse, as
I soon found to my cost. Tired as I was before, I could
have walked a good deal further, but no sooner did I rise
again to my feet, than an inexpressible weakness over-
came me, and I felt that I could go no further. This
my man soon perceived, and proposed making a fire and
having a cup of tea, and then, if I felt better, we might
proceed. This I agreed to ; so, entering the woods, we
dug a hole in the snow, and in half an hour had a fire
blazing in it, that would have roasted an ox ! In a short
time a panful of snow was converted into hot tea ; and,
as I sat sipping this, and watching the white smoke as it

wreathed upwards from the pipe of my good-natured guide, I never felt rest more delightful.

The tea refreshed us so much that we resumed our journey, intending, if possible, to reach Port Neuf during the night; and as we calculated that we had walked between fifteen and eighteen miles, we hoped to reach it in a few hours. Away, then, we went, and plodded on till dark without reaching the post; nevertheless, being determined to travel as long as we could, we pushed on till near midnight, when, being quite *done up*, and seeing no sign of the establishment, we called a council of war, and sat down on a lump of ice to discuss our difficulties. I suggested, that if we had not already passed the post, in all probability we should do so, if we continued to travel any further in the dark. My companion admitted that he entertained precisely the same views on the subject; and, furthermore, that as we both seemed pretty tired, and there happened to be a nice little clump of willows, intermixed with pine trees, close at hand, his opinion was, that nothing better could be done than encamping for the night. I agreed to this—and the resolution being carried unanimously, the council adjourned, and we proceeded to make our encampment. First of all, the snow was dug away from the foot of a large pine with our snow-shoes, which we used as spades; and when a space of about ten feet long, by six broad, was cleared, we covered it with pine branches at one end, and made a roaring fire against the tree at the other. The snow rose all around to the

height of about four feet, so that when our fire blazed
cheerily, and our supper was spread out before it upon
my green blanket, we looked very comfortable indeed, and
what was of much more consequence, *felt* so.   Supper
consisted of a cup of tea, a loaf of bread, and a lump
of salt butter.   After having partaken largely of these
delicacies, we threw a fresh log upon the fire, and rolling
ourselves in our blankets, were soon buried in repose.

Next morning, on awaking, the first thing I became
aware of was the fact that it was raining, and heavily
too, in the shape of a Scotch mist.   I could scarcely
believe it, and rubbed my eyes to make sure, but there
was no mistake about it at all.   The sky was gray, cold,
and dismal, and the blanket quite wet !   "Well," thought
I, as I fell back in a sort of mute despair, " this is certainly precious weather for snow-shoe travelling !"   I
nudged my sleeping companion, and the look of melancholy resignation which he put on, as he became gradually aware of the state of matters, convinced me, that
bad as yesterday had been, to-day would be far worse.
When I got upon my legs, I found that every joint in
my body was stiffer than the rustiest hinge ever heard
of in the annals of doors ! and my feet as tender as a
chicken's, with huge blisters all over them.   Bezeau,
however, though a little stiff, was otherwise quite well,
being well inured to hardships of every description.
It is needless to recount the miseries of the five miles'
walk that we had to make before arriving at Port
Neuf, over ground that was literally next to impassable.

About nine o'clock we reached the house quite exhausted, and remained there for the rest of the day. Here we were hospitably entertained, by the Canadian family inhabiting the place, the three following days; during which, it rained and thawed so heavily, that we could not venture to resume our journey. On the 16th, the weather became colder, and Bezeau announced it as his opinion that we might venture to proceed. Glad to be once more on the move—for fears of being arrested altogether, by the setting in of spring, had begun to beset me—I once more put on my snow-shoes; and, bidding adieu to the hospitable inmates of Port Neuf, we again wended our weary way along the coast. Alas! our misfortunes had not yet ceased. The snow was much softer than we anticipated, and the blisters on my feet, which had nearly healed during the time we staid at Port Neuf, were now torn open afresh. After a painful and laborious walk of eight or nine miles, we arrived at a small house, where a few enterprising men lived, who had penetrated thus far down the gulf to erect a saw-mill. Here we found, to our infinite joy, a small, flat-bottomed boat, capable of carrying two or three men; so, without delay, we launched it, and putting our snow-shoes and provisions into it, my man and I jumped in, and pulled away down the gulf; intending to finish the twenty miles that still remained of our journey by water. We were obliged to pull a long way out to sea, to avoid the ice which lined the shores, and our course lay a good deal among drifting masses, Half-an-hour after we em-

barked, a snow-storm came on, but still we continued to
pull along, preferring any thing to resuming the snow-
shoes.

After a few hours' rowing, we rested on our oars, and
refreshed ourselves with a slice of bread and a glass of
rum, which latter, having forgotten to bring water with
us, we were obliged to drink pure.   We certainly cut a
strange figure, while thus lunching in our little boat,—
surrounded by ice, and looking hazy through the thickly
falling snow, which prevented us from seeing very far
ahead, and made the mountains on shore look quite
spectral.

For about five miles we pulled along in a straight
line, after which the ice began to trend outwards, and
finally brought us to a stand-still, by running straight
out to sea.   This was an interruption we were not at all
prepared for, and were rather undecided how to proceed.

After a little confabulation, we determined to pull out, and see if the ice did not again turn in the proper direction; but after pulling straight out for a quarter of a mile, we perceived, or imagined we perceived, to our horror, that the ice, instead of being stationary, as we supposed it to be, was floating slowly out to sea with the wind, and carrying us along with it. No time was to be lost, so wheeling about, we rowed with all our strength for the shore; and after a pretty stiff pull gained the solid ice. Here we hauled the flat up out of the water with great difficulty, and once more put on our snow-shoes.

Our road still lay along shore, and, as the weather was getting colder, we proceeded along much more easily than heretofore. In an hour or two the snow ceased to fall, and showed us that the ice was *not* drifting, but, that it ran so far out to sea, that it would have proved a bar to our further progress by water at any rate. The last ten miles of our journey now lay before us; and we sat down, before starting, to have another bite of bread and a pull at the rum bottle; after which, we trudged along in silence. The peculiar compression of my guide's lips, and the length of step that he now adopted, showed me that he had made up his mind to get through the last part of the journey without stopping; so, tightening my belt, and bending my head forward, I plodded on, solacing myself as we advanced, by humming " Follow, follow, over mountain— follow, follow, over sea !" &c. About four or five o'clock in the afternoon, upon rounding a point, we were a little

excited by perceiving evident signs of the axe having
been at work in the forest,—and a little further on discovered, to our inexpressible joy, a small piece of ground
inclosed, apparently, as a garden. This led us to suppose
that the post could not be far off, so we pushed forward
rapidly ; and upon gaining the summit of a small eminence, beheld, with delight, the post of Isle Jeremie.

This establishment, like most of the others on the St
Lawrence, is merely a collection of scattered buildings,
most of which are store-houses and stables. It stands in
a hollow of the mountains, and close to a large bay,
where sundry small boats and a sloop lay quietly at
anchor. Upon a little hillock, close to the principal
house, stands a Roman Catholic chapel ; and behind it,
stretches away the broad St Lawrence, the south shore
of which is indistinctly seen on the horizon. We had
not much inclination, however, to admire the scenery
just then ; so, hastening down the hill, my man rushed
into the men's house, where, in five minutes, he was
busily engaged eating bread and pork, and recounting
his adventures to a circle of admiring friends ; while I
warmed myself beside a comfortable fire in the hall, and
chatted with the gentleman in charge of the establishment.

At Isle Jeremie, I remained about six weeks; or rather,
I should say, belonged to the establishment for that time;
as during a great part of it I was absent from the post.
Mr C——, soon after my arrival, went to visit the
Company's posts lower down the St Lawrence, leaving

me in charge of Isle Jeremie ; and, as I had little or nothing to do, in the way of business, (our Indians not having arrived from the interior,) most of my time was spent in reading and shooting.

It was here that I took my first lessons in navigation—I mean in a practical way ; as for the scientific part of the business, that was deferred to a more favourable opportunity,—and, truly, the lessons were rather rough. The way of it was this :—Our flour at Isle Jeremie had run out. Indians were arriving every day calling loudly for flour, and more were expected ; so Mr C—— told me, one fine morning, to get ready to go to Tadousac in the boat, for a load of flour. This I prepared to do at once, and started after breakfast in a large boat, manned by two men. The wind was fair, and I fired a couple of shots with my fowling-piece, as we cleared the harbour, in answer to an equal number of salutes from two iron cannons that stood in front of the house. By the bye, one of these same guns had a melancholy interest attached to it a few months after this. While firing a salute of fourteen rounds, in honour of the arrival of a Roman Catholic bishop, one of them exploded while the man, who acted as gunner, was employed in ramming home the cartridge, and blew him about twenty yards down the bank. The unfortunate man expired in a few hours. Poor fellow !—he was a fine little Canadian, and had sailed with me, not many weeks before, in a voyage up the St Lawrence. But to return. Our voyage, during the first few days, was prosperous enough, and I amused

myself in shooting the gulls which were foolish enough
to come within range of my gun, and in recognising
the various places along shore where I had rested and
slept, on the memorable occasion of my snow-shoe trip.
But when did the St Lawrence prove friendly for an
entire voyage? Certainly not when I had the pleasure
of ploughing up its rascally waters! The remainder of
our voyage was a succession of squalls, calms, contrary
winds, sticking on shoals for hours, and being detained
on shore, with an accompaniment of pitching, tossing,
oscillation and botheration, that baffles all description.
However, time brings the greatest miseries to an end ;
and, in the process of time, we arrived at Tadousac,—
loaded our boat deeply with flour,—shook hands with
our friends,—related our adventures,—bade them adieu,
—and again found ourselves scudding down the St Lawrence, with a snoring breeze on our quarter. Now this
was truly a most delectable state of things, when contrasted with our wretched trip up ; so we wrapped our
blankets round us, (for it was very cold,) and felicitated
ourselves considerably on such good fortune. It was
rather premature, however ; as, not long after, we had a
very narrow escape from being swamped. The wind,
as I said before, was pretty strong, and it continued so
the whole way ; so that, on the evening of the second
day, we came within sight of Isle Jeremie, while running
before a stiff breeze, through the green waves, which
were covered with foam. Our boat had a drooping
nose, and was extremely partial to what the men

termed "drinking;" in other words, it shipped a good deal of water over the bows. Now it happened, that while we were straining our eyes ahead, to catch a sight of our haven, an insidious squall was creeping fast down behind us. The first intimation we had of its presence was a loud and ominous hiss, which made us turn our heads round rather smartly; but it was too late,—for with a howl, that appeared to be quite vicious, the wind burst upon our sails, and buried the boat in the water, which rushed in a cataract over the bows, and nearly filled us in a moment, although the steersman threw her into the wind immediately. The sheets were instantly let go, and one of the men who happened to be a sailor jumped up, and seizing an axe, began to cut down the main-mast, at the same time exclaiming to the steersman, "You've done for us now, Cooper." He was mistaken, however, for the sails were taken in just in time to save us; and, while the boat lay tumbling in the sea, we all began to bail, with any thing we could lay hands on, as fast as we could. In a few minutes the boat was lightened enough to allow of our hoisting the foresail; and, about half an hour afterwards, we were safely anchored in the harbour. This happened within about three or four hundred yards of the shore; yet the best swimmer in the world would have been drowned ere he reached it, as the water was so bitterly cold, that when I was bailing for my life, and, consequently, in pretty violent exercise, my hands became quite benumbed and almost powerless.

Shortly after this, I was again sent up to Tadousac, in charge of a small batteau, of about ten or fifteen tons, with a number of shipwrecked seamen on board. These unfortunate men had been cast on shore about the commencement of winter, on an uninhabited part of the coast, and had remained without provisions or fire for a long time, till they were discovered by a gentleman of the Hudson's Bay Company, and conveyed over the snow in sleighs, to the nearest establishment, which happened to be Isle Jeremie. Here they remained all winter, in a most dreadfully mutilated condition, some of them having been desperately frozen. One of the poor fellows, a negro, had one of his feet frozen off at the ankle, and had lost all the toes and the heel of the other, where the bone was laid bare for about an inch and a half. Mr C——, the gentleman who had saved them, did all in his power to relieve their distress ; amputating their frozen limbs, and dressing their wounds, while they were provided with food and warm clothing. I am sorry to say, however, that these men, who would have perished had it not been for Mr C——'s care of them, were the first, upon arriving at Quebec the following spring, to open their mouths in violent reproach and bitter invective against him ; forgetting that, while their only charge against him was a little severity in refusing them a few trifling and unnecessary luxuries, he had saved them from a painful and lingering death. In a couple of days we arrived at Tadousac, the second time, to the no small astonishment of my brother scribbler residing there; and after reloading our craft, we directed our course once more down the gulf. This time the wind was also favourable, but, unfortunately, a little too strong; so we were obliged, in the evening, to come to an anchor in Esquimain River. This river has good anchorage close to the bank, but is very deep in the lead, or current; this, however, we did not know at the time, and seeing a small schooner close to shore, we rounded to a few fathoms outside of her, and let go our anchor. Whirr! went the chain—ten! twelve! sixteen! till at last forty fathoms ran out, and only a little bit remained on board, and still we had no bottom. After attaching our spare cable to the other one, the anchor at last grounded. This, however, was a dangerous situation to remain in, as, if the wind blew strong, we would have to run out to sea, and so much cable would take a long time to get in; so I ordered my two men, in a very pompous, despotic way, to heave up the anchor again; but not a bit would it budge. We all heaved at the windlass, still the obstinate anchor held fast,—again we gave another heave, and smashed both the handspikes. In this dilemma, I begged assistance from the neighbouring schooner, and they kindly sent all their men on board with new handspikes; but our refractory anchor would *not* let go, and at last it was conjectured that it had got foul of a rock, and that it was not in the power of mortal man to move it. Under these pleasant circumstances, we went to bed, in hopes that the falling tide might swing us clear before morning. This turned

out just as we expected,— or, rather, a little better,—
for next morning, when I went on deck, I found that we
were drifting quietly down the gulf, stern foremost, all
the sails snugly tied up, and the long cable dragging at
the bows! Towards evening we arrived at Jeremie,
and I gladly resigned command of the vessel to my
first lieutenant.

One afternoon, near the middle of April, I sat sunning myself in the verandah, before the door of the
principal house at Isle Jeremie ; and watched the fields
of ice, as they floated down the Gulf of St Lawrence,
occasionally disappearing behind the body of a large
pig, which stood upon a hillock close in front of me,
and then reappearing again as the current swept them
slowly past the intervening obstacle. Mr C——, with
whom I had been leading a very quiet, harmless sort
of life for a couple of weeks past, leant against a wooden
post, gazing wistfully out to sea. Suddenly he turned
towards me, and with great gravity, told me that as
there was nothing particular for me to do at the establishment, he meant to send me down to Seven Islands,
to relieve the gentleman at that post of his charge :
adding, that as he wished me to set off the following
morning at an early hour, I had better pack up a few
things to-night. Now this order may not seem, at the
first glance, a very dreadful one ; but taking into consideration that Seven Islands is one hundred and twenty
miles below the post at which I then resided, it does
appear as if one would wish to think about it a little

before starting. Not having time to think about it, however, I merely, in a sort of bantering desperation, signified my readiness to undertake a voyage to any part of the undiscovered world, at any moment that he (Mr C——) might think proper, and then vanished, to prepare myself for the voyage. It was optional with me whether I should walk through one hundred and twenty miles of primeval and most impassable forest, or paddle over an equal number of miles of water. Preferring the latter, as being at once the less disagreeable and more expeditious method, I accordingly, on the following morning, embarked in a small Indian canoe, similar to the one in which I had formerly travelled with two Indians, in the North-West. My companions were, a Canadian, who acted as steersman,—a genuine Patlander, who ostensibly acted as bowsman, but in reality was more useful in the way of ballast, —and a young Newfoundland dog, which I had got in a present from Mr B——, while at Tadousac.

When we all got into our allotted places, the canoe was quite full; and we started from Isle Jeremie in good spirits, with the broad, sun-like face of Mike Lynch looming over the bows of the canoe, and the black muzzle of Humbug (the dog) resting on its gunwale.

It is needless to describe the voyage minutely. We had the usual amount of bad and good weather, and ran the risk several times of upsetting; we had also, several breakfasts, dinners, suppers, and beds in the forest; and, on the afternoon of the third day, we arrived at Goodbout, an establishment nearly half-way between the post I had left, and the one to which I was bound. Here we staid all night, proposing to start again on the morrow. But the weather was so stormy, as to prevent us, for a couple of days, trusting ourselves out in a frail bark canoe. Early on the third morning, however, I took my place as steersman in the stern of our craft, (my former guide being obliged to leave me here,) and my man Mike squeezed his unwieldy person into the bow. In the middle lay our provisions and baggage, over which the black muzzle of Humbug peered anxiously out upon the ocean. In this trim, we paddled from the beach, amid a shower of advice to keep close to shore, in case the *big-fish*—alias, the whales—might take a fancy to upset us. After a long paddle of five or six hours, we arrived at Pointe des Monts, where rough weather obliged us to put ashore. Here I remained all night, and slept in the light-house,—a cylindrical building of moderate height, which stands on a rock off Pointe des Monts, and serves to warn sailors off the numerous shoals with which this part of the gulf is filled. In the morning, we fortunately found an Indian with his boat, who was just starting for Seven Islands; and after a little haggling, at which Mike proved himself quite an adept, he agreed to give us a lift for a few pounds of tobacco. Away, then, we went, with

> " A wet sheet and a flowing sea,
> And a wind that follow'd fast."

ploughing through the water in beautiful style.

The interior of our boat presented a truly ludicrous, and rather filthy scene. The Indian, who was a fine-looking man of about thirty, had brought his whole family — sons, daughters, brothers, sisters, wife, and mother,—and a more heterogeneous mass of filthy, dark-skinned humanity I never before had the ill-luck to travel with. The mother of the flock was the most extraordinary being that I ever beheld. She must have been very near a hundred years old, as black and wrinkled as a singed hide, yet active and playful as a kitten. She was a very bad sailor, however, and dived down into the bottom of the boat the moment a puff of wind arose. Indians have a most extraordinary knack of diminishing their bulk, which is very convenient some-times. Upon this occasion, it was amusing to watch them settling gradually down, upon the slightest appearance of wind, until you might almost believe they had squeezed themselves quite through the bottom of the boat, and left only a few dirty blankets to tell the tale. Truly, one rarely meets with such a compact mass of human ballast. If, however, a slight lull occurred, or the sun peeped out from behind a cloud, there was immediately a perceptible increase in the bulk of the mass, and gradually a few heads appeared, then a leg, and soon a few arms; till, at last, the whole batch were up, laugh-ing, talking, singing, eating, and chattering, in a most uproarious state of confusion! After the usual amount of storms, calms, and contrary winds, we arrived in safety at the post of Seven Islands, where I threw my worthy

friend, Mr A——, into a state of considerable surprise
and agitation, by informing him, that in the individual
before him he beheld his august successor !

The establishment of Seven Islands is any thing but
an inviting place, although pretty enough on a fine day ;
and the general appearance of the surrounding scenery
is lonely, wild, and desolate.   The houses are built on a
low sandy beach, at the bottom of the large bay of Seven
Islands.   The trees around are thinly scattered and very
small.   In the background, rugged hills stretch as far
as the eye can see ; and in front, seven lofty islands,
from which the bay and post derive their name, obstruct
the view, affording only a partial glimpse of the open sea
beyond.   No human habitations exist within seventy
miles of the place.   Being out of the line of sailing,
no vessels ever visit it, except when driven to the bay for
shelter ; and the bay is so large, that many vessels come
in and go out again without ever having been seen.
Altogether, I found it a lonely and desolate place, during
a residence of nearly four months.

An extensive salmon fishery is carried on, at a large
river called the Moisie, about eighteen miles below the
post, where the Company sometimes catch and salt upwards of eighty and ninety tierces of fish.

During my sojourn there, I made one or two excursions to the fishery, a description of which may perhaps
prove interesting to those versed in the more practical
branches of ichthyology.

It was a pretty morning in June when Mr A—— and

I set out from Seven Islands on foot, with our coats (for
the weather was warm) slung across our backs, and
walked rapidly along the beach, in the direction of the
river Moisie. The weather was very calm, and the mosquitoes, consequently, rather annoying ; but, as our pro-
gressive motion disconcerted their operations a little, we
did not mind them much. The beach all the way was
composed of fine hard sand, so that we found the walk
very agreeable. A few loons dived about in the sea, and
we passed two or three flocks of black ducks, known in
some parts of the country by the name of " old wives ;"
but, having brought no gun with us, the old ladies were
permitted to proceed on their way unmolested. The land
all along presented the same uniform line of forest, with
the yellow sand of the beach glittering at its edge ; and,
as we cleared the islands, the boundless ocean opened
upon our view.

In about four hours or so, we arrived at the mouth of
the Moisie, where the first fishery is established. Here
we found that our men had caught and salted a good
many salmon, some of which had just come from the
nets, and lay on the grass, plump and glittering, in their
pristine freshness. They looked very tempting, and we
had one put in the kettle immediately, which, when we
set to work at him a couple of hours afterwards, certainly
did not belie his looks. The salmon had only commenced
to ascend the river that day, and were being taken by
fifties at a haul in the nets. The fishery was attended
by three men, who kept seven or eight nets constantly

in the water, which gave them enough of employment—
two of them attending to the nets, while the third split,
salted, and packed the fish in large vats. Here we spent
the night, and slept in a small house about ten feet long
by eight broad, built for the accommodation of the fishermen.

Next morning we embarked in a boat belonging to a
trapper, and went up the river with a fair wind, to visit
the fisheries higher up. On the way we passed a seal-
net belonging to the owner of the boat, and at our request he visited it, and found seven or eight fine seals
in it: they were all dead, and full of water. Seal-nets
are made the same as salmon-nets, except that the mesh
is larger, the seal having a pretty good-sized cranium of
his own. After a good deal of unravelling and pulling,
we got them all out of the net, and proceeded onward
with our cargo.

The scenery on the river Moisie is pleasing: the banks
are moderately high, and covered to the foot with the
richest and most variegated verdure; while here and
there, upon rounding some of the curvatures of the
stream, long vistas of the river may be seen, embedded
in luxuriant foliage. Thirteen or fourteen miles up the
river is the Frog Creek fishery, at which we arrived late
in the afternoon, and found that the man superintending
it had taken a good many fish, and expected more. He
visited his nets while we were there, but returned with
only a few salmon. Some of them were badly cut up
by the seals, which are the most formidable enemies of

fishermen, as they eat and destroy many salmon, besides breaking the nets. We were detained here by rain all night, and slept in the small fishing-house.

Travelling makes people acquainted with strange beds as well as strange bed-fellows; but I question if many people can boast of having slept on a bed of *nets*. This we were obliged to do here, having brought no blankets with us, as we expected to have returned to the Point fishery in the evening. The bedstead was a long low platform, in one end of the little cabin, and was big enough to let four people sleep in it—two of us lying abreast at one end, and two more at the other end, feet to feet. A large salmon-net formed a pretty good mattress; another, spread out on top of us, served as a blanket; and a couple of trout-nets formed excellent pillows. From this *piscatorial* couch we arose early on the following morning, and breakfasted on a splendid fresh salmon; after which we resumed our journey. In a couple of hours we arrived at the Rapid fishery, where I found that my old friend Mike, the Irishman, had caught a great number of salmon. He was very bitter, however, in his remarks upon the seals, which it seems had made great havoc among his nets during the last two days. A black bear, too, was in the habit of visiting his station every morning; and, sitting on a rock not far off, watched his motions with great apparent interest while he took the fish out of the nets. Mike, poor man, regretted very much that he had no gun, as he might perhaps shoot "the baste." Bears are very destructive at times to the salted salmon, paying visits during the night to the vats, and carrying off and tearing to pieces far more than they are capable of devouring.

While inspecting the nets here, we witnessed an interesting seal-hunt. Two Indians, in separate canoes, were floating quietly in a small eddy, with their guns cocked, ready to fire at the first unfortunate seal that should show his head on the surface of the stream. They had not waited long when one popped up his head, and instantly got a shot, which evidently hurt him, as he splashed a little, and then dived. In a minute the Indian reloaded his gun, and paddled out into the stream, in order to have another shot the moment the seal rose for air ; this he did in a short time, when another shot was fired, which turned him over apparently lifeless. The Indian then laid down his gun, and, seizing his paddle, made towards the spot where the seal lay. He had scarcely approached a few yards, however, when it recovered a little and dived, much to the Indian's chagrin, who had approached too near the head of a small rapid, and went down, stern foremost, just at the moment his friend the seal did the same. On arriving at the bottom, the animal, after one or two kicks, expired, and the Indian at last secured his prize. After this, we embarked again in our boat ; and the wind *for once* determined to be accommodating, as it shifted in our favour, almost at the same time that we turned to retrace our way. In a few hours we arrived at the fishery near the mouth of the river, where we found supper just ready.

After supper, which we had about eight o'clock, the night looked so fine, and the mosquitoes in the little smoky house were so troublesome, that we determined to walk up to the post ; so, ordering one of the men to follow us, away we went along the beach. The night was fine, though dark, and we trudged rapidly along. It was very tiresome work, however, as, the tide being full, we were obliged to walk upon the soft sand. Every thing along the beach looked huge and mystical in the uncertain light; and this, accompanied with the solemn boom of the waves, as they fell at long intervals upon the shore, made the scene quite romantic. After five hours' sharp walking, with pocket handkerchiefs tied round our heads to guard us from the attacks of mosquitoes, we arrived at Seven Islands between one and two in the morning.

Not long after this, a boat arrived with orders for my companion, Mr A——, to pack up his worldly goods, and set sail for Tadousac. The same day he completely gutted my dwelling-house ; and, after packing up nearly every moveable it contained, bade me adieu and set sail. In a few minutes the boat vanished behind a point of land, and I turned to look at my now deserted home.

The situation in which I found myself was a novel, and, to say truth, not a very agreeable one. A short way off stood a man watching contemplatively the point round which the boat had just disappeared ; and this man was my only companion in the world !—my Friday, in fact. Not another human being lived within sixty miles of our solitary habitation, with the exception of the four men at the distant fishery. In front of us, the mighty Gulf of St Lawrence stretched out to the horizon, its swelling bosom unbroken save by the dipping of a sea-gull or the fin of a whale. Behind, lay the dense forest, stretching back, without a break in its primeval wildness, across the whole continent of America to the Pacific Ocean; while above and below lay the rugged mountains that form the shores of the Gulf. As I walked up to the house, and wandered like a ghost through its empty rooms, I felt inexpressibly melancholy, and began to have unpleasant anticipations of spending the winter on this lonely spot.

Just as this thought occurred to me, my dog Humbug bounded into the room, and, looking with a comical expression up in my face for a moment, went bounding off again. This incident induced me to take a more philosophical view of affairs. I began to gaze round upon my domain, and whisper to myself that I was " monarch of all I surveyed." All the mighty trees in the wood were mine—if I chose to cut them down ; all the fish in the sea were mine—if I could only catch them ; and the palace of Seven Islands was also mine. The royal feeling inspired by the consideration of these things induced me to call in a very kingly tone of voice for my man (he was a French Canadian), who politely answered, " Oui, Monsieur." " Dinner !" said I, falling back in my throne, and contemplating, through the palace window, our vast dominions !

On the following day a small party of Indians arrived, and the bustle of trading their furs, and asking questions about their expectations of a good winter hunt, tended to disperse those unpleasant feelings of loneliness that at first assailed me.

One of these poor Indians had died while travelling, and his relatives brought the body to be interred in our little burying-ground. The poor creatures came in a very melancholy mood to ask me for a few planks to make a coffin for him. They soon constructed a rough wooden box, in which the corpse was placed and then buried. No ceremony attended the interment of this poor savage ; no prayer was uttered over the grave ; and the only mark that the survivors left upon the place was a small wooden cross, which those Indians who have been visited by Roman Catholic priests are in the habit of erecting over their departed relatives.

The almost total absence of religion of any kind among these unhappy natives, is truly melancholy. The very name of our blessed Saviour is almost unknown by the hundreds of Indians who inhabit the vast forests of North America. It is strange that, while so many missionaries have been sent to the southern parts of the earth, so few should have been sent to the northward. There are not, I believe, more than a dozen or so of Protestant clergymen over the whole wide northern continent; and, alas ! many even of that small number are slothful, inefficient men, and one or two are absolutely *unworthy* of their high and responsible situation. For at least a cen-

tury these North American Indians have hunted for
the white men, and poured annually into Britain a co-
pious stream of wealth.   Surely it is the duty of *Christian* Britain, in return, to send out faithful servants of
God to preach the gospel of our Lord throughout their
land.

The Indians, after spending a couple of days at the
establishment—during which time they sold me a great
many furs—set out again to return to their distant wigwams.   It is strange to contemplate the precision and
certainty with which these men travel towards any part
of the vast wilderness, even where their route lies
across numerous intricate and serpentine rivers.   But
the strangest thing of all is, the savage's certainty of
finding his way in winter through the trackless forest, to
a place where, perhaps, he never was before, and has
only had a slight description of.   They have no com-
passes, but the means by which they discover the cardinal
points is curious.   If an Indian happens to become confused with regard to this, he lays down his burden, and,
taking his axe, cuts through the bark of a tree, from the
thickness or thinness of which he can tell the north point
at once, the bark being thicker on that side.

For a couple of weeks after this, I remained at the
post with my solitary man, endeavouring by all the
means in my power to dispel ennui ; but it was a hard
task.   Sometimes I shouldered my gun and ranged about
the forest in search of game, and occasionally took a
swim in the sea.   I was ignorant at the time, however,

that there were sharks in the Gulf of St Lawrence, else
I should have been more cautious. The Indians afterwards told me that they were often seen, and several
gentlemen who had lived long on the coast corroborated
their testimony. ' Several times Indians have left the
shores of the gulf in their canoes, to go hunting, and
have never been heard of again, although the weather at
the time was calm; so that it was generally believed that
sharks had upset the canoes and devoured the men. An
occurrence that afterwards happened to an Indian renders this supposition highly probable. This man had
been travelling along the shores of the gulf with his
family, a wife and several children, in a small canoe. Towards evening, as he was crossing a large bay, a shark
rose near his canoe, and, after reconnoitring a short
time, swam towards it, and endeavoured to upset it. The
size of the canoe, however, rendered this impossible ; so
the ferocious monster actually began to break it to pieces,
by rushing forcibly against it. The Indian fired at the
shark when he first saw it, but without effect ; and, not
having time to reload, he seized his paddle and made for
the shore. The canoe, however, from the repeated attacks of the fish, soon became leaky, and it was evident
that in a few minutes more the whole party would be at
the mercy of the infuriated monster. In this extremity
the Indian took up his youngest child, an infant of a few
months old, and dropped it overboard ; and while the
shark was devouring it, the rest of the party gained the
shore.

I sat one morning ruminating on the pleasures of solitude in the *palace* of Seven Islands, and gazed through the window at my solitary man, who was just leaving an old boat which he had been repairing, for the purpose of preparing dinner. The wide ocean, which rolled its waves almost to the door of the house, was calm and unruffled, and the yellow beach shone again in the sun's rays, while Humbug lay stretched out at full length before the door. After contemplating this scene for some time, I rose, and was just turning away from the window, when I descried a *man*, accompanied by a *boy*, walking along the sea-shore towards the house. This unusual sight created in me almost as strong, though not so unpleasant, sensations as were awakened in the bosom of Robinson Crusoe when he discovered the foot-print in the sand. Hastily putting on my cap, I ran out to meet him, and found, to my joy, that he was a trapper with whom I was acquainted ; and, what added immensely to the novelty of the thing, he was also a *white* man and a gentleman ! He had entered one of the fur companies on the coast at an early age, and, a few years afterwards, fell in love with an Indian girl, whom he married ; and, ultimately, he became a trapper. He was a fine good-natured man, and had been well educated ; and to hear philosophical discourse proceeding from the lips of one who was, in outward appearance, a regular Indian, was very strange indeed. He was dressed in the usual capote, leggins, and moccasins of a hunter.

" What have you got for dinner?" was his first question, after shaking hands with me.

"Pork and pancakes," said I.

" Oh," said the trapper, " the first salt, and the latter made of flour and water?"

" Just so ; and, with the exception of some bread and a few ground peas in lieu of coffee, this has been my diet for three weeks back."

" You might have done better," said the trapper, pointing towards a blue line in the sea; " look, there are fish enough if you only took the trouble to catch them."

As he said this, I advanced to the edge of the water, and there to my astonishment discovered, that what I had taken for sea-weed, was a shoal of kippling, so dense that they seemed scarcely able to move.

Upon beholding this, I recollected having seen a couple of old hand-nets in some of the stores, which we immediately sent the trapper's son (a youth of twelve) to fetch. In a few minutes he returned with them; so, tucking up our trousers, we both went into the water and scooped the fish out by dozens. It required us to be very quick, however, as they shot into deep water like lightning, and sometimes made us run in so deep, that we wet ourselves considerably. Indeed, the sport became so exciting at last, that we gave over attempting to keep our clothes dry; and in an hour we returned home, laden with kippling, and wet to the skin.

The fish, which measured from four to five inches long,

were really excellent, and lent an additional relish to the pork, pancakes, and *pease coffee!*

I prevailed upon the trapper to remain with me during the following week; and a very pleasant time we had of it, paddling about in a canoe, or walking through the woods, while my companion told me numerous anecdotes, with which his memory was stored. Some of these were grave, and some comical; especially one, in which he described a bear-hunt that he and his son had on the coasts of Labrador.

He had been out on a shooting expedition, and was returning home in his canoe, when, on turning a headland, he discovered a black bear walking leisurely along the beach. Now the place where he discovered him was a very wild, rugged spot. At the bottom of the bay rose a high precipice, so that bruin could not escape that way; along the beach, in the direction in which he had been walking, a cape, which the rising tide now washed, prevented his retreating; so that, the only chance for the brute to escape was, by running past the trapper within a few yards of him. In this dilemma, the bear bethought himself of trying the precipice; so, collecting himself, he made a bolt for it, and actually managed to scramble up thirty or forty feet, when bang went the boy's gun; but the shot missed, and it appeared as if the beast would actually get away, when the trapper took a deliberate aim and fired. The effect of the shot was so comical, that the two hunters could scarcely re-load their guns for laughing. Bruin, upon receiving the shot, covered his head with his fore-paws, and, curling himself up like a ball, came thundering down the precipice head over heels, raising clouds of dust, and hurling showers of stones down in his descent, till he actually rolled at the trapper's feet ; and then, getting slowly up, he looked at him with such a bewildered expression, that the man could scarcely refrain from laughter, even while in the act of blowing the beast's brains out.

This man had also a narrow escape of having a *boxing* match with a moose-deer or elk. The moose has a strange method of fighting with its fore-feet ; getting up on its hind-legs and boxing, as it were, with great energy and deadly force. The trapper, upon the occasion referred to, was travelling with an Indian, who, having discovered the track of a moose in the snow, set off in chase of it, while the trapper pursued his way with the Indian's pack of furs and provisions on his shoulders. He had not gone far when he heard a shot, and the next moment a moose-deer, as large as a horse, sprang through the bushes and stood in front of him. The animal came so suddenly on the trapper, that it could not turn ; so, rising up with a savage look, it prepared to strike him, when another shot was fired from among the bushes by the Indian, and the moose, springing nearly its own height into the air, fell dead upon the snow.

About a week after his arrival, the trapper departed, and left me again in solitude.

*   *   *   *   *   *   *

The last voyage.—There is something very sad and melancholy in these words—the last. The last look ; the last word ; the last smile ; even the last shilling, have all a peculiarly melancholy import ;—but the last *voyage*, to one who has lived, as it were, on travelling ; who has slept for weeks and months under the shadow of the forest trees ; and dwelt among the wild romantic scenes of the wilderness, has a peculiar and thrilling interest.   Each tree I passed on leaving, shook its boughs mournfully, as if it felt hurt at being thus forsaken. The very rocks seemed to frown reproachfully, while I stood up and gazed wistfully after each well-known object for the last time.   Even the wind seemed to sympathise with the rest ; for, while it urged the boat swiftly away from my late home, like a faithful friend holding steadfastly on its favouring course, still it fell occasionally, and rose again in gusts and sighs, as if it wished to woo me back again to solitude.   I started on this, the last voyage, shortly after the departure of my friend the trapper, leaving the palace in charge of an unfortunate gentleman who brought a wife and five children with him, which rendered Seven Islands a little less gloomy than heretofore.   Five men accompanied me in an open boat ; and on the morning of the 25th August, we took our departure for Tadousac :—and, truly, nature appeared to be aware that it was my *last* voyage ; for she gave us the most unkind and harassing treatment that I ever experienced at her hands.

The first few miles were accomplished pleasantly

enough. We had a fair breeze, and not too much of it; but, towards the afternoon, it shifted and blew directly against us, so that the men were obliged to take to the oars—and, as the boat was large, it required them all to pull, so that I was obliged to become steersman.

The men were all French Canadians; a merry, careless, but persevering set of fellows, just cut out for the work they had to do; and, moreover, accustomed to it. The boat was a clumsy affair, with two sprit-sails, and a jigger or mizzen; but, notwithstanding, she looked pretty well at a distance, and, though incapable of progressing very fast through the water, she could stand a pretty heavy sea. We were badly off, however, with regard to camp gear, having neither tent nor oiledcloth to protect us, should it rain. Indeed all we had to guard us from the inclemency of the weather at night was one blanket each man; but, as the weather had been fine and settled for some time back, we hoped to get along pretty well.

As for provisions, we had pork and flour, besides a small quantity of coffee made from burnt pease, which I treasured up as a great delicacy.

Our first encampment was a good one. The night, though dark, was fine and calm, so that we slept very comfortably upon the beach; every man with his feet towards the fire, from which we all radiated like the spokes of a wheel. But our next was not so good. The day had been very boisterous and wet, so that we lay down to rest in damp clothes, with the pleasant reflection that we had scarcely advanced ten miles. The miseries of our fifth day, however, were so numerous and complicated, that it at last became absurd! It was a drizzly damp morning to begin with. Soon this gave way to a gale of contrary wind, so that we could scarcely proceed at the rate of half a mile an hour ; and, in the evening, we were under the necessity either of running *back* five miles to reach a harbour, or of anchoring off an exposed lee-shore. Preferring the latter course, even at the risk of losing our boat altogether, we cast anchor, and, leaving a man in the boat, we waded ashore. Here things looked very wretched indeed. Every thing was wet and clammy. Very little fire-wood was to be found, and when it was found, we had the greatest difficulty in getting it to light. At last, however, the fire blazed up; and, though it still rained, we began to feel, *comparatively speaking*, comfortable.

Now, it must have been about midnight when I awoke, wheezing and sniffling with a bad cold, and feeling uncommonly wretched,—the fire having gone out, and the drizzly rain having increased ; and while I was endeavouring to cover myself a little better with a wet blanket, the man who had been left to watch the boat rushed in amongst us, and said that it had been driven ashore, and would infallibly go to pieces if not shoved out to sea immediately. Up we all got, and, rushing down to the beach, were speedily groping about in the dark up to our waists in water, while the roaring breakers heaved the boat violently against our breasts. After at least an hour of this work, we got it afloat again, and returned to our beds, where we lay shivering in wet clothes till morning.

We had several other nights nearly as bad as this one, and once or twice narrowly escaped being smashed to pieces among rocks and shoals, while travelling in foggy weather.

Even the last day of the voyage had something unpleasant in store for us. As we were nearing the mouth of the river Saguenay, the tide began to recede; and, ere long, the current became so strong, that we could not make head-way against it; we had no alternative, therefore, but to try to run ashore, there to remain until the tide should rise again. Now it so happened, that a sand-bank caught our keel just as we had turned broadside to the current, and the water, rushing against the boat with the force of a mill-race, turned it up on one side, till it stood quivering, as if undecided whether or not to roll over on top of us. A simultaneous rush of the men to the elevated side decided the question, and caused it to fall squash down on its keel again, where it lay for the next four or five hours, being left quite dry by the tide. As this happened within a few miles of our journey's end, I left the men to take care of the boat, and walked along the beach to Tadousac.

Here I remained some time, and then travelled through the beautiful lakes of Canada, and the United States, to New York. But here I must pause. As I said before, I write not of civilised, but of savage life ; and, having now o'er-shot the boundary, it were as well that I should close.

On the 25th of May 1847, I embarked in the good ship New York, for England.

The merry " Yo, heave ho !" of the sailors, as they worked the windlass and capstan, rang loudly out, while I stood upon the deck with several other passengers, watching them as they cleared the noble vessel from her moorings. In half an hour we left the wharf, and gently floated down the Hudson ; while the trees and houses on the shore, receding slowly from our view, passed away like a shadow.

The air was light and warm, and the sun unclouded, as we floated slowly out to sea, and ere long the vessel bathed her swelling bows in the broad Atlantic.

Gradually, as if loath to part, the wood-clad shores of America grew faint and dim ; and, as I turned my eyes, for the last time, upon the distant shore, the blue hills quivered for a moment on the horizon, as if to bid us all a long farewell, and then sank into the liquid bosom of the ocean.

THE END.

71271